Relax, there will be no test.

History can ruin a good vacation. But *Europe 101* boils down European history and art. The tangle of people and events that makes your sightseeing more meaningful—from the pyramids to Picasso, from Homer to Hitler—is sorted into a fascinating and orderly parade. Today's tourist sights were yesterday's history. And the better you understand that past, the more fun those sights will be.

Europe 101 gives you a practical background to help you understand your sightseeing. It connects yesterday's Europe with today's sights—art, museums, buildings, and people. Throughout the book, you'll find lists of sights that tie your new understanding of Europe right into your upcoming trip plans. This unique approach to art and history, supplemented with maps, time lines, and illustrations, makes this "professor in your pocket" an essential tool in any thinking tourist's preparation for Europe.

Beyond their formal university education in European history, art, and culture, the authors have spent a total of eighty months roaming Europe, on their own and as tour guides. They understand what the average traveler needs to know to appreciate the sights and culture. And, just as important, they know what isn't important.

Now, for the first time, you can enjoy a fun-to-read, practical book that prepares you for Europe's history, art, and culture.

EUROPE 101
History and Art for the Traveler

FOURTH EDITION

Rick Steves
and
Gene Openshaw

GRAPHICS AND MAPS BY
DAVID C. HOERLEIN

John Muir Publications
Santa Fe, New Mexico

Other JMP travel guidebooks by Rick Steves
  Europe Through the Back Door
  Asia Through the Back Door (with John Gottberg)
  2 to 22 Days in Europe
  2 to 22 Days in France (with Steve Smith)
  2 to 22 Days in Germany, Austria, and Switzerland
  2 to 22 Days in Great Britain
  2 to 22 Days in Italy
  2 to 22 Days in Norway, Sweden, and Denmark
  2 to 22 Days in Spain and Portugal
Also by Rick Steves and Gene Openshaw
  Mona Winks: Self-Guided Tours of Europe's Top Museums

John Muir Publications, P.O. Box 613, Santa Fe, NM 87504

Fourth edition. Third printing March 1993

Library of Congress Cataloging-in-Publication Data
Steves, Rick, 1955-
    Europe 101: history and art for the traveler/Rick Steves and
  Gene Openshaw: graphics and maps by David C. Hoerlein.—4th ed.
      p.   cm.
    Includes index.
    ISBN 0-945465-22-X
    1. Europe—Civilization. 2. Europe—Description and travel—
  1971-   —Guide-books. 3. Historic sites—Europe—Guide-books.
  I. Openshaw, Gene. II. Title. III. Title: Europe one-o-one.
  CB203.S734   1990
  914.04'559—dc20   90-15481
                                                                CIP

Typeface: Trump Mediaeval
Typesetter: Copygraphics, Inc.
Printer: McNaughton & Gunn, Inc.

Distributed to the book trade by:
W. W. Norton & Company
New York, New York

Contents

To those
who couldn't care less
about history and art . . .
that they might care more.

Owner's Manual

Why We Wrote This—
And How It Will Help You

Most history is about as exciting as somebody else's high school yearbook—a pile of meaningless faces and names. This history is different. *Europe 101* has a specific purpose—to prepare you for your trip. We have thrown out the dreary dates and meaningless names. What is left is simple, fast moving, and essential to your understanding of Europe.

Europe 101 strips history naked and then dresses it up with just the personalities and stories that will be a part of your travels. Take Frederick the Great, for instance. "Great" as he was, he's just Frederick the So-So to the average tourist, so he isn't mentioned in this book. Louis XIV, however, gets special attention because nearly every traveler visits his palace at Versailles or its many copies throughout Europe. When you understand Louis he becomes a real person who puts his leotards on one leg at a time just like you and me, and his palace comes alive. Unprepared, bored tourists will wonder why you are having so much fun in "just another dead palace."

Art, like history, can be confusing and frustrating. *Europe 101* carefully ties each style of art to its historical era and relates it to your trip. You can't really appreciate baroque art through "Better Homes and Gardens" eyes. You need a baroque perspective.

Those who know and love art but can't get to Europe gnash their teeth while unappreciative tourists race through the Louvre just to see Mona's eyes follow them across the room. Museums can be a drag or they can be unforgettable highlights—depending on what you know. *Europe 101* will prepare you. After reading this book you'll step into a Gothic cathedral, excitedly nudge your partner, and whisper, "Isn't this a great improvement over Romanesque?" Europe, here you come!

No apologies. This book will drive art snobs nuts. Its gross generalizations, sketchy dates, oversimplifications, and shoot-from-the-hip opinions will really tweeze art highbrows. All we want to do is give smart, Europe-bound people who slept through their history and art classes a good, practical way to catch up and understand Europe.

Europe 101 is carefully organized to make Europe's history, art, and culture more meaningful and fun. When used properly, it's your professor in a pocket.

Take a minute to understand the layout. The body of the book (Part I) is the essential story of Europe's history and art organized chronologically through the prehistoric, ancient, medieval, Renaissance, early modern, and modern worlds. Each chapter ends with a time line and a map that lets you visualize how history and art interrelate. The best and most accessible examples of this art and history are listed throughout the book in recommended sightseeing highlights boxes. These lists are based on fame, accessibility, visitor friendliness, and arbitrary whims because, heck, it's our book. They are listed in roughly descending order of importance. The last chapters of the book (Part II) paint a more detailed landscape of areas of special interest to tourists.

To get the most out of your reading, borrow an art history picture book with good color prints from the library. Refer to it as we introduce you to our culture's finest art.

Because much of this book will relate to your travel plans, take notes. Read with pen in hand and fill those margins. You can be your own tour guide.

Now spend a few minutes dreaming about your upcoming trip, go over the itinerary in your head, and then turn the page and dive in.

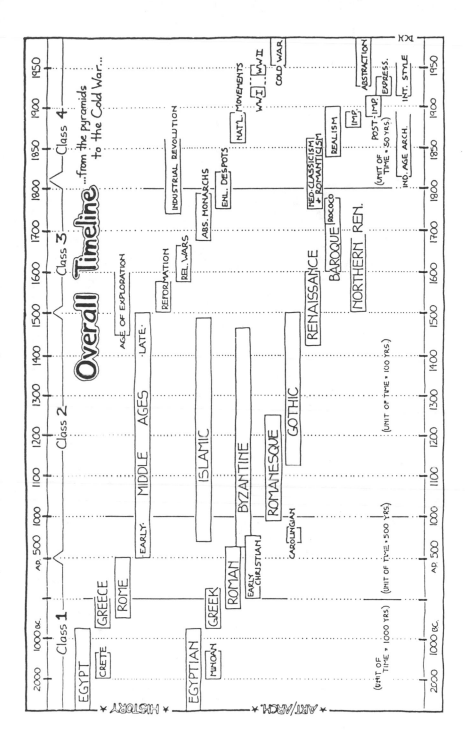

Overall Timeline

...from the pyramids to the Cold War...

Class 1 — Class 2 — Class 3 — Class 4

HISTORY

- EGYPT
- CRETE
- GREECE
- ROME
- EARLY MIDDLE AGES · LATE ·
- AGE OF EXPLORATION
- REFORMATION
- REL. WARS
- INDUSTRIAL REVOLUTION
- ABS. MONARCHS
- ENL. DESPOTS
- NAT'L. MOVEMENTS
- WW I
- WW II
- COLD WAR

ART/ARCH.

- EGYPTIAN
- MINOAN
- GREEK
- ROMAN
- EARLY CHRISTIAN
- BYZANTINE
- ISLAMIC
- CAROLINGIAN
- ROMANESQUE
- GOTHIC
- RENAISSANCE
- NORTHERN REN.
- BAROQUE
- ROCOCO
- NEO-CLASSICISM + ROMANTICISM
- REALISM
- IMP.
- POST-IMP.
- IMP.
- EXPRESS.
- ABSTRACTION
- INT. STYLE
- IND. AGE ARCH.

XX

(UNIT OF TIME = 1000 YRS.)
(UNIT OF TIME = 500 YRS.)
(UNIT OF TIME = 100 YRS.)
(UNIT OF TIME = 50 YRS.)

2000   1000 BC.   AD. 500   1000   1100   1200   1300   1400   1500   1600   1700   1800   1850   1900   1950

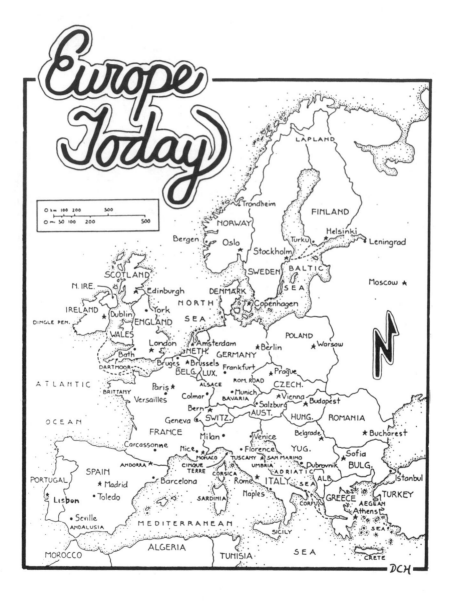

Part I
Europe's History and Art

Prehistoric Europe

Civilization was born when nomads settled. Before this, there was no tourism. Uncivilized man, armed with crude stone tools and fire, survived by hunting wild animals and gathering plants and fruit. Life was nomadic, a constant search for new food.

But even prehistoric nomads with the munchies had art. In the primitive art of prehistoric Europe, cave paintings and statuettes are magic symbols, not simply decorations. A cave dweller thought he or she could gain control over animals by capturing their likeness. The paintings and statues were like voodoo dolls: you created a likeness with just enough details to make it recognizable and then stuck pins (or whatever) into it to influence the creature from afar. (It's questionable how much game was actually caught by this method, yet the same theory is used today when Americans strike their TV sets to influence the Super Bowl.)

Paleolithic Art (40,000 B.C. – 8000 B.C.)

Europe's first art came during the latest in a series of ice ages, when people lived in tents and lean-tos on the bare, icy plains and hunted wild, woolly mammoths. The finest examples of their art, on cave walls at Altamira, Spain, and Lascaux, France, date back to around 12,000 B.C. The startlingly realistic drawings of animals are made with charcoal, ocher, and other natural pigments. Some of these paintings look like modern art. In fact, many modernists have adopted primitive techniques. The Altamira and Lascaux caves are closed to tourists due to the heat and humidity generated by modern crowds. The best prehistoric cave painting still open to tourists is the Grotte de Font-de-Gaume, in France's Dordogne region.

Cave Painting—12,000 B.C.
Painted by cavemen 14,000 years ago, this is more realistic than half the paintings in Europe's modern art galleries.

This "hunter style" of art is found throughout Europe. Ancient drawings of animals and, occasionally, drawings of the hunters themselves have been chiseled and sanded onto rocks or dug into hillsides.

As the ice fields slowly receded from northern Europe (beginning around 9000 B.C.), prehistoric life changed. The frozen plains were replaced by forests and plants. Food gathering, farming, and herding became more profitable. The wandering hunter tribes began to settle down. Europe entered a new era.

Historians divide prehistory into "ages" to show man's progression from stone tools and crude possessions to more sophisticated metals. The main Stone Age periods are the Paleolithic ("lithos" means stone in Latin), the end of the Ice Age, 40,000-8000 B.C.; Mesolithic, 8000-4500 B.C.; and Neolithic, 4500-2000 B.C. Then came the use of metals—the Copper Age, 3000-1800 B.C.; the Bronze Age, 1800-500 B.C.; and so on, until Roman times. These very rough categories are determined by many other cultural features besides what the tools in use were made of.

Not all of Europe progressed at the same rate. Scandinavia, enveloped in ice long after the Continent had turned to forest, lagged behind the rest of Europe. Its inhabitants employed a more primitive technology for longer. Many present-day tribes—the Bushmen of Africa, Australia's Aborigines, the Eskimos, and England's punk-rockers—still employ Stone Age technology.

Neolithic Art (4500 B.C.–2000 B.C.)

As art passed from Paleolithic ("Old" Stone Age) to Neolithic ("New" Stone Age), it became less realistic. Figures became more stylized and simplified. The artwork symbolized what it was supposed to represent in order to make the magic work; it wasn't an exact, realistic rendering.

This trend is especially evident in the small "Venus" statues so popular in the ancient world. Because the future of humanity depended on the fertility of the earth, people worshiped "Mother Nature," who took the form of a fertile woman. Paleolithic Venuses were realistic portrayals of a female. As time went on, though, artisans began to exaggerate some of Venus's most feminine features—breasts, hips, butt, and genitals. By late Neolithic times, Venuses were more stylized still: a "Venus" might just be a stick with two lumps for breasts.

The Venus of Willendorf—30,000 B.C.
This 4-inch-high limestone fertility symbol was one of many such statues made by prehistoric Europeans who worshiped Mother Nature. This Pillsbury Dough Girl was found in present-day Austria.

The most impressive remains of Neolithic culture are the massive, megalithic ("big stone") ruins, such as Stonehenge in England. Built of stones weighing as much as 400 tons, these structures amazed Europeans of the Middle Ages, who figured the stones must have been placed by a race of giants.

Megalithic tombs, similar in purpose to the pyramids of ancient Egypt, were burial chambers for the great warrior-aristocrats of the time, carrying them into the next life. Warriors were buried with all their possessions, a boon for modern-day archaeologists. Found throughout Europe, megalithic tombs are most common in France, which has several thousand.

Some stones—called menhirs—were designed to stand alone, as statues. They are often decorated with a relief carving of a stylized human being.

The final type of megalithic structure, the sanctuary, is the most impressive and mysterious. It usually comprised a circle of stones, possibly arranged for astronomical observations. For example, Stonehenge's pillars are placed so that the rising sun on the longest day of the year (the summer solstice) filters through and strikes the altar stones. An avenue of stones that could accommodate huge crowds leads up to the sanctuary. The purpose of the structures is still a mystery, but we can imagine solemn, somewhat terrifying rituals to honor a very powerful god—a god symbolized by the huge slabs of rock on an open moor.

Stonehenge, England
One of ancient Britain's many wonders, Stonehenge is a
4,000-year-old celestial calendar made of giant stones (artist's
reconstruction).

In England, the building of megaliths extended into the Bronze Age (1800-500 B.C.). The people of this era were farmers and herders. They had increasing contact and trade with the more civilized Mediterranean world. Because these people were entombed with their belongings, today's museums display a wealth of both ceremonial and commonplace objects—weapons, pottery, jewelry, statuettes (Venus figures), and masks—that show a remarkable level of handicraft skill.

The trend toward stylization in art continued when metalwork was developed. It culminated in the highly abstract, intricate, ornamental designs used for decoration by the Celts, the ancient peoples of Britain and France who were conquered by the Romans around the time of Christ.

The magic symbolism of primitive art evolved, under Egyptian influence, into the free, naturalistic, decorative art of the Greek civilizations.

Gradually, the scrambling of Europe's prehistoric nomads took on a pattern. People met at the most fertile places in the best season. Their interaction sparked the birth of civilization.

People saw the advantages of farming their own plants and raising their own animals in a choice spot. Eventually, more people farmed and fewer hunted. By 10,000 B.C., groups began settling in the most fertile and livable areas—near rivers.

This transition from hunter-gatherer to farmer-herder led to cooperation and leisure time, two elements key to the rise of civilization. As we know, people living together and dealing with mutual problems need to cooperate. This cooperation, or social organization, enabled early societies to accomplish giant projects, such as building irrigation and drainage systems, that no one could do alone. This interaction nurtured governments, a greater exchange of knowledge and ideas, the development of common languages, the rudiments of writing to preserve this new knowledge, and paid vacations.

Domestic people were more productive than nomads. In the off-season they had time on their hands—time to sing songs, tell stories, make decorative pottery, organize religion, and construct permanent buildings.

By 7000 B.C., small independent cities had appeared. Present-day Iraq, Iran, and the Middle East, ideally located and with a good cli-

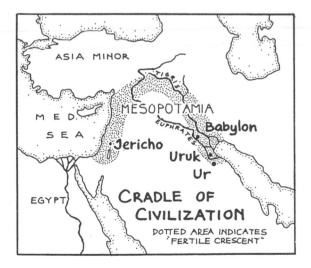

mate, were the birthplace of Western civilization. At the "Crossroads of the World," where Asia, Europe, and Africa met, this area (known as Mesopotamia) was perfect for receiving and spreading through trade all the world's knowledge. This was the age of Jericho, followed by Ur, Uruk, Lagash, and Babylon, each in its time the hub of the known world.

Prehistoric Europe:

Stonehenge and Avebury circles, England
Cave paintings at Les Eyzies-de-Tayac, Dordogne, France
Cave paintings at Pileta caves, near Ronda, Spain
Lascaux II (re-creation), near Les Eyzies, France
Menhirs and Dolmens, Gulf of Morbihan, Brittany, France
Artifacts in many museums, especially National Museums in
    Copenhagen, Vienna, and London

The Ancient World
3000 B.C.–A.D. 500

The year 3000 B.C., when writing appeared, marks the beginning of recorded history—a historic event that reached its culmination in this book. Egypt was united in 3000 B.C., establishing a great civilization that thrived for 2,000 years.

Egypt

Even if you don't visit Egypt, it's worth knowing about because of its influence on Greek culture and because of the large number of Egyptian artifacts in Europe today.

But consider visiting Egypt. Only a ninety-minute flight or an all-day boat ride from Athens, Egypt is just about the most exciting side trip you can plug into your European adventure, well worth the diarrhea.

Egypt is the Nile. From an airplane, the river looks like a lush, green ribbon snaking through an endless sea of sand. By learning to harness the annual flooding of the Nile—its water and its fertilizing silt—ancient Egyptians prospered. The Nile's "blessing," combined with relative isolation from enemy civilizations, brought Egyptians contentment and political stability.

For most of its history, Egypt was politically stable. The Egyptian leader, the pharaoh, was believed to be a living god. Pharaohs ruled a pro status quo Egypt virtually unchallenged for 2,000 years.

The pharaoh's religion stressed preparation for the afterlife. In those days you could "take it with you." Pyramids, built over a period of decades by hordes of slaves, were giant stone tombs designed to preserve a king's body and possessions so they would arrive safely in the afterlife. Many pharaohs even took their servants with them alive—for a while. The walls were painted with images of earthly things in case the pharaoh's real goodies didn't make it (a primitive forerunner of baggage insurance).

The Great Pyramids and the Sphinx—2500 B.C.
Just outside of Cairo. These, like much Egyptian art, were funerary—intended for the dead and their baggage back in the days when you could take it with you.

Egypt's art changed little from 3000 through 1000 B.C., reflecting this political stability and obsession with an afterlife. Much Egyptian art is funerary, built for the tombs of the wealthy and found on the Nile's west bank, where the sun dies each night and people were buried.

Saqqara (c. 2700 B.C.) is the original pyramid. It is a "step pyramid," designed as a series of funerary buildings stacked one on top of the other. The three Great Pyramids at Giza (c. 2500 B.C.) are the most visited of the pharaoh's stairways to heaven—and well worth seeing. These are far from the only pyramids, however. You'll find dozens of them as you explore the Nile region.

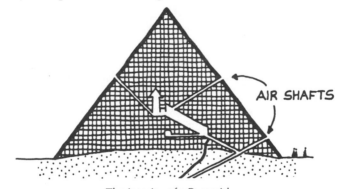

The Interior of a Pyramid
The pyramids were huge tombs designed to hold the dead pharaoh and his eternal luggage until he entered the hereafter. Notice the air shafts, which let the soul fly out of the tomb. Even though pyramids were booby-trapped and carefully designed to foil grave robbers, most were robbed.

Eventually, grave robbers broke into most of the pyramids. Time and time again, pharaohs woke up in heaven with absolutely nothing, so rulers decided to stop marking their tombs with pyramids and instead hid them in the "Valley of the Kings," near Luxor. Mounted patrols guarded these hidden waiting rooms for the Eternity Express. Many have been opened only recently, revealing incredible riches and art that looks brand-new even though it's more than 3,000 years old. Tutankhamen ("Tut" to his friends) was just a mediocre pharaoh, an ancient Gerry Ford, who achieved fame only because his tomb was discovered intact. Many more unmarked and hidden pharaohs' tombs wait in silence and darkness.

Egyptian Art

The distinguishing characteristics of Egyptian art—two-dimensionality, strong outlines, and rigid frontality—are explained by Egyptian religion and politics. Egyptian art was symbolic, intended to preserve likenesses of things and people for the afterlife and to explain the divinity of the pharaoh and the relationships of the gods. It was more important to be symbolically accurate than to be lifelike.

It's dangerous to equate "good" art with "lifelike" art. Often artists with great technical skill purposely distorted a subject to make an emotional, social, intellectual, or artistic point. Understand the artist's purpose before judging his work.

The Egyptian artist was a master at realistically portraying details. But he would paint or sculpt only the details most essential to recognize the subject. Egyptian art is picture symbols—like our "Deer Crossing" road signs—showing things from the most characteristic or easy-to-recognize angle. For example, heads are shown in profile.

Egyptian Wall Painting
Looking as though he was just run over by a pyramid, this 2-D hunter is flat, as is most Egyptian art.

Painters were more like mapmakers. They created unrealistic but recognizable scenes. Fish and birds were shown as if a biologist had "stretched them out," trying to capture every identifying trait. This was so effective that scientists today can identify the species of most of the animals found in Egyptian drawings.

When an Egyptian died, his soul had to make a long journey to the Egyptian paradise. No normal soul could make this hairy journey without pit stops. A statue or painting of the deceased qualified as a rest stop. If you were rich, it was worth having your statue on display everywhere you could, to improve your chances of providing your soul with a rest stop on its long journey to salvation.

These were mug shots for eternity—chin up, no funny faces, nothing fancy. Statues were bold, stiff, frontal, and designed according to a rigid set of proportions. For instance, the head might be half the height of the body and a forearm as long as a shin. This canon of proportions remained unchanged for centuries.

If any pharaoh made it to heaven it was Ramses II, the one who wrangled with Moses and the Israelites. Not only did he have more statues than anyone else but he even had his name chiseled over the names of many earlier pharaohs' statues—just in case his soul (in search of a rest stop) could read.

In the world of politics, Egyptians used symbolic pictures to explain the relationship of the god-king pharaohs to their inferiors. For example, portraying a pharaoh as twice as tall as his subjects, while not "lifelike," accurately represented his social and political status. Each god and pharaoh had an identifying symbol. A beard was a sign of power. Even a statue of Queen Hatshepsut, history's first woman ruler, has a beard chiseled on.

The one striking exception to Egypt's 2,000 years of political, religious, and artistic rigidity was the reign of the Pharaoh Akhnaton (1350 B.C.). We owe our knowledge of this period to the recent discovery of the tomb of Akhnaton's son-in-law and successor, Tutankhamen. Akhnaton was history's first monotheist. He startled the conservative nobility and priesthood of his time by lumping the countless gods of the Egyptian pantheon into one all-powerful being, Aton.

In paintings dating back to his lifetime, we see the royal family painted with a new artistic freedom, with more natural, lifelike, personal settings—a "family portrait" with Akhnaton, his wife, Nefertiti, and their children. Tut's wife is shown, as big as the king, straightening his collar. There is a naturalism and gaiety in these pictures that is radically different from the stiff symbolism of earlier years.

Nefertiti (Berlin)—1350 B.C.
Much of Egypt's greatest art is in Europe, including this masterpiece of Nefertiti, Akhnaton's wife, in Berlin. Early European archaeological teams were allowed to take home their favorite find.

Akhnaton—1350 B.C.
Akhnaton, Egypt's great nonconformist and Tut's father-in-law, promoted individuality. During his reign, we see the first real change in 2,000 years of Egyptian art. Note the exaggerated personal features and the sensual curves in this pharaoh's likeness.

Yet after this brief period of freedom, the old rigidity returned. When Egypt finally declined as an economic power—a victim of conquest by enemies with more efficient weapons—its artistic legacy to the rising Greek world was the technical mastery of a formal religious style. Herodotus, an ancient Greek historian, said of the Egyptians, "They are religious to excess, far beyond any other race of men."

The statues, wall paintings, coffins, mummies, and tombs you'll see in Europe's museums attest to the Egyptians' obsession with the afterlife. The statues are symbolic, representing a god or an abstract idea.

Amen-Ra was the King of the Gods, the god of the sun. He is usually shown as a man with a beard, a double-plumed headdress, and a scepter in his right hand.

Anubis, with the head of a jackal, was the Messenger of the Gods whose job was conducting the souls of men to the underworld after death. Horus, God of the Sky, has a hawk's head. The pharaoh was believed to be Horus on earth.

The strict hierarchy of Egyptian society is seen in symbols. A leopard skin is a sign of priesthood. Anyone barefoot belongs to an inferior class. Important people are shown as bigger than commoners. The stony-faced statues of pharaohs are full of symbolism to show their divine power. A two-layered crown meant this pharaoh ruled a united Egypt.

Egypt's two halves were represented by a lotus and a papyrus plant. When a pharaoh united Egypt, the art of his reign included a symbol of the lotus and papyrus intertwined.

Symbolic Crowns of Egypt
Upper and Lower Egypt were symbolized by crown types. The left crown is of Lower Egypt, the middle is Upper Egypt's, and the one on the right depicts the unity of both under one pharaoh—symbolized by the intertwined lotus and papyrus.

Even Egyptian writing, called hieroglyphs, used pictures to symbolize ideas. They combined two elements: (1) pictures that stood for sounds (phonograms), such as the letters of our alphabet, and (2) pictures representing things and ideas (ideograms), such as the characters used in ancient Chinese writing.

Hieroglyphs were a complete mystery to modern scholars until the discovery of the Rosetta Stone (now in London's British Museum) allowed them to break the code. One hieroglyph you'll see a lot of is

Rosetta Stone (British Museum, London)
The inscription repeated the same message in three
different languages, helping modern scholars to break
the code of ancient Egyptian hieroglyphics.

the ankh, which symbolizes life, in Egyptian art. Statue figures are
shown clutching the ankh as though trying to hold onto life.
Hieroglyphs are essentially pictures, as shown below.

WATER	MAN	ANKH
SUN	WOMAN	MOUTH
EARTH	SON	EVERYTHING
HOUSE	DO, MAKE	OF RULER

The Pre-Greek World

Minoans

The Minoans of Crete created the most impressive pre-Greek civilization. Theirs was a delicate, sensual, happy-go-lucky society that
worshiped an easygoing Mother Earth goddess. The Minoans were
more concerned with good food and dance than with the afterlife.
Life here was an ancient Pepsi commercial.

An isolated location on the island of Crete (a twelve-hour boat
ride west of Athens) and their great skill as traders enabled Minoans
to thrive from 2000 through 1400 B.C. They built their great palaces,
Knossus and Phaestus, without fear of attack, and so the palaces were
open and unfortified. They installed graceful and elegant decorations,
including tapered columns, that created an atmosphere of intimacy
and coziness.

Their art was so free and easy, it's fun to speculate that the laidback Minoans might have influenced the relaxed art style of Akhnaton's Egypt.

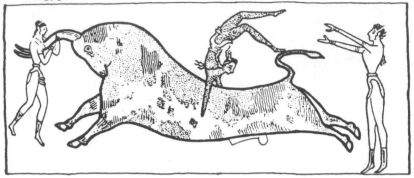

Bull Dance Fresco—1500 B.C.
This painting on wet plaster from the isle of Crete shows the grace of the easygoin' Minoan civilization that so mysteriously vanished. Located in the fine little Minoan museum in Heraklion, Crete.

In 1400, the Minoan civilization vanished without a hint of preceding decline. The great palaces became ghost towns overnight, and no one knows why. Some people think that the eruption of Santorini (home of Atlantis?) caused a tidal wave that swept the Minoan civilization into oblivion. Today, the island of Santorini is just the lip of a crater (lined with tourists), and the ruins of the Minoan civilization on Crete attract crowds from all over the world.

The Minoans definitely influenced the pre-Greek tribes who lived on the mainland. You can see the unique, inverted Minoan column in the famous "Lion Gate" of the ruined Mycenaean capital,

The Lion Gate (Mycenae, Greece)—1250 B.C.
This gateway to the Mycenaean citadel shows the heavy, fortified style of this militaristic society from Trojan War times. The ancient Greeks, thinking no people could build with such huge stones, called Mycenaean architecture "Cyclopean." Mycenae is two hours south of Athens by bus (artist's reconstruction).

Mycenae (two hours by bus from Athens). Greek legend has it that the Minoans ruled the early Greeks, demanding a yearly sacrifice of young Greeks to the dreadful Minotaur (half bull, half man) at the palace of Knossus. The Minoans' domination, however, was probably more cultural than political.

The Greek Dark Ages (1200–800 B.C.)

The death of the Minoan civilization left only the many isolated, semibarbaric tribes of Greece to fight things out. The period from 1200 through 800 B.C. is often called the "Dark Age." What we know about this Greek period comes largely from the poems and songs passed down over generations and eventually recorded by Homer in the ninth century B.C. in the _Iliad_ and the _Odyssey._

The _Iliad_ tells of the Greeks' attack on Troy (on the west coast of present-day Turkey) and how they finally won by sneaking into the city in the belly of a huge wooden horse. The _Odyssey_ describes the Greek warrior Ulysses' long journey home after that war. However mythical these stories might be, they reveal the Greeks' desire to establish order in their warring world. The Trojan War is representative of all the wars of this period, and Ulysses' return home to a world filled with anarchy and lawlessness represents the long and difficult unification and rise of classical Greece.

Classical Greece

The incredible output of art, architecture, and philosophy during the "Golden Age" of Greece set the pace for all of Western civilization to follow. Astonishingly, all this was achieved within the space of a century in Athens, a city of 80,000! It was the flowering of many centuries of slow economic and cultural growth.

By 800 B.C., the bickering tribes of the Greek peninsula had settled down, bringing a new era of peace, prosperity, and unification. Great traders, the Greeks shipped their booming new civilization, with its ideas and riches, to every corner of the Mediterranean. As the Greek population multiplied, they established colonies as far away as France, Spain, and Italy. Many Greek ruins remain in those countries today.

A growing sense of unity (Pan-Hellenism) developed among the Greek-speaking peoples. They developed a common alphabet. They held the first Olympic Games in 776 B.C., during which wars were halted and athletes from all over Greece competed. They increased political unity through both conquest and alliance. The foundation of the unity, however, was the small, self-contained city-state.

Parthenon Metope Panel (British Museum, London)
This mythical battle between humans and half-human centaurs symbolized Greece's triumph over barbarism and chaos.

The individual city-state, or polis (as in "metropolis"), was a natural product of Greece's mountainous landscape and its many islands, which isolated people from their neighbors. The ideal city-state was small enough to walk across in a day but large enough to meet all the cultural and economic needs of its people. It was an independent mini-nation.

Landowners ruled in a generally democratic style. A city-state's typical layout included a combination fortress/worship site atop a hill called the acropolis ("high city"). The agora, or marketplace, sat at the base of the hill, with the people's homes and farms gathered around. An important feature of the agora was the stoa, a covered colonnade or portico used as a shady meeting place—ideal for discussing politics.

Athens in the Golden Age (450–400 B.C.)

Athens was one such polis (with the basic acropolis-agora layout) that rose, through alliance, industry, trade, and military might, until it dominated the Greek world. Cursed with poor, rocky soil, Athens turned to craftsmanship and trade for its livelihood. Able leaders stimulated industry by recruiting artisans from throughout the Greek world. By 500 B.C., Athens was the economic and cultural center of a loosely unified Greece.

Old Athens Today
This is the historic core of Athens: the acropolis (city on the hilltop), the agora (old market at the foot of the hill), and Plaka (the extent of the nineteenth-century town and now the tourist, hotel, restaurant, shopping, and nightlife center).

Persia (present-day Iran and Iraq) posed a threat from the East. Persians ruled Ionia (modern-day Turkey's west coast), a center of high Greek culture. Here, the elegance and riches of Persia and the culture of the Anatolian civilizations mixed with the creative imagination of the Greeks. The Greeks united under Athenian leadership to protect themselves against the Persian threat. By using their superior navy, the Greeks defeated the Persians, making Athens the protector and policeman of the Greek peninsula.

In less than 100 years, Athens had risen from a stable, small-crafts city-state to the cultural, political, and economic center of an empire. Athens demanded payment, or tribute, from the other city-states for her defense of the peninsula. The new wealth in Athens set off a cultural volcano whose dust is still settling.

After the Persian War, the Athenians immediately set about rebuilding their city, which had been burned by the invaders. Grand public buildings and temples were built and then decorated with the greatest painting and sculpture ever. Giant amphitheaters were built to house dramatic, musical, and poetic festivals. During all this cultural growth and public building, the average citizen remained hard-working and simple, living modestly but comfortably.

The Acropolis, Athens
(artist's reconstruction)

In schools and in the agora, under the shade of the stoa, the Greeks debated many of the questions that have occupied the human mind. Both Plato (who wrote down many of Socrates' ideas) and his student Aristotle organized schools of philosophy. Plato (c. 380 B.C.) taught that the physical world is only a pale reflection of true reality (the way a shadow on the wall is a poor version of the three-dimensional, full-color world we see) and that rational thinking is the path to understanding the true reality. Aristotle (c. 340 B.C.), an avid biologist, emphasized study of the physical world rather than the unseen one. These two divergent ideas resurfaced again and again, especially in Christian theology centuries later. St. Augustine was a neo-Platonist, and Thomas Aquinas was a student of Aristotle.

The Greeks studied the world and man's place in it. They weren't content with traditional answers and old values. (In fact, similar ideas were popping up all over the world at this time. Buddha in India, Confucius in China, and the Old Testament prophets in Palestine were all trying to relate everyday life to some larger scheme of things.)

The "Golden Mean" was a new ideal that stressed the importance of balance, order, and harmony. This was a virtue pursued both by individuals—for example, someone who was both an athlete and a scholar—and in art and architecture.

Life Slice—Ancient Greece

Imagine a Greece without rubble, without ruins; when statues had arms, and buildings had roofs; when the gray marble columns were painted bright colors; when flesh and blood people went around saying "Know thyself." There was a time when ancient Greece was alive—farming, trading, voting, and going to the theater.

Farming was a tough row to hoe in rocky Greece so the Greeks learned to trade with people in more fertile areas. Greeks produced wine, olive oil, and crafts like pottery which they traded for grain. They had lots of slaves. As many as a third of the people in Athens were slaves.

As well as being slave owners, the ancient Greeks were great democrats. Greece was divided by mountains and water into many small, self-governing, democratic city-states run by the common vote of the citizens. In Athens, any landowning adult male could vote. (Thomas Jefferson added that you had to be white.)

With all their slaves and wealth, the Golden Age Athenians still lived quite simply. For dress, men and women wore a simple, loose tunic and a heavier wool wrapping for decoration and warmth.

Athenians tried to live the "golden mean," a balance between body and mind. The children learned the three "Rs," music, and athletics. The favorite leisure activities were sports and the theater.

Greek Theater, Epidaurus, 350 B.C.

Architecture

Greek art is known for its symmetry, harmony, and "classic" simplicity. It strikes a happy medium (a golden mean) between the rigidly formal Egyptian art and the unrestrained flamboyance of later (Hellenistic) art.

In architecture, this ideal of "nothing to excess" is best seen in Greek temples. There were two different styles, or "orders," Doric and Ionic. Although the easiest way to identify these styles is by their columns, the columns themselves are only the tip of this architectural iceberg.

Doric columns are strong and simple, following the earliest styles of temple building. (The Doric tribe, of whom the Spartans were a member, was known for its austere life-style.)

A Greek temple was a house for a god's statue. The people worshiped outside, so its exterior was the important part and the interior was small and simple. The earliest temples were built of mud brick and wood. When stone came into use, the Greeks used the old style with the new material. The stone columns were shaped like timber supports, and formerly wooden beam ends, now in stone, divided the square panels on the eaves. The tops, or "capitals," of Doric columns are also simple—just little sailors' caps of stone between the column and the roof they support.

The Parthenon, in Athens, is the greatest Doric temple, a masterpiece of Greek order and balance. The columns are thick but much more graceful than those of the massive Egyptian temples. These Doric columns swell slightly in the middle to give the impression that the roof is compressing them just a little.

The designers of the Parthenon used other eye-pleasing optical illusions. The base of the temple, which appears flat, actually bows up in the middle to overcome the illusion of sagging that a straight horizontal line would give. (If you and your partner stand on the same step at opposite ends, you'll see each other only from the waist up.) Also, the columns bend inward just a hair. If you extended them upward more than a mile, they would come together. These design

The Parthenon (Athens)—450 B.C.
A "classic" example of Doric simplicity. It stood nearly intact until the seventeenth century, when it was destroyed by an explosion during a Venetian-Turkish war. Today its greatest threat is twentieth-century pollution.

elements give a more harmonious, cohesive feel to the architectural masterpiece of Greece's Golden Age.

Whereas Doric beauty was somewhat austere, the later Ionic style reflected grace, ease, and freedom while retaining balance and simplicity. An Ionic column is slenderer than a Doric column and has deeper vertical grooves. The capital, with its scroll-like curls sticking out of either side, is more decorative. These curls give the impression of "spleening" (from the author's private word reserve) under the weight of the roof. This style reflects a conscious effort to decorate and beautify the temple, but the ornamentation almost never needs an excuse. It's never extravagant or superfluous.

A third order, the Corinthian, was developed during the Hellenistic period and was passed on to Roman architecture, where it is often seen side by side with Doric and Ionic. The Corinthian is the next step in the path from simplicity to decoration. A Corinthian column's flowery capital of acanthus leaves doesn't even pretend to serve an architectural purpose; it is blatantly ornamental.

As temples evolved to more graceful styles, columns became slenderer. There was a canon of proportions: Doric columns were to be eight times as tall as their base width, Ionic were to be ten times as tall as their base width, and Corinthian were to be eleven times as tall as their base width.

Temples of all the orders had similar features. Fluted, or grooved, columns are an architectural echo of the days when the columns were logs with their bark gouged out. Columns were made of stacked slices of stone, each with a plug to keep it in line. They hold up the roof and provide a pleasant, shady stoa under the broad eaves. The capitals shorten the distance needed to bridge the columns.

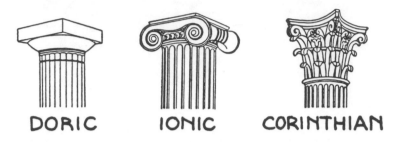

DORIC   IONIC   CORINTHIAN

Classical Architecture—Doric, Ionic, and Corinthian
The easiest way to identify the classical "orders" is by the columns. Doric is the earliest, simple and stocky. Ionic is fancier, thinner, with more pronounced grooves and a rolled capital. Corinthian (Roman style) is the most ornate, with a leafy capital. As temples evolved, columns grew slenderer and more widely spaced.

In the old days, when timbers spanned the roof, the ends of the beams divided the roof into little, fun-to-fill-with-carving squares called metopes. When builders began to use stone, the metopes were retained. The pediment is the triangular gable that was the artistic focus of the ancient sculptors. They filled these narrow, awkwardly shaped spaces with some of ancient Greece's best art. The frieze, the panel under the eaves, was usually filled with low-relief carvings of mythological battles and scenes. The famous Elgin Marbles, now in the British Museum, are the sculptures that decorated these three parts of the Parthenon—metope, pediment, and frieze.

Much post-Greek architecture, as well as that of the present day, utilizes the classical orders for decoration.

Sculpture and Painting

The Greeks believed that the human body expressed the human spirit, and sculptors tried to catch it in all its naked splendor. Even gods were depicted as having human bodies. The trick was to sculpt a body that was realistic but also posed, balanced, idealized, and beautiful. We see in Greek sculpture the same evolution from rigidity to graceful balance to exuberance that we saw in Greek architecture. The early Greek archaic period (750–500 B.C.) is like the formal Egyptian style, where statues of people were like schematic diagrams, preserving only the essential details of the subject in a stiff, frontal pose. It looks as though the sculptor couldn't let his model move for fear of missing some important detail.

This posed frontality is seen in the Greek "kouros," statues of naked young men from the sixth century B.C. They are strongly outlined and remarkably realistic—but not lifelike. A kouros looks like a human but like no human in particular because there are no individual details. The body appears to have been made on an assembly line, with universally interchangeable parts.

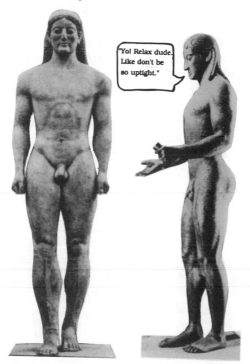

Archaic-style Greek "Kouros," or Boy—ca. 570 B.C.
Moving from the stiff, Egyptian-type frontality of the Archaic period toward the balance and naturalism of the "Golden Age," the Greek kouros (boy) at right has begun to lose his rigidity.

Greek society honored individuality and admired the human body. This attitude, combined with technical mastery of the skills of sculpture, freed the subject from those archaic, rigid poses. Artists began to relax their subjects and portray life more realistically.

Sculptors showed subjects from side angles and from three-quarters angles, capturing movement and balancing new slants. Artists paid closer attention to detail. Robes drape down naturally from the statues, and the intricate folds become beautiful in themselves.

Remember that most "Greek" statues we see are chalky, lifeless Roman copies with blank stares and Vatican fig leaves. When you read ancient descriptions of lost originals or look at the few surviving Greek originals, you'll be impressed by their vibrancy. Athens' National Museum of Archaeology, by far the greatest museum for ancient Greek art, has many good examples of each stage of Greek sculpture.

Painting was revolutionized in the same way by the discovery of foreshortening. (You foreshortened the last time you drew receding lines to turn a square into a three-dimensional box.) Now a subject could be shown from any angle—not just from the most convenient frontal pose. The artist could record things as they happened, even putting his individual stamp on the work by showing it from his personal perspective.

In their day, Greek painters were more famous than their sculpting counterparts. The best Greek painting you are likely to see will be on the vases that fill art museums from Oslo to Lisbon. (The vases were used to hold oil or wine rather than flowers.) Enjoy a rare peek into the everyday good times of the Greeks by studying the paintings on their vases.

Geometric-style Vase
This earliest stage of Greek art (700 B.C.) shows wasp-waisted figures pulling their hair out to symbolize their sadness at this funeral procession.

Even with this exciting, new found freedom in their technical mastery of the arts, the Golden Age of Greece is best characterized by the Golden Mean: restraint and a strong sense of harmony.

The famous statue _Discus Thrower_ illustrates this balance. It's a remarkable study in movement, yet the body is captured at a moment of nonmovement just before he hurls the discus. The human form is posed but natural, perfectly balanced, with nothing in the extreme; it reflects the Golden Mean. Previously, the body had been the sum of its parts. Now, it was an organic whole.

Golden Age, _The Discus Thrower,_ by Myron—450 B.C.
The anatomy is realistic and the statue is relaxed enough to "move." But the pose—caught at the moment just before the discus gets thrown— is still perfectly balanced. Like most great Greek statues, the original is long gone. This is a Roman copy of a Greek statue with a Catholic fig leaf.

The brief Golden Age of Greece (150 B.C.) was the balancing point between archaic and Hellenistic Greece. Both society and its art evolved from aristocratic, traditional, stiff, and archaic (c. 600 B.C.) to democratic, original, realistic, and wildly individual (c. 300 B.C.). But the balance dissolved when radical individuality arrived along with the Hellenistic age.

Praxiteles, _Venus de Medici_ (Uffizi Gallery, Florence)
Greek art evolved to a Golden Age balance. This masterpiece by probably the greatest Greek sculptor served as the ideal of classical beauty through the ages. Nineteenth-century tourists used to swoon in ecstasy at her loveliness.

Laocoön (Vatican Museum)—1st Century A.D.
A textbook example of the Hellenistic style, it is so exuberant it seems ready to jump right off its pedestal. The classical composure is lost. Unearthed near Rome in 1506, this work astounded and inspired Michelangelo and the Renaissance sculptors.

Hellenism (330 B.C.–First Century A.D.)

The ideas of the small Greek peninsula were spread single-handedly throughout the Mediterranean and Near East by one man—Alexander the Great. Alexander ushered in the Hellenistic period. "Hellene" is Greek for "Greek."

As Athens declined in power through costly wars with Sparta and other neighboring city-states, the Macedonians to the north (present-day Yugoslavia) swept in. Their leader was 20-year-old Alexander, a former student of Aristotle. By the time Alexander died, at the age of 32, he had created the largest empire ever, stretching as far east as India. (What have you accomplished lately?) He was a military genius, a great administrator, and a lover of Greek culture. Alexander went to bed each night with two things under his pillow: a dagger and a copy of the _Iliad_. But although he might have conquered Greece politically, Greece ruled Alexander's empire culturally.

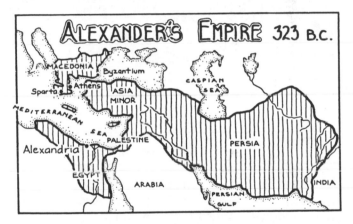

During the Hellenistic era, Greek was the common language of most of the civilized world. Cities everywhere had Greek-style governments and schools, and their citizens observed Greek holidays and studied Greek literature. Public squares throughout the Mediterranean looked Greek. Alexandria (Egypt) was the intellectual center of the world, with more than a million people, a flourishing arts and literature scene, and the greatest library anywhere. No ship was allowed to enter the port without surrendering its books to be copied.

Hellenistic sculpture reflected the exuberance of Hellenistic civilization. The statuary of the period was dramatic, emotional, and "unbalanced," showing rough-and-tumble scenes such as the one depicted in the Laocoön. A typical example is a tangle of battling gods and giants literally falling out of the relief scene and onto the monumental stairway they are supposed to decorate. In this period, freestanding statues replaced the well-ordered up-against-the-wall reliefs of the earlier ages.

Altar of Zeus (Berlin's Pergamon Museum)—170 B.C.

When Alexander died in 323 B.C., his political empire crumbled. But the Greek civilization fostered during his rule lived on for centuries. This Hellenistic culture was obsessed with an anchorless creativity. The "cynics" were history's first hippies, rejecting all authority and institutions, and the mood was "back to basics," focusing on the individual. As the Romans began to conquer these lands and people, they found them easy to administer, with a ready-made centralized government and economy. They were more "civilized" than their Roman conquerors. The Romans absorbed what was profitable into their own culture, and civilization took one more step westward.

Five Favorite Greek Ruins

Greece has a lifetime of crumbled old ruins to explore. It's very important, as you plan your Greek itinerary, not to assume that everything built before Christ is worth your energy. Be selective. Don't burn out on the mediocre. Choose as much antiquity as you can absorb—and then concentrate on absorbing the sun, food, and drink of a country with many dimensions.

Here are our five favorite Greek ruins. If you can see these, don't worry about the rest.

Athens' Acropolis

This is the biggie. The city of Athens might be overrated, but its acropolis is not.

The Parthenon—the climax of the acropolis and Greece's finest Doric temple—is worth really studying. The fine acropolis museum is helpful for your mental reconstruction of the original magnificence of this historic hilltop.

Below the acropolis is the ancient agora, ancient Athens' civic center and market. Most important among many sights here is the Temple of Hephaistos, or Theseum, the best-preserved classical Greek temple anywhere.

The Theseum, Athens—450 B.C.
In Athens' agora, where Socrates, Plato, and Aristotle hobnobbed, you'll find the best-preserved Greek temple anywhere.

Delos

Without Delos, Athens' acropolis might not have been built. During Greece's "Golden Age," the treasury of the Athens-dominated Greek alliance was located on this little island near Mykonos. The Athenians financed the architectural glorification of their city by looting this treasury.

Delos, an easy half-day side trip from Mykonos, was the legendary birthplace of Apollo and therefore the most sacred Cycladic island.

Today it is uninhabited except for daily boatloads of visitors. See the famous "Lions of Delos," wander through nearly a square mile of crumbled greatness, and climb to the island's summit for a picnic. From the peak of Delos you'll enjoy a grand, 360-degree view of the Greek Isles, with the Fort Knox of ancient Greece at your feet.

Olympia

For more than a thousand years the Olympic Games were held, not coincidentally, in Olympia. What was once the most important sanctuary of Zeus in all of Greece is now a thought-provoking and popular tourist attraction.

Most tourists sail to Greece from Italy. The boat (free with a Eurailpass) lands in Patras, and the hordes stampede on into Athens. Be different. Head south from Patras to Olympia and then explore the Peloponnesian interior on your way to Athens.

Olympia's Temple of Zeus was one of the great tourist traps of the ancient world, boasting a then-world-famous 40-foot statue of Zeus by the great sculptor, Phidias. It was one of the Seven Wonders of the Ancient World.

Olympia can still knock you on your discus. Get there very early (before the tour buses do), and buy a guidebook and use it, along with the Olympia Museum, to refill the stadium with 40,000 fans and resurrect the wonders of these sacred stones. Line up on the starting block and burst into the world of ancient Greece.

Delphi

Once upon a time, Zeus, the king of all the gods, threw out two eagles. Where they met after circling the earth was called the world's navel, or belly button. This was the center of the universe and the home of the Oracle of Delphi in the days of Socrates.

In Delphi, the gods communicated with mortals through a priestess. This made Delphi politically powerful, religiously righteous, and very rich.

Today, its staggering setting does more than its history to make this four-hour side trip from Athens worthwhile. Along with plenty of photogenic ruins to explore, Delphi has one of Greece's best archaeological museums.

Ephesus

The ruins of Asia Minor's largest metropolis and the home of the Ephesians of New Testament fame are our favorites.

Ephesus is actually on the Turkish mainland, only a ninety-minute boat ride from what is possibly the most beautiful Greek island, Samos.

Ephesus was at its peak at about 100 B.C., when it was the capital of the Roman province of Asia and had a population of about 250,000. You can explore a giant, 25,000-seat outdoor theater, park your chariot outside a stadium that held 70,000, and hike up the marble-cobbled main street lined with buildings that are in a perfect state of ruin, with fragile remnants somehow surviving century after century. You can even sit on a 2,000-year-old toilet.

A trip to Efes (Turkish for Ephesus) is a great excuse to sample a slice of Turkey. Remember, if you're looking for cultural thrills, the difference culturally between Turkey and Greece is much greater than that which separates Greece and the United States.

Athens' National Museum of Archaeology

It's useful to preface a visit to the ancient wonders of Greece with a visit to the National Archaeological Museum in Athens.

Athens, like Mexico City and Cairo, has hoarded the lion's share of its artistic heritage under one grand roof. Take this museum as seriously as you can. Trace the evolution of Greek art, study a guidebook, take a guided tour, and examine the ancient life-styles painted on the vases. With a rudimentary knowledge of Greek art you can, for example, date to the decade statues you've never seen before—with a little background you can see more than rubble in the ruins.

Beware. Greece is the most touristed but least explored country in Europe. It seems that at any time, 90 percent of its tourists are crowding into its top ten or twelve sights. In these places, more than just about anywhere else in Europe, you should expect trouble finding rooms without reservations. Do what you can to minimize tourist crowd problems.

Greece is peppered with ancient sights, each offering something unique. But as with Gothic cathedrals, German castles, or paintings in a big museum, you can't and shouldn't try to see and appreciate them all. Practice selective savoring.

Ancient Greek Sights:

Minoan ruins of Knossos and museum, Iraklion, Crete, Greece
Mycenae, south of Athens
Athens' acropolis and agora
Delphi, site of oracle
Olympia, site of first Olympic games
Delos (near Mykonos), treasury of Athenian League
Paestum, just south of Naples
Agrigento, Sicily
Epidavros, Peloponnese, Greece
Aphrodisias, Turkey
Acrotiri, Santorini, Greece

Top Museums of Ancient Greece:

National Museum, Athens
British Museum (Parthenon sculpture), London
Louvre (Venus de Milo), Paris
Vatican Museum (Laocoön), Rome
Pergamon Museum, Berlin, Germany

Victory of Samothrace (Louvre, Paris)

Rome

Rome is history's supreme success story. By conquest, assimilation, and great administration, Rome rose from a small Etruscan town to the ruling seat of the Western world.

Rome lasted for about a thousand years, from 500 B.C. through A.D. 500. In a nutshell, it grew for 500 years, peaked for 200, and fell for 200. For the first 500 years, Rome was a republic; for the second 500, an empire. Today, armies of tourists endure the hot Roman sun and battle its crazy traffic to see what's left of that greatest of civilizations.

The Etruscan "She-Wolf" (Capitol Museum, Rome)—500 B.C.
Long after the Etruscans sculpted this statue, Romulus and Remus were scooted under, and it became the symbol of Rome. You'll see copies of this everywhere, but the original "She-Wolf" is in the museum on Capitol Hill in Rome.

Legend says that Rome was founded in 753 B.C. by twin brothers, Romulus (hence "Rome") and Remus. They are said to have been orphaned as babies and raised by a she-wolf before starting the greatest empire ever. This story must have seemed an appropriate metaphor for the Romans, explaining how such a "civilized" people (as they considered themselves) could have grown out of such "barbarian" surroundings.

Rome was situated at the first bridge on the Tiber River, as far upstream as boats could navigate. Rome linked the advanced Etruscan civilization to the north with the agriculturally rich Greek colonies to the south.

The Etruscans thrived in much of northern Italy during Greece's Golden Age. We know little about this civilization other than what we have learned from recent excavations of Etruscan tombs. Discoveries indicate that the Etruscans were peaceful, religious, easygoing, and prosperous craftspeople and merchants. With a good map, you can track down many interesting Etruscan sights between Rome and Florence.

Etruscan Museums and Sites:

Tarquinia necropolis
Orvieto museum
Cerveteri tombs and frescoes
Volterra
Vatican Museum, Rome
Carlsberg Glyptothek, Copenhagen
Louvre, Paris

In 509 B.C., the local Romans threw out their Etruscan king, establishing a plutocratic (rule by the rich) "republic." From the start, war was the business of state, and Rome expanded. The Roman conquests were cemented by a well-organized, generally enlightened, benevolent rule. People knew that when they were conquered by Rome they had joined the winning team, that political stability would replace barbarian invasions, and that they would enjoy free trade and public building projects—roads, baths, aqueducts, theaters, and great games. With contented subjects, the empire continued to expand. By 260 B.C., it included Italy, and by 100 B.C., Rome controlled the entire Mediterranean world.

Roman Triumphal Arch
Emperors milked their military victories for propaganda purposes. Grand triumphal arches glorified their exploits. Today you'll find these arches scattered from Germany to Morocco.

This giant empire strained a government that had been designed to rule only a small city-state. During the last century B.C., Rome, while still growing and prospering, had to deal with civil strife, class struggles, corrupt politicians, and the corrosive individuality of Hellenism.

Julius Caesar, an ambitious general, cunning politician, and charismatic leader, outmaneuvered his rivals and grabbed the reins of Rome in about 50 B.C. Supported by his armies, Caesar suspended the constitution and replaced the "republic" with the "empire." His dictatorial rule restored order and reformed the government.

He further consolidated his power by naming a month, July, after himself. He ran through many reforms but underestimated the conservatives in the senate and those who loved the old republic. He was assassinated (Et tu, Brute?), and a struggle followed between would-be dictators and republicans. A decade later the political vacuum was filled by Julius's adopted son, Caesar Augustus. (This family name became a title—Caesar, Tsar, Kaiser.)

Caesar Augustus—A.D. 1
Here, the first emperor, Augustus (founder of the Pax Romana), demonstrates his complete control and mastery of the empire.

Pax Romana—The Roman Peace (A.D. 1–200)

Augustus, known as the architect of the Roman Empire, established a full-blown monarchy and ushered in the "Pax Romana." This "Roman peace" was two hundred years of relative peace and prosperity with an enlightened and generally benevolent rule throughout the vast empire. Augustus, like Julius, named a month in his own honor. He was more sensitive to the senate and its traditions but still reformed the government, restored temples, undertook huge public building projects, and even legislated morality. He declared himself the "pontifex maximus" (high priest) and boasted that he "found Rome a city of brick and left it a city of marble."

The Pax Romana's unprecedented political stability was made possible by a smooth succession of leaders. Historically, accession to the throne was hereditary, but, also historically, emperors' sons made lousy rulers. The great rulers of the second century (Nerva, Trajan, Hadrian, and Antoninus) had no blood sons but, instead, adopted as a son the man they deemed most capable of ruling. Then, when they died, the "son" inherited the throne—and ruled well. This worked fine until Marcus Aurelius had a blood son, Commodus. As emperor,

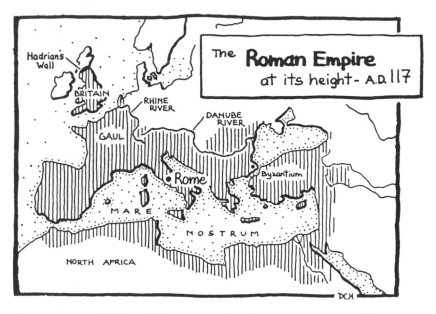

Roman maps called the Mediterranean "Our Sea" (Mare Nostrum). The empire stretched as far north as the Danube and Rhine rivers and the southern border of Scotland. At this time, the word "Rome" meant the entire civilized world.

this palace brat who ran around dressed in animal skins and carrying a club as if he were Hercules, ushered in a period of instability and decline.

The Pax Romana saw a well-governed Rome reach its zenith, stretching from the Nile to the Danube, the Rhine to the south border of present-day Scotland, where the Romans decided to "call it an empire" and built Hadrian's Wall from coast to coast across northern England. Everywhere the Roman army went it built roads, aqueducts, and cities on a grid plan. Roman maps labeled the Mediterranean "Mare Nostrum" (Our Sea). Trade thrived. The word "Rome" became universal, referring not only to the city but also to the whole civilized world.

The Pantheon, with its famous and lovely skylight, is probably the one sight that will give you the best feel for the magnificence and splendor of Rome. This concrete structure is 142 feet high and 142 feet wide. A domed temple dedicated to all Roman gods, it was the wonder of its time and inspired Renaissance artists. The huge domes of the Florence cathedral and St. Peter's in Rome were modeled on this early architectural triumph.

Life Slice — Ancient Rome

Let's look at a "typical" well-to-do Roman citizen and his family over the course of a day.

In the early morning, Nebulus reviews the finances of the country farm with his caretaker/accountant/slave. At midmorning he is interrupted by a "client," one of many poorer people dependent upon him for favors. The client, a shoemaker, wants permission from the government to open a new shop. He asks Nebulus to cut through red tape for him. Nebulus promises to see a lawyer friend in the basilica about the matter.

After a light lunch and siesta, he walks to the baths for a work-out and steam. There, he discusses plans for donating money to build a new aqueduct for the city.

Back home, his wife, Vapid, tends to the household affairs. The servants clean the house and send clothing to the laundry. Usual dress is a simple woolen tunic—two pieces of cloth, front and back, sewn together at the sides. But tonight they will attend a dinner party. She will wear silk, with a wreath of flowers. Nebulus will wear his toga—a 20-foot-long white cloth wrapped around the body and draped over one shoulder. It's heavy and hard to put on, but it's the rage.

The children, Raucus and Ubiquitous, say good-bye to the pet dog and bird and head off to school in the Forum. On the way, they stop at the bakery for fresh-baked bread. Once with the teacher, fun ends. They learn their basic three R's—or else. Discipline is severe. They'll be whipped if they step out of line. When they get older, they may study literature, Greek, and rhetoric—public speaking. (The saving grace of this dreary education is they don't have to take Latin!)

At the evening dinner party, Vapid marvels over the chef's creation— ham filled with honey, pasted in flour and baked. Romans love good food and wine. Beef and cow's milk are considered inferior to pork and goat's milk. The wine is the finest the world has to offer—Roman merchants use wine as a staple trading product. They toast each other with wine glasses and clay goblets bearing inscriptions like "Fill me up," "Little water, undiluted wine," and "Love me, baby!"

The Roman orgy has become legend, but the legend is merely legendary. For the most part, they advocated moderation and sexual fidelity. If anything, stuffiness and business sense were the rule at such affairs. The family unit was considered sacred.

Roman Religion

Religion permeated Roman life. The gods were powers you bargained or dealt with. If you wanted a favor, you prayed and sacrificed to the proper god, either at home on a small altar or at the local temple. For guidance, you might see a seer who would rip open an animal to check the shape of the entrails for predictions of the future.

Jupiter was the king of the gods, based—like all the Roman gods—on his Greek counterpart, Zeus. Each profession had its patron god or goddess. For example, Betty Crocker would pray to Vesta—the goddess of the hearth. There was no moral obligation to worship the gods; you did it to gain a favor. Here's one prayer that has survived: "I beseech you to avenge the theft committed against me. Punish with a terrible death whoever stole these articles—six tunics, two cloaks, etc."

Roman Portrait Busts—Three Generations
The Romans worshiped the father. Since portrait busts were important in their religion, portraiture was one area of art where they excelled. Here we see three generations of heads—sculpted in 50 B.C., 40 B.C., and 20 B.C.—all plugged into a body done in A.D. 15. The museum on Rome's Capitol Hill has more heads than a Grateful Dead concert in a cabbage patch.

Roman Art

The Romans were not great artists. Although the Greeks loved beauty and intellectual stimulation, the Romans were engineers and administrators. Their artistic accomplishments were big and functional, designed for accommodating the masses with roads, colosseums, and baths rather than portraying beautiful gods. If offered a choice of a ticket to a symposium on the nature of truth or a ticket to a gladiatorial battle to the death, a Roman would have gone for the gore.

Rome's greatest contributions to history are in law and engineering. Her legal and administrative traditions were the basis for all Western governments that followed. In engineering, the Romans developed the use of the arch and concrete, enabling them to build the largest and most complex structures of their time.

By developing the round arch, Rome was able to build circles around the Greeks.

Pont du Gard, Roman Aqueduct (South France)
A giant, 2,000-year-old water system, built without mortar, near Nimes in southern France.

Maybe it's lucky that the Romans weren't great innovators in art. As a result, they admired, preserved, and copied the precious Greek art that otherwise might have been lost or destroyed. In fact, most of the examples of Greek Golden Age sculpture you'll see during your trip are excellent Roman copies. The originals are long gone, but every high-class Roman wanted quality copies of Greek originals in his villa. These fill today's museums.

Roman art and architecture are characterized by utility and grandeur. (An ancient Roman in modern America would consider a Los Angeles freeway interchange a great work of art.) The Romans focused on functionality and purpose. Decoration was secondary.

The Colosseum is a perfect example. Built in A.D. 80, with 50,000 numbered seats, Romans could fill and empty this stadium as quickly and smoothly as we do ours. It could be flooded to give sports fans mock naval battles. "Sails" could be drawn across the top to turn it into a giant, shaded, domed stadium.

The Colosseum's essential structure was Roman, built with arches, barrel vaults, and concrete. The three orders of Greek

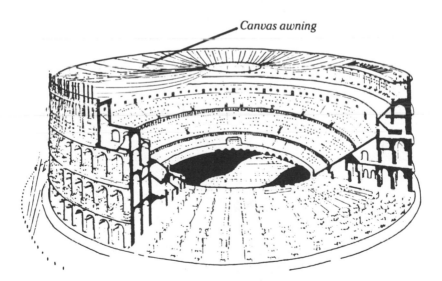

Canvas awning

The Roman Colosseum (Rome)—A.D. 80
A good example of Roman engineering accommodating the needs of the masses. To double the seating capacity, they put two theaters together to make an amphitheater. A canvas awning could be drawn across the top to make it a "domed" stadium. Built with barrel vaults and concrete, it could fill with, hold, and empty out 50,000 fans in as orderly a manner as our football stadiums do today. Opening day was celebrated with the slaughter of 5,000 animals.

columns on the exterior—Doric, Ionic, and Corinthian—have nothing to do with support. They are just niceties pasted on for looks and because Greek things were in vogue at the time of construction. The Colosseum is a fitting symbol of Roman art—Roman practicality with a Greek facade.

On opening day at the Colosseum, Romans enjoyed the slaughter of 5,000 animals. About 1,200 years later, the Colosseum was appreciated only as a quarry offering free, precut stones to anyone who could carry them away. Today tourists respect the Colosseum as a monumental symbol of a monumental civilization.

Roman Busts

One art form in which the Romans actually surpassed the Greeks was in the making of portraits. The Greeks were concerned with sculpting or painting idealized human "10s" without distinguishing individual characteristics. But Roman ancestor worship and family solidarity required realistic portraits of the father and his ancestors. Also, when it became a law that the emperor was to be worshiped as a god, portraits of him were necessary.

Roman portraiture (especially the common "bust," a statue showing just the chest up, minus arms) reached a new level of naturalism.

Emperor Vespasian—A.D. 75

Of course, many portraits were idealized and prettied up despite their stern dignity, but many are startling portraits of downright ugly people. We have a living history in the busts of the famous emperors: they come alive as people, not just faceless names from the past. Go to a museum in Rome and look Nero in the eye.

When Rome faded as a political empire, much of her art lay dormant, ignored until the renaissance (rebirth) of classical ideals a thousand years later.

The Fall of Rome

The third century is known as the "Age of Iron and Rust," a period of socioeconomic breakdown and the beginning of Rome's end. Taxation rose to oppressive levels, cities shrank and became disorderly, prices increased 1,000 percent over twenty years, and barbarians were closing in on the borders. Like most ancient civilizations, Rome had a false economy based on slavery and booty. When Rome stopped expanding, the flow of booty and slaves that had fueled the empire for so long dried up. The army was no longer a provider; it was an expensive problem. Politically, the government was more like a banana republic than a great empire. During one fifty-year period, eighteen Roman emperors were assassinated.

A Roman Emperor during the Fall—A.D. 250
As Rome began to fall, so did its art. This relatively crude work shows a boy emperor nervously awaiting assassination.

Rome's tumble was a gradual process delayed by two strong rulers. Diocletian, recognizing that the empire was overextended, split it into an eastern half and a western half. Later, Constantine (A.D. 285-340) moved the capital eastward to present-day Istanbul, which he named Constantinople—in his honor. He ruled the eastern half, while Rome was left holding the crumbling West.

In a further attempt to save the falling Roman Empire, Constantine made Christianity not only legal but also the official religion of Rome. We often forget that for its last 150 years Rome was officially Christian. People debate whether Constantine sanctioned the religion in a pragmatic move to gain the support of a growing, prosperous, and potentially law-abiding minority or whether he really had, as he claims, a Christian vision that helped him win a battle. (The huge Arch of Constantine next to the Colosseum marks his victory.) His mother was a devout Christian, famous within the church for her search for the actual cross of Jesus. Whatever the reason for Constantine's big switch, the fact is that in the year A.D. 300 you could have been killed for being a Christian, and in A.D. 400, after a later emperor made Christianity the only legal religion, you could have been killed for not being a Christian. As you travel today, you'll see plenty of early Christian art. The good shepherd (a guy carrying a lamb on his shoulders) as well as fish are common symbols. The Vatican museum has a huge collection of such art.

But Rome's downfall was inevitable. In 476 the last emperor pulled the plug, and the Roman Empire's long terminal illness was over.

Rome's ghost lived on, however. Her urban nobility fled from the cities, establishing themselves as the landed lords of medieval Europe's feudal countryside. Latin, the Roman language, was the language of the educated and ruling classes throughout the Middle Ages. And the Roman Catholic church inherited the empire's administrative finesse and has been ruled by a "pontifex maximus" ever since.

Ancient Cultures Exhibits and Museums:

National Museum of Archaeology, Athens
The Vatican Museum, the Vatican (Rome)
National Museum, Rome
The Louvre's "Oriental Antiquities" Wing, Paris
British Museum, London
Kunsthistorisches, Vienna
Dahlem Museum, Berlin
Ny Carlsberg Glyptothek, Copenhagen
Pergamon Museum, Berlin

Roman Art and Architecture in Italy:

Colosseum, Forum, and Circus Maximus, Rome
Pantheon, Rome
Ostia Antica, Rome's ancient seaport
Pompeii and Herculaneum, south of Naples
Hadrian's Villa, Tivoli, Italy
Theater and Arena, Verona

Tombs and mummies preserved corpses and possessions for the afterlife. Stiff, unrealistic, standing-at-attention statues and paintings. (Statues and mummies in British Museum and Vatican Museum.)

Top Roman Sights outside of Italy:

Pont du Gard, near Avignon, South France
Colosseum, theater, arena, etc., Nimes and Arles, France
Aqueduct, Segovia
Aquae Sulis spa and museum, Bath, England
Hadrian's Wall, England
Theater and arch, Orange, South France
Porta Nigra, Trier
Ephesus, Turkey
Diocletian's Palace, Split, Yugoslavia

Top Museums of Ancient Rome:

Vatican Museum, Rome
National Museum, Rome
Capitoline Museum, Rome
E.U.R. museum, Rome (great model of ancient Rome)
Louvre, Paris
Römisch-Germanisches Museum, Köln, Germany

Time Line of the Ancient World

You've just absorbed 3,500 years of history and art. That wasn't so bad, was it? Now, before you shake the dust of the Ancient World off and plunge into the Dark Ages, take a look at the following chronological review.

You can look at the march of history two ways—horizontally and vertically. Before you lie down, let us explain. The time line shows civilizations moving horizontally (left to right) as they travel through time. But it also shows vertical history—related events that occur at the same approximate date. Look both ways (one way at a time, of course) to see how civilizations and artistic trends interact and relate.

Horizontally, we can see how each of the ancient cultures influenced the following one. The early Mesopotamian cities came first, followed by the stable agricultural civilization of Egypt. The Minoans from Crete catapulted the early Greek culture, influencing the mainland Mycenaeans who slowly progressed—economically and politically—into the Golden Age of Greek culture. Alexander the Great spread this culture by conquest throughout the Hellenistic world, where it was later adopted by the growing Roman Empire. The sacking of Rome marks the end of the ancient world.

Notice that while culture moved progressively westward from Mesopotamia to Rome, Central and Northern Europe remained populated by barbarian tribes wallowing in the Stone Age.

Looking at vertical history, we see that political events (the upper half of the time line) intertwine with art and architecture trends (lower half). For example, look up and down the chart around the year 500 B.C. and see how the Greek era of productive colonization and the successful war against Persia (in the upper half) financed the building of the acropolis and the Golden Age of art (lower half).

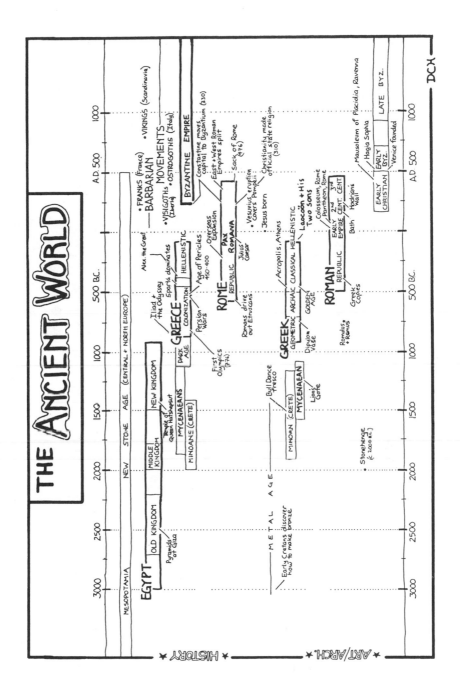

THE ANCIENT WORLD

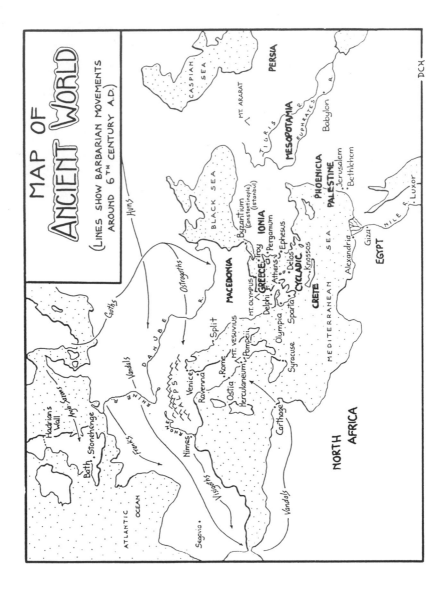

MAP OF ANCIENT WORLD

(LINES SHOW BARBARIAN MOVEMENTS AROUND 6TH CENTURY A.D.)

Temple of Neptune (Paestum, south of Naples)—450 B.C.
You don't need to go to Greece to see great Greek ruins. Five hundred years before
Christ, southern Italy was Magna Graecia, Greater Greece.

The Middle Ages
A.D. 500 – 1500

A thousand years separate the ancient and the modern worlds. This period, called the Middle Ages, lasted from about 500 to 1500. To keep things simple, let's call the first half of the Middle Ages the Dark Ages (from A.D. 500 to 1000) and the second half the High Middle Ages (from A.D. 1000 to 1500).

The castles and cathedrals that fill the average tourist's scrapbook are the great accomplishments of medieval Europe. To most travelers, these are very big and very old—period. But when you understand the religious fervor that built these cathedrals and the brutality that built the castles, they come alive. Let's spark the spirit of the old churches and fill the castles' armor with real people.

The Dark Ages (A.D. 500-1000)

By 500, Rome was gone and three realms filled the power vacuum: the Christian church, the Byzantine Empire, and the "barbarian" peoples of Northern Europe. Although they originally threatened Roman culture, each was ultimately instrumental in preserving it, helping to bridge the ancient and modern worlds.

The Church

Two of these realms, the church and the Byzantine Empire, are actually extensions of the old Roman Empire, dating from the reign of the great Emperor Constantine (A.D. 300). In trying to revive his fading empire, Constantine recognized the rights of the Christian church, a body that had grown, despite persecution, into one of the stabilizing institutions of the empire. Later, Christianity became Rome's official state religion.

The church bridged the ancient and modern worlds by carrying Rome's classical learning and administration through the Middle

Ages, passing it along to the rising secular world during the Renaissance. The church organized itself according to Roman hierarchies. Roman governors became Christian bishops, senators became cardinals, scholars became priests, and the pope even adopted the supreme title originally held by the emperor—Pontifex Maximus. This Roman administration lived on long after the final collapse of Imperial Rome.

The Dark Ages, 500-1000

Monasteries preserved classical literature and the Latin language in Dark Age Europe. When Benedict set up what later became the most influential monastic order of the Middle Ages, he scheduled a daily program of monk duties, combining manual labor with intellectual tasks such as translating and copying ancient texts, including works that were purely secular and even heretical.

Until the popes got the church organized into a central system (around A.D. 1000), the loose chain of monasteries was the "center" of Christianity. Monks ran the mail system, carrying ecclesiastical business from kingdom to barony.

Monks were also the keepers of technological knowledge about clocks, water wheels, accounting, wine-making, foundries, gristmills, textiles, and agricultural techniques. The later Cistercian monasteries were leaders of the medieval industrial revolution of the later Middle Ages.

The church preserved some of Rome's sheer grandness. Its great wealth, amassed from tithes and vast landholdings, was invested into huge church buildings, decorated as ornately as anything Rome had

Intellectual life survived the Dark Ages in monasteries. Copying and translating Greek and Roman writings were common tasks for monks.

The Romanesque-style Monastery at Cluny, France (artist's reconstruction). This was the largest church in medieval Europe at a time when monasteries were also great political and economic centers. Now it is mostly in ruins.

ever seen. The pomp and pageantry of the church rituals you might see in your travels is reminiscent of the glorious days of Caesar. For a taste of Caesar's Rome, visit the lavish Christian basilicas of Rome (such as Santa Maria Maggiore). As you stand in the shade of the huge ruined arches of the Basilica Maxentius in the Roman Forum, remember that houses of justice such as this one served as the architectural model for almost all Christian churches for the next two millennia.

The Byzantine Empire

The eastern Roman Empire, often called the Byzantine Empire, was the other great preserver of Roman culture. In a second desperate attempt to invigorate his failing empire, Constantine, in around A.D. 330, moved his capital from Rome to the new city of Constantinople (modern-day Istanbul). In a sense, this was the real end of Rome. The center of the civilized West packed up and moved eastward, where it remained for a thousand years while Europe struggled to establish itself. The emperor and his court, scholars, and artists all moved to the East, leaving the self-proclaimed emperors in Rome with no real power outside Italy.

Byzantine Mosaic (Ravenna)—A.D. 550
The art that remains of this era is generally mosaic—made from patterns of small stones and glass. Mosaics, popular in ancient Rome, survived in Rome's sister city, Constantinople. Ravenna and Venice have many mosaics and architectural treasures from the Byzantine glory days.

We think of the Eastern Empire as Byzantine rather than Roman because it quickly took on an Eastern flavor. Its language, literature, and art were Greek. The church followed "Eastern Orthodox" ways, eventually splitting with the pope's Latin church.

Nevertheless, the Byzantine Empire had a great influence on the West. Throughout the Middle Ages, the emperor in Constantinople was considered by Christians and barbarians all over Europe to be the civilized world's supreme ruler. Constantinople was the world's leading city for centuries. It provided a model of the unified and glorious Europe that so many kings and popes had dreamed of.

St. Mark's Basilica in Venice is covered with intricate Byzantine-style mosaics. Imagine paving a football field with contact lenses.

When the Crusades put the East and West in contact, the long forgotten classical Roman and Greek knowledge returned to Europe. After Constantinople was finally overrun by the Turks, scholars and artists fled to the West, where their knowledge added to the growing spirit of the Renaissance.

Constantinople, today's Istanbul, is an exciting brew of ancient past and cosmopolitan present, Moslem East and Christian West.

Byzantine Sights:

Many churches and mosaics, Ravenna, Italy
St. Mark's, Venice
Hagia Sophia and much more, Istanbul
Mystra; near Sparta on the Peloponnesian Peninsula, Greece
Meteora pinnacle monasteries, Greece
Charlemagne's Chapel, Aachen, Germany
Sacré-Coeur, neo-"Byzantine"-style church, Paris
Mt. Athos monasteries (for men only), Greece
Many churches in Athens

Barbarian Europe

The third realm of the Dark Ages was a scattered and chaotic compost pile of barbarian tribes from which modern Europe was to sprout. There was no effective government and no sense of state, just small autonomous tribes and peasant communities. Local life was isolated, fragmented, dreary, illiterate, superstitious, and self-sufficient at best. Thoughts of a pie-in-the-sky afterlife concerned people more than secular growth. Money, trade, and progress had little to do with the "Dark" Ages (as we, with such an opposite outlook, have termed those times).

Quietly, the seeds of modern Europe were planted. There was no nation of "France" or "England," but there were barbarian tribes of Franks and Angles. The Dark Ages saw the emergence of local nations no longer dominated by Roman culture. The Franks were becoming France, and "Angle-land" was to become England.

Life in the Dark Ages

The Fall of Rome was like a great stone column falling across the Continent, burying Europe and scattering civilization like so much dust. It was 500 years before dazed Europeans began to pick themselves up from the rubble and build a new world. In the meantime, they lived lives of hardship, fear, and ignorance.

During the Dark Ages, as the philosopher Hobbes described it, life was "nasty, brutish and short" (and so was Hobbes). Skeletons unearthed by archaeologists show a people chronically undernourished due in part to ineffective farming techniques. Infant and child mortality rates soared. Wise elders of a village might have been only in their thirties.

Whatever civilization the Romans had brought to the "barbarians" of Northern Europe died. Roads and cities, pillaged as quarries by local peasants, crumbled. There were few large towns and little trade; the economy was based on subsistence farming clustered around small villages. A bad harvest was a sentence for famine and death to a community isolated from outside help.

The Roman communication grapevine withered as fewer and fewer people learned to read and write. Priests and monks alone were literate or capable of simple arithmetic at a time when letters and numbers were believed by the unlearned to have magical powers. (Our modern word "clerk"—someone who works with words or numbers —comes from "cleric.")

Feudalism

Dark Age Europe had no central governing authority: "king" was more an honorary title than a position of power. Government was in the hands of local nobles, barons, dukes, knights, and petty lords.

The people of medieval Europe developed a strict social and economic system called "feudalism" in an attempt to give their chaotic world some order and security. Feudalism carefully defined the duties of each class—like chessmen, who can move only a certain way—with each class dependent on the other for its livelihood. The peasants pledged part of their crop to a local noble who in turn gave them land to work and the promise of protection and a system of justice. This noble was in the service of a more powerful noble, and so on up to the king—the theoretical pinnacle of the feudal hierarchy.

The currency of feudalism was loyalty and land. A lower nobleman (vassal) promised loyalty (fealty) to a higher-up (lord) in return

Feudal terms:

fealty = loyalty

fief = land, in return for fealty

lord = man above on feudal ladder

vassal = man below on feudal ladder

king = top rung of feudal ladder

serfs = near slaves who worked the land of the lowest lord. This was **manoralism**. The manor house was the lord's palace.

knight = moves up two and over one. Worth about as much as a bishop.

for use of some land (a fief). One man's vassal was another man's lord. A strict code of honor cemented this two-way deal.

The feudal nobility played war for kicks. On sunny afternoons the knights suited up, trampled their peasants' crops, and raided the neighboring nobles' domains in an attempt to kidnap the lord. Most of medieval Europe toiled to survive while sons of the rich spent their leisure hours playing chivalrous games. The perennial pawns in this feudal chess game were, of course, the peasants.

Nobles hardly lived lives of luxury, though. Their castles were crude structures—cold, damp, and dark, with little privacy or warmth. Nobles were illiterate—and proud of it. They looked down on educated people. The younger sons and daughters of nobles (who received no inheritance) were forced to become clergy. The rest lived lives that revolved around war, training for war, hunting, and feasting. Their feasts often became week-long bouts of drinking and rowdiness. Medieval life was "regulated by a calendar of feasts which governed the relations between the living and the dead, old and young, men and women—blending technology, magic, work, religion, work-days and feast days into a satisfying whole" (Friedrich Heer, *The Medieval World).*

The Dark Age Peasant Supporting His Lord
A few people lived high on the medieval hog, but the vast majority of Europeans were serfs—bound to the land, barely subsisting, illiterate, superstitious, and waiting for a glorious life after death.

As if economic hardships weren't enough, the people of the Dark Ages had other things to fear. The "barbarian" invasions from Scandinavia (the Vikings), Hungary (Magyars), Central Asia (Huns), and Spain (Moslems) threatened Europe from all sides. The Dark Ages were a time of migration of tribes fleeing from danger and resettling in more hospitable lands. It wasn't until centuries later that the invaders were defeated or absorbed and Europeans stopped finishing off their prayers with "and deliver us from the Norsemen, amen."

They also had to contend with demons, devils, spirits of the woods and rocks, mischievous saints, and a jealous god. Magic and local folklore intertwined with Christianity. Witches were burned. A sword could be put on trial for falling off the wall as if a spirit had inhabited it. The hideous gargoyles that adorn Romanesque churches are pictures straight out of the imagination of these superstitious and frightened people.

Justice was meted out in "trials by ordeal." The accused might have been forced to grab a red-hot iron or to pull a stone from a caldron of boiling water. If he was unharmed or the wound healed miraculously in a few days, he was innocent. If not, he was really punished. A woman accused of being a witch might have been bound and thrown into a lake. If she drowned, she was believed to be inno-

Trial by Ordeal

The ancient "Trial by Ordeal" survived well into the Middle Ages. Here, two bishops lead a queen barefoot over a red-hot grate to determine whether she has been true to her husband (left). Notice the hand of God "overseeing" things.

cent. If she floated, she was believed to be guilty and burnt accordingly. These ordeals were usually held in or near the church, with a priest in attendance.

Look at a ninth-century "history book" and you can see the mix of magic, fear, fantasy, harshness, and ignorance of the Dark Ages. The years are boiled down to a few terrible and miraculous events, all told matter-of-factly. Some excerpts:

"Account of the year A.D. 837: A gigantic whirlwind broke out and a comet appeared, emitting streams of light three cubits long before the amazed spectators. The pagans devastated Walicrum and abducted many women there, taking also huge sums of money.

"The year 852: The steel of the pagans grew white hot: an excessive heat of the sun: famine followed: there was no fodder for the beasts, but the feeding of pigs flourished.

"The year 853: Great hunger in Saxony with the result that many ate horses.

"The year 857: A great plague with swelling of the bladder raged among the people and destroyed them with horrible festering, so that their limbs dropped off and fell away before death."

The church was the refuge from this awful and fearful world. God was a god of power, like an earthly noble, to fight the forces of evil. God's weapons were prayer, the Mass, and other rituals, which, in the minds of the peasants, had magical power. Romanesque churches stood like strong castles in the war against Satan. To the peasant, the

church was a refuge from his dreary life and a hint of the glories that awaited him in heaven. If anywhere religion was "the opiate of the masses," it was in medieval Europe.

The church dominated every aspect of medieval life. A sin was a crime and vice versa. The religious authorities were the civil authorities. Tithes were taxes. God brought prosperity and He brought plagues. The Bible was the final word on all matters—scientific, economic, social, and political.

The popular religion didn't change much with the coming of Christianity; it simply labeled old folk gods with new names. Christian churches were built on holy pagan sites. The "good spirits" of folklore became the "saints" of the church, powers to be bargained with for earthly favors. The church calendar, which established holy days (hence the word "holiday"), patterned itself after old pagan feast days. Even today, we celebrate Christmas much as the Druids of Britain celebrated the winter solstice, with trees and mistletoe.

We usually assume Europe was Christian from the time of the Roman Emperor Constantine, but that's not the case. The Christian faith was slow to penetrate the northern countries, and total conversion was interrupted by the Viking and Hungarian invasions in the eighth and ninth centuries. Not until 1000 could Europe be considered thoroughly Christian.

Viking Sights:

National Museum, Copenhagen, Denmark
Jorvik Exhibit, York, England
Ships at Bygdoy, Oslo, Norway
Ships at Roskilde, Denmark
Lindholm Hoje, Aalborg, Denmark

Candles in the Wind—Dark Age Bright Spots

The flickering flame of civilization was kept alive through the Dark Ages by a few brave individuals. They preserved the learning of the classical world for a later era, when economic prosperity allowed it to blaze again in society at large.

Of course, the whole world wasn't in a Dark Age. In Central America, the Mayans and Toltecs were building great cities and doing complex astronomical work. In China, the T'ang dynasty was flourishing. Many of the technological inventions that spurred

Burg Eltz, on Germany's Mosel River

Europe's recovery from the Dark Ages came from China—paper, clockwork, looms, spinning wheels, and gunpowder.

On the fringes of Europe, other cultures kept Greco-Roman learning alive. We've seen how the Byzantine Empire lasted until early Renaissance times and was always a stronghold of culture during Europe's Dark Ages.

The Islamic countries, from the Middle East to North Africa to Spain, fostered science and literature while Europe was still groping for the light switch. In Baghdad (modern Iraq), the Abbasid dynasty of caliphs created an enlightened court for poets, astronomers, mathematicians, and Greek scholars. This court, from around A.D. 800, the era of Charlemagne, is immortalized in *Thousand and One Arabian Nights*.

Even within Europe, not all areas were in complete darkness. Italy, closest to the source of Roman influence, kept in touch with the classical world even after its fall to the barbarians. It was always linked by trade with the enlightened Byzantine world. Italy was even united briefly with the Eastern Empire under the Emperor Justinian (A.D. 550). The churches of Ravenna from this period are as magnificent as anything in Istanbul.

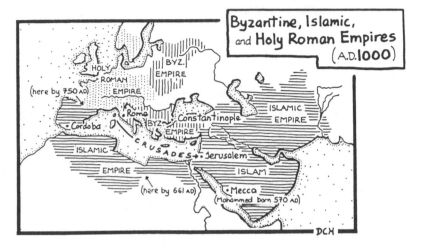

Byzantine, Islamic, and Holy Roman Empires (A.D. 1000)

Spain and the Moors (711-1492)

When most of Spain and Portugal fell to the Moors, Moslem invaders from North Africa, the region's importance as an intellectual center increased. Islam was a strict religion, but its record on tolerating other religions was better than that of medieval Christianity. In Spain, both Christians and Jews were allowed freedom and relative equality (for a fee). The interaction among the three cultures sparked inquiry and debate and produced some of the Middle Ages' finest scholars.

In 950, the library at Cordoba, Spain, held some 600,000 manuscripts (in the same year there were only 5,000 manuscripts in all of France). As Christians gradually reconquered Iberia, they opened Arab libraries throughout Spain. This wealth of knowledge from ancient Greece and Rome was translated into Latin and made available to Europe during the later Middle Ages.

All over Spain and Portugal, but especially in Cordoba and Granada (the last Moslem stronghold), you'll see impressive buildings that remind us of the Moors' leading medieval civilization.

Ireland

Fleeing the barbarian chaos of Continental Europe as Rome fell, missionary monks carried civilization to the western fringe of the known world. Ireland was the northern intellectual capital. When St. Patrick (c. 400s), a Christian monk from Romanized England, established his faith in Ireland, he found many excellent schools run by the native Celtic tribes that taught classical subjects. Patrick's successors kept these schools open, mixing Christianity into the curriculum. Latin learning was reinfused into England and the Continent (as far inward as Switzerland) by Irish missionaries. Be sure to visit Cashel, near Tipperary, which was an impressive ecclesiastical center of Ireland during this period.

Page from *Book of Kells* (Trinity College, Dublin)
The "illuminated manuscript" was Dark Age Europe's greatest pictorial art form. (See the *Book of Kells* at the British Museum, also.)

The *Book of Kells* (Trinity College, Dublin) and the *Lindisfarne Gospels* (British Museum) are the best examples of this Irish flowering from A.D. 500-900. Both are illuminated (illustrated) gospels showing classical, Celtic, and even Byzantine influences.

Charlemagne—The Mini-Renaissance of A.D. 800

Throughout this period, popes and kings were trying to restore Europe to the glorious days of a unified Roman empire. One light in the Dark Ages was the reign of Charlemagne (SHAR-luh-mayn)— "Charles the Great," King of the Franks. He united most of the Western Christian world, from Germany to Sicily, and established what we call the Carolingian Empire, the largest since Rome. He worked closely with the pope, both leaders realizing that cooperation was essential to wielding power effectively. To underline this alliance, establish himself as the protector of Christendom, and remind Europe that the greatness of classical Rome could once again be hers, Charlemagne was crowned emperor by the pope in Rome on

Christmas, A.D. 800. Drowsy Europe quivered and drooled with excitement at this mini-Renaissance, or "Roman revival."

Charlemagne's capital city of Aix-la-Chapelle (present-day Aachen, Germany—well worth a visit) became the first capital of "Europe." Trade and communication increased, and the court became a cultural center where artists and scholars worked to revive Roman ideals. Academia flourished, and classical works were studied and copied. It's said that Charlemagne could read a little (a rarity at the time) and went to bed each night with a slate to practice his writing.

Charlemagne personally set about to improve the lot of his people. He instituted trial by judge, replacing the barbaric "ordeal"; he revised the monetary system, built schools and churches, and advanced the Christian faith. Perhaps most important, his foot became the standard form of measurement—the "foot"—or so goes the legend.

Charlemagne was the top-dog ruler, but the Franks who succeeded him were wieners. When he died, the empire was divided among his three sons into realms that became Germany, France, and the smaller countries. His successors returned to their quarreling ways, and as they bickered, the light flickered out.

Later kings in Germany and Austria claimed to rule a revived "Holy Roman Empire" like Charlemagne's, but their kingdoms—as Voltaire pointed out—were neither holy, nor Roman, nor an empire. It was to be a long time before Europe enjoyed rule under another leader of Charlemagne's stature and shoe size.

The reign of Charlemagne was a turning point in the early Middle Ages. Before his time, it seemed that darkness might dominate forever. Afterward, hope in the restoration of learning and civilization was restored.

Despite the "Carolingian Renaissance," these were still the Dark Ages. Charlemagne was an enlightened but ruthless leader. He was responsible for the conversion of the pagan German tribes to Christianity. His chosen instrument of persuasion was the same used by later Crusaders—the sword. He invaded Germany, conquered it tribe by tribe, and gave the leaders a choice—convert or die. Apparently it was not an easy choice, as many chose martyrdom and guerrilla resistance. Charlemagne responded by chopping down the sacred tree trunk said by pagan myth to support the world. (The pagan world didn't tumble with it, however.) The Franks built "churches" that were really military outposts in the conquered lands. Resistance died hard, and the resisters died even harder; it's said that Charlemagne once ordered the decapitation of 4,500 pagans in one day.

The High Middle Ages (A.D. 1000-1500)

At the turn of the first millennium, A.D. 1000, Europe began waking up. It made some basic economic, political, and ideological changes that culminated a few centuries later in the Renaissance. For the previous five hundred years, progress could have been graphed as a straight, horizontal line. Now that line soared upward, carrying Europe into the modern age.

Barbarian invasions were no longer a great threat, and people settled down. Feeling secure, Europeans built and planned for the future. Natural power sources were harnessed by the windmill and water wheel. Agricultural advances such as improved plows and harnesses and crop rotation increased productivity. Fewer farmers were needed to feed the society. Towns grew up, offering the newly upwardly mobile peasant (a "numppie"?) an exciting alternative to life under his feudal master. Urbanization increased trade and improved communication. Europeans were no longer hopelessly isolated in a dark feudal struggle for subsistence. Europe perked up, experiencing the same enthusiasm that marked the United States' westward movement. Land was cleared and roads and bridges were built as Europe flexed its muscles.

Romanesque Art (A.D. 1000-1200)

Churches, churches! Most tourists reach the saturation point after a few weeks on the road. Any small town's biggest, most central building is its church. After a while they all begin to look alike, but they aren't. If you can recognize the distinguishing features of Europe's churches, they become more than just handy places to take shelter from the rain.

It's hard to overestimate the importance of the church in medieval life. Typically the only stone structure in town and a landmark for miles around, the church was the political, religious, and even the recreational center of the town. The lavish churches, surrounded by bleak hovels, offered the medieval peasant a glorious promise—and a pleasant escape from the almost endless drudgery of feudal life.

The art and architecture of this period reflect Europe's desire for stability and security in a chaotic and warring world. The churches were powerful and defiant beacons of religious truth in a largely heathen Europe—outposts in the territory of darkness.

The Romanesque style is the first real "European" art form. It is "Roman"-esque because it employs Roman features, columns and rounded arches, which create an overall effect of massiveness and

Basilica Aemilia (Roman Forum)—179 B.C.
The floor plan of these pre-Christian law courts became the model for churches throughout the Middle Ages. Notice the central nave (where the tourists are walking) flanked by narrower side aisles.

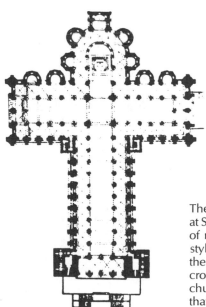

The floor plan of the pilgrimage Cathedral at Santiago de Compostela (Spain) is typical of many European churches—a basilica-style main hall with transepts added to give the rectangular basilica the shape of a Latin cross. Note: a "cathedral" is not a type of church architecture. It's simply a church that's a governing center for a local bishop.

strength. These buildings, mostly churches, are like dark fortresses with thick walls, towers, big blocks of stone, few windows, dark interiors, and a minimum of decoration. Slowly, the massive "tunnel" vaults lightened up into the graceful ribbed vaults of the Gothic style.

The grand "basilica" pattern of the Romanesque church is rooted in ancient Rome. The pagan temples of Rome were designed to house only the image of the god, not crowds of worshipers. But the main ritual of Christianity was the Eucharist, a large group "meal" represented by sharing a little bread and wine. This required a large meeting hall.

So when Christianity became Rome's adopted religion, new churches were modeled not after her temples but after the largest Roman secular structures: Roman law courts, or basilicas. The same basilica floor plan that you'll see in the Roman Forum (Basilica Aemilia) was used in nearly every medieval church.

A basilica has a long central hall (nave) with narrower halls on either side and, at the far end, a semicircular area (apse) for the altar. An aisle that forms a cross with the main hall, called a transept, was often added so that the building looked more Christian, but the basic pre-Christian basilica plan remained.

This floor plan was ideal for accommodating large congregations, especially the massive processions of pilgrims who came to worship Christian relics (such as a piece of Jesus' cross or the body of a saint). Pilgrims would walk up one side aisle, around the altar, and out the other aisle, worshiping at each chapel along the way. Columns separated the walkways (ambulatories) from the long central nave where the congregation stood (sitting in church hadn't been invented yet).

Romanesque Architecture (Towns or Churches):

Durham Cathedral, England
Aix-la-Chapelle (Charlemagne's church and relics), Aachen, Germany
Bayeux Tapestry, Bayeux, France
Vezelay Cathedral, France
Santiago de Compostela, Spain
Cathedral of Pisa (Leaning Tower and Baptistry), Italy
Worms and Speyer cathedrals, Germany
Basilique St.-Sernin and Augustins Museum, Toulouse, France
Carcassonne, southern France
Sarlat town, southern France
Dom (cathedral), Trier, Germany

Medieval churches always faced eastward. The portal (entry) is therefore the "west portal," the transepts point north and south, and the altar is at the east end. Memorizing the terms used in the last few paragraphs will make you an informed medieval churchgoer.

Santiago de Compostela—
Europe's First "Tourist Attraction"
This Romanesque church in northwestern Spain houses the body of St. James and was a very popular pilgrimage site. Europe's first "tourist guidebook" was written to direct medieval pilgrims during their long journey to Compostela. Today, it's just as majestic as ever but visited by very few tourists.

Religious Art

Although the floor plan of churches was essentially Roman, the Romanesque decorations were strictly Christian. Through most of the Middle Ages, sculpture and painting were used only to embellish architecture, and art was the church's servant. Not until the Renaissance were painting and sculpture created for art's sake.

Theologians wondered, "What is art's place in the church?" The Bible stated explicitly that no "graven images" should be made for worshiping. Did that include paintings? Craftings of nature? Illustrated Bible stories? The debate lasted for centuries. By A.D. 600, it was generally agreed that art had great value in worship as a way of educating and inspiring the masses of illiterate Christians. Remember, most Middle Age Europeans couldn't read, write, or speak Latin, the language used in church services. They went to church to "read" the stories of their religion as told in sculpture, stained glass, and tapestries.

Romanesque Church (Vezelay, France)
Vezelay, halfway between Paris and Switzerland, is the textbook example of Romanesque architecture. First, look through the doors and notice the round ("Roman"-esque) arches in the nave (central hallway). In the tympanum, the semi-circular area above the door, you'll typically find a Romanesque church's most interesting sculpture. Notice how cluttered these narrative reliefs look—a far cry from the bold, freestanding statues of ancient Rome and the coming Renaissance.

Pope Gregory the Great said, "Painting can do for the illiterate what writing does for those who can read." So we modern tourists, also "illiterate" with regard to Europe's languages, can still see the religious stories told in church art.

The images carved into the walls and doors of churches were every bit as effective as the priest's sermon. Typically, devout peasants could look at scenes of lost souls, naked and chained, being dragged off to Hell. On Jesus' right would be the blessed—faces looking to heaven, hands obediently folded, comfortable with their opiate: a promise of a happy afterlife if they shut up and obeyed. Escapist theology was as attractive to feudal peasants in medieval Europe as it is to twentieth-century peasants in Central America.

Sometimes you have to look close to see these sermons in stone built right into the church. Architecture, the designing of God's house, was the most respected medieval art form. Painting, sculpture, stained glass, tapestries, and so on, were okay because they embellished the house of God. Statues were tucked into niches carved in the church wall. Stories were told in "low-relief," protruding only slightly from the wall or surrounding material (as opposed to "freestanding" statues).

A church's most interesting and creative sculpture is often found in the tympanum (the arched area above the door) or hiding in the capitals of the columns along the nave. Sculptors were allowed a little craziness here, and it's fun to see their grotesque fantasies peeking through the capital's leaves or the weird gargoyles and their buddies filling nooks and sticking out of crannies.

Gargoyles and Their Buddies
The medieval superstitions of Europe sneaked into Romanesque and Gothic churches on rooftops and in inconspicuous corners. These gave the anonymous medieval sculptors a chance to have some fun.

Because medieval art is mostly Christian art, realism and classical beauty took a back seat to getting the message across. Artists concentrated on inspiring and uplifting the peasants by boiling their subjects down to the essential details—just what was necessary to get the point of the story across. They often ignored nature and painted the commonly accepted stereotype of what they thought something should look like. Pictures became symbols that stood for ideas and actions rather than representations of real things. A lion was meant to be a symbol of the resurrection, not a lesson in zoology.

Classical techniques that made art realistic were forgotten. Medieval art was stiff, unreal, and two-dimensional. Figures looked as if they'd been cut out of paper and pasted into random groups. Background, shading, depth, and proportion didn't matter. Scenes were often overcrowded.

But remember, art doesn't have to be realistic or "original" to be good. It would be easy to write medieval art off as lousy art, but we must always consider art in the context of its period and its function.

The Bayeux Tapestry
Actually embroidery, this 900-year-old narration of the important Battle of Hastings (when the Normans of France invaded and began their conquest of England) is just about the best example you'll see of Romanesque "painting." Here, realism takes a back seat to narration. Bayeux, a pleasant town, is only two hours by train from Paris.

This art had narrative and religiously symbolic purposes. The artist wanted to teach and inspire the viewer. Being "freed" from the constraints of realism enabled the medieval artist to experiment with new (and often bizarre) color schemes, compositions, and proportions, sometimes exaggerating them to enhance the spiritual effect.

The final product, although far from "classical," is impressive, inspirational, and beautiful on its own terms.

Medieval art, like Chinese, Byzantine, and Egyptian art but unlike our culture's art, had no need to be original. A donor would commission an artist to create a replica of an existing piece of art, possibly with finer materials but with no demand for particular originality. The artist would have no problems with copying someone else's work. It's like our notion of music. For your wedding you hire an organist and a singer not to come up with new music but to redo nicely something you already know you like.

While most medieval art was religious, there was plenty of secular castle art. Unfortunately, little survives. While churches and church art were respected, protected, and saved, secular stuff was destroyed or simply tossed out like an old poster.

Crusades (1100-1250)

This new progressive spirit showed itself in the aggressive "holiness" called the Crusades, a subject you will see and hear plenty about in your sightseeing.

The Crusades were a series of military expeditions promoted by various popes and kings to protect the holy city of Jerusalem from Moslem invaders. Although they began as religious missions, nearly anyone could find a self-serving reason to join these holy wars of prophets and profits.

The East enjoyed luxuries dreamed about by many Europeans. The Crusades opened new and lucrative trade routes to the Orient. Supply routes set up for the wars remained afterward as purely economic and cultural links between Northern Europe and Italy and between Italy and Byzantium. The nobles enjoyed this opportunity to conquer new land for fiefs, while their knights sought adventure, glory, and spoils in the Crusades. The pope's prestige and authority

Richard the Lionhearted and Saladin, two of the greatest medieval knights, are shown jousting in this medieval illustration. Richard was a renowned Crusader.

seemed to soar with each Moslem killed, and Christians chased salvation by converting "heathens" and protecting Jerusalem.

Although the Crusades finally failed with the Moslem capture of Jerusalem (and, later, Constantinople), they did have a great effect on Europe, giving it a broader, more cosmopolitan outlook. They opened a floodgate of new ideas from the East and brought back many classical ideas that the West had lost during the Dark Ages. The Crusaders also learned important stone-working skills that helped Europeans build the great castles and churches of the Middle Ages. And the majestic flavor of sacred Byzantine art showed up very clearly in Western art.

Venice emerged from the Crusades the big winner. Europe's appetite had been whetted by the East's luxury goods, and sea-trading Venice established itself as the dominant intermediary. The Venetians prospered, expanding to control the entire Adriatic area politically and to become Europe's economic powerhouse until new trade routes to the East were developed several hundred years later. Today Venice's past glory decays elegantly and her lavish architecture reflects her former lucrative position at the crossroads of East and West.

Knights, Ladies, Love, and War

King Arthur and the Knights of the Round Table—Lancelot, Galahad, Perceval, and the crew—are the ideal of medieval life, where men are always chivalrous and women are always kidnapped by dragons. How appropriate that this symbol of glorious chivalry is a myth: Arthur and the knights are pure fiction based on a minor historical figure. Nevertheless, the myth played a big role in medieval thinking.

Knights of the Middle Ages followed an unwritten code of honor—chivalry—that demanded valor in battle and service to their king, God, and ladylove. Originally intended for knights alone, it was quickly accepted by all nobility in Europe, whose lives revolved around war, religion, loyalty, and (sometimes) love.

Knights were warriors who pledged their fighting skills to some powerful lord in return for land, a title, or money. Knights on horseback were much more important than the average mercenary foot soldier. With the invention of stirrups, the rider could "dig in" and put force behind the lance he carried. A single knight could charge and break the ranks of dozens of foot soldiers. Dressed in a heavily armored suit (so heavy that, if he fell off, he was as helpless as a turtle on his back), a mounted knight was like a tank among infantry.

Later descendants carried the title of "knight" earned by their warrior forefathers even when they themselves took no part in war. The code of chivalry still applied to these gentlemen of high society. In fact, the word for "gentleman" in several languages (French, _chevalier_; Spanish, _caballero_; Italian, _cavaliere_), like the word _chivalry_ itself, comes from the Latin word for "horseman."

When there were no real wars in which they could demonstrate their courage and skill, knights held tournaments, fighting each other in teams or individually. The most common event, the joust, sent two knights charging at each other on horseback, each determined to unseat the other by using his lance. Sure enough, many knights died in these "sporting" contests. In later tournaments an attempt was made to try to minimize injury by using blunted or wooden weapons, saving the sport but diminishing the danger (like modern fencing). Still, as late as 1559, France lost a king (Henri II) when a wooden splinter pierced his visor during a joust.

Medieval pageantry and contests such as jousting are reenacted energetically in many of Europe's colorful festivals. Try to work a few of these festivals into your itinerary.

The heroic deeds of knighthood were proclaimed in story and song by troubadors, wandering poet-singer-storytellers of the Middle Ages. These men were not journalists by any means; they didn't tell of real men performing real deeds. Instead, they created an ideal world of loving knights and lovely ladies. Their stories set the pattern of behavior for medieval lords and ladies.

"Camelot"—Henry, Eleanor, and Courtly Love

The closest Europe ever came to a real "Camelot" was the court of King Henry II and Queen Eleanor of Aquitaine, rulers of England and France during the short-lived Angevin Empire (1150-1200). Henry was the perfect Arthur—strong and intelligent, with a dominating personality. Eleanor was the refined, strong-willed, and beautiful Guinevere—with a healthy dose of political savvy thrown in. Their son, Richard the Lionhearted, was, by contemporary accounts, all the Knights of the Round Table rolled into one.

Their court was Europe's center for troubadors and young knights, for days spent in jousting and nights under the stars listening to stories and songs.

It was here that a new element was added to the old warrior's code of chivalry—love. The knight of this period had to be not only valiant in war but gentle in love as well. The new code was known as "courtly love."

Love was a radical notion in a society where marriages were arranged by parents primarily for monetary and political gain. It was the brainchild of highly educated ladies of the court tired of being treated as bargaining chips in the marriage game. They insisted that both parties, the man and the woman, had to consent for a marriage to be valid.

Queen Eleanor had strong personal reasons for opposing arranged marriages with courtly love. She and Henry had become estranged when Henry took a mistress (no big deal) and insisted on being seen with her in public (big deal). She was also aware of the fate of a young kinswoman, Alais, who had been given to young Richard for a bride. Because Richard was away on Crusade, Henry thought nothing of taking Alais for his own, keeping her a prisoner for 25 years. At his death, she was freed—only to be married off to a lesser courtier.

Women were considered impure and dangerous to men, the descendants of the first woman, Eve, who had caused Adam to sin against God. As one twelfth-century poet put it, "If I had the eloquent tongue of Ovid, still I could not put into words how cunning an evil woman is, how treacherous, how shrewd, how destructive."

The new code of chivalry demanded that the knight serve his lady first; next in importance came service to God and king. In tournaments and battles, it was customary for the knight to wear a token of the lady, perhaps a kerchief or a flower.

The main theme of the troubadors' songs of love (_chansons d'amour_) was unconsummated love. The knight is head over heels for the lady, but, alas, she is married or somehow beyond his reach. Nevertheless, the knight accepts this hopeless situation, pining for his true love and doing all in his power to please her, while knowing she can never be his. The songs alternate between the ecstasy of love and the bitterness of longing.

In the court of Queen Eleanor, "rules" of love were drawn up to "educate" the young men about how they should act toward the lady. Knights had to give up their baser passions, thinking always of what would please their lady. Here are some of the court's "Twelve Rules of Love" (from a twelfth-century book, _The Art of Courtly Love_):

Marrying for money should be avoided like a deadly pestilence.
Thou shalt keep thyself chaste for the sake of thy beloved. [A radical idea for the time.]

In practicing the solaces of love thou shalt not exceed the desires of thy lover.

Thou shalt not be a revealer of love affairs.

Thou shalt be in all things polite and courteous.

Thou shalt be obedient in all things to the command of ladies, and strive in the service of Love.

Historical fact shatters any illusions that Henry and Eleanor created a real-life Camelot. But Chivalry lived on. The "Man of Steel and Velvet" was an ideal for gentlemen long after knighthood lost its warring function. The seventeenth-century English gentleman and the *gentilhomme* of France owed much to the medieval code. The duel replaced the tournament as a test of courage.

The last gasp of true romantic chivalry in literature was the tragicomic fictional figure of Don Quixote (written in 1610). Ridiculed by his contemporaries, he held fast to the old ideals, jousting with windmills when there were no other true knights left to fight.

Castle Life

"Like a tortoise fighting a stone"—that was medieval warfare when impregnable castles dotted Europe's landscape. War was a drawn-out, costly struggle as one side laid siege to the other. The only good thing

to be said was that casualties were few and far between. Boredom was the common enemy of attacker and attacked.

The medieval castle was a simple stone structure consisting of a central "keep," or main building, surrounded by a wall. The keep was usually built on a hill, cliff, or mound of earth. The wall enclosed the

The Siege
Medieval Castles Gave Defenders the Edge
Any decent castle was a real pain to attack. Some castles were simply avoided, written off as unconquerable. The "starve 'em out siege" approach was the most common. Some of these sieges lasted several years, until hunger or boredom won out. The advent of gunpowder ended the days when the best offense was a good castle.

castle yard where the people lived. This "motte (mound) and bailey (yard)" pattern was the basis of all medieval castles.

Later castles were much bigger, with more rings of walls as much as twenty feet thick (and more baileys). The Crusaders had been impressed by the massive castles and walled cities of the Byzantines and applied many of their techniques to the motte and bailey plan.

Outside the wall was the moat, a ditch filled with water (they only put alligators in them in fairy tales). The main gate was made of oak, plated with iron, and often protected by a portcullis, or iron grille. Above the gate were twin towers, often four stories high, with small windows for shooting at the enemy.

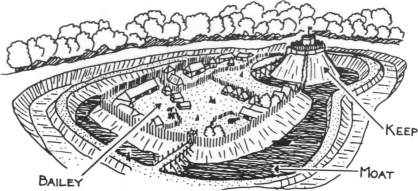

Motte and Bailey
Not attorneys at law but the basis for all medieval castles—a keep (motte) and yard (bailey) surrounded by a wall.

The keep was the headquarters and home of the lord, used as a dining hall, ballroom, and as a last bastion when the outer walls fell in an attack. Despite their impressive architecture, castles were cold, damp, and uncomfortable. A lord who commanded thousands had fewer creature comforts than a twentieth-century suburban dog.

The Siege, Military Patience

Against such a formidable structure, an attacker's main weapon was hunger. The enemy camped around the castle and waited—waited for supplies to run out. This often took years, and given the poor communication and supply lines of the period, the attacker might well run out of supplies first.

During a siege of Carcassonne (Europe's greatest walled fortress city) in southern France, the city ran desperately low on food and was about to surrender. The attackers, after waiting for years, were losing patience and about to give up too. In a stroke of genius, the queen of the city fed the last of the food to the last pig and threw the pig over the wall. When the invaders saw how well fed the pig was, they figured the people inside had plenty of food, so they packed up and headed home.

But the patience of military men wears thin, and later on, castles were stormed with a number of ingenious weapons. Catapults, powered by tension or counterweights, were used to fling huge boulders or red-hot irons over the walls. Under cover of archers armed with crossbows and 6-foot longbows, armies would approach the castle and fill the moat with dirt. Then they would wheel up the "storming towers," built of wood and covered with fire-resistant wet hides, and climb over the walls. They battered weak points in the wall and gate with a wood-and-iron battering ram. And as a last resort, they might have even tried tunneling beneath the walls.

The defenders poured boiling water and burning pitch onto the invaders. From the turrets, archers fired arrows and flung missiles. Others were stationed along the walls to overturn ladders and storming towers. Once the attackers got inside the castle, battle was fierce hand-to-hand combat. More likely, though, the defenders simply retreated behind the next inner wall to start the process over again.

So it went, and would go still, except that the sword outlasts the sheath and new weapons always overcome old defenses. When the Turks besieged Constantinople in 1453, they had a new weapon—a

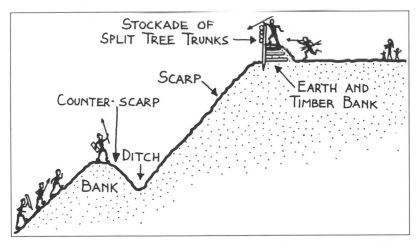

Early castles evolved from primitive ditch and stockade fortifications. Sites offering a natural fortification, like a hilltop surrounded by a river, were preferred. As ditches became moats and stockades became stone walls, castles took the form we think of today.

19-ton cannon that fired 1,500-pound rocks more than a mile in the air. The era of gunpowder had arrived, and the castle walls of Europe fell. Within a century, the siege style of warfare that had gone on almost unchanged for 2,000 years was a thing of the past.

Many of the castles you'll see in Europe today never had a military function. After 1500, lords built castle-forts for protection and castle-palaces for domestic life. In the romantic era of the 1800s, many castles, like those of Bavaria's Mad King Ludwig, had no practical purpose and were merely fantasy abodes.

Azay le Rideau (Loire Valley Chateau, France)

Top Medieval Castles:

Burg Eltz and Cochem Castle on the Mosel, Germany
Reifenstein Castle, Vipiteno, North Italy
Many along the Rhine (like Rheinfels and Marksburg, etc.) from
    Mainz to Koblenz
Tower of London
Chateau Chillon, Lake Geneva, Switzerland
Langeais, Loire Valley, France
Chinon, Loire Valley, France
Beynac, Dordogne, France
Warwick, England
Carcassonne, France

Birth of Nation-States

During the High Middle Ages, Europe began dumping feudalism in favor of larger political units. Cities didn't fit into the rural feudal mold. Merchants were natural allies of a national government, which offered political stability, uniform laws, coinage and measurements, freer trade, and independence from the whims of feudal lords.

An hour's cruise down the Rhine River, lined with castles (each a separate "kingdom" in its day), tells the story. In earlier times, a trading ship might have crossed thirty-five "national" boundaries and paid thirty-five customs duties just to take a load downstream. The urbanites welcomed a king who could keep the peace between the feuding feudal nobles, creating a larger political unit more conducive to efficient business and trade.

The time was coming for the emergence of national monarchs heading large states. England and France appeared in something like their modern form. When William the Bastard (of Normandy) crossed the English Channel in 1066 and became William the Conqueror, he set up a strong central government and forced a greater unification of England's feudal lords.

England became part of the Angevin Empire, which, by the time of Henry II and Queen Eleanor of Aquitaine, stretched from Scotland south through western France to the Pyrenees. However, when Henry's son, Richard the Lionhearted, died, England returned to fragmented rule by local nobles. These nobles cemented their newly recovered autonomy by forcing the new King John to sign the Magna Carta (1215), which constitutionally guaranteed their rights. This set the stage for hundreds of years of power struggles between strong kings and strong nobles (who later formed a Parliament).

The French bits of the shattered Angevin Empire were conquered and united, and France emerged as Europe's superpower.

Church versus State

The popes joined the kings in the European power sweepstakes. Throughout the Middle Ages, kings and popes played "tug of war" with temporal power. After A.D. 1000, on the crest of a spiritual revival, a series of energetic popes reformed the church, the monasteries, and the communications networks, establishing the papacy as a political power to rival the kings.

In many ways, the medieval church operated like a "nation" without borders. It owned lots of land, taxed through tithes, influenced political decisions on all levels, and attracted Europe's most talented men to work in her service. Local kings and princes were threatened by and jealous of this rich and powerful so-called spiritual organization that meddled so deeply in their material realm.

This pope-king thing came to a head in the debate over who had the right to appoint bishops. The pivotal battle of wills was between Pope Gregory VII and "Holy Roman Emperor" Henry IV of Germany. The powerful German king appointed a bishop against the pope's will and was excommunicated. Despite his military might, Henry learned that his people supported him only if he was in good with the pope. Fighting for his political life, he "went to Canossa" (Italy, 1077) to beg forgiveness of the pope. The famous image of him kneeling for hours in the snow outside Gregory's window reminded later leaders that the pope was supreme.

Note that earlier, the church and nobles shaped European history. Now, popes and kings have joined in. Later, we'll see how the city class (French Revolution) and the working class (Socialist Revolution) were dealt onto the card table of European history.

Gothic Art (1150-1400)

The combination of church wealth, political stability, and a reawakened spiritual fervor brought Europe a new artistic style— Gothic. Centered in rich, stable northern France, this style replaced the gloomy, heavy Romanesque with an exciting lightness and grace.

Ste.-Chapelle (Paris)—1246. Supine view.

From the first page of the Bible, it's clear that light is divine. Abbot Suger, who "invented" the Gothic style in 1144 at St. Denis outside Paris (it has been rebuilt and is not really worth visiting today), wanted to create a cathedral of light. The rest of Europe followed suit; building churches with roofs held up by skeletons of support, freeing the walls to become window holders. Now when Christians went to church they were no longer surrounded only by the stone of the earth; they were also bathed in the light of heaven.

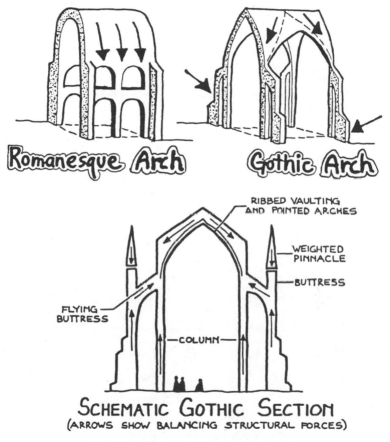

SCHEMATIC GOTHIC SECTION
(ARROWS SHOW BALANCING STRUCTURAL FORCES)

The Basic Arches of Medieval Architecture
Romanesque buildings were barrel vaulted. They required massive wall support, so windows had to be kept small. The next style, Gothic, featured rib vaults (pointed arches arranged in a crisscross manner) supported by flying buttresses. Gothic churches were bigger, brighter, and taller than the earlier Romanesque. Pointed arches distributed the roof weight outward, while buttresses pushed in. Walls were freed to become giant window holders. Enter stained glass.

Gothic architecture began with certain technical improvements over Romanesque. In a Romanesque church, the heavy stone roof was simply arched over the supporting pillars like a bridge. These pillars had to be fortified into massive walls to support the weight, leaving only tiny windows and a dark place of worship.

Gothic architects discovered better ways to distribute the weight of the roof. Gothic builders were masters at playing one form against another to create a balanced harmonious structure.

The most distinctive Gothic feature is the pointed arch, which can reach higher while minimizing the increased weight on the supports. The weight of the roof presses outward rather than down. (If a church with rounded arches falls, it falls downward. If a church with pointed arches falls, the weight of the roof is sent outward, and the church falls outward.)

Using pointed arches in a crisscross pattern that spans diagonally from column to column increases the strength still more. To counteract the outward pressure, Gothic architects reinforced the walls with buttresses. "Flying" buttresses, visible on the exterior of many cathedrals, project away from the church several meters, offering even greater support while taking up even less wall space. In the end, the church was supported by a skeleton of columns, ribs, pointed arches, and buttresses. The roof became taller than ever.

Here's the steeple. . . see all the people
It takes 13 tourists to build a Gothic church—six columns, six buttresses, and one steeple.

Stained glass became a booming new medium for artists and an excellent opportunity for more narrative art to be "read" by the devout but illiterate peasants.

Over time, Gothic churches became more elaborately decorated. The ribs of the kitty-corner arches (vaulting) were often exaggerated beyond their function until they became simply decorations, called tracery. As Gothic style evolved, this tracery became fantastically elaborate and complex and was often covered with gold. The most overripe stage in the evolution of this style is called "flamboyant" (flamelike) Gothic. The English version of this style, perpendicular Gothic, is what you can see in the Henry VII Chapel in London's Westminster Abbey.

King's College Chapel (Cambridge, England)
The Gothic style evolved into a very ornate "flamboyant," or flamelike, stage known as "perpendicular" in England. Here we see nearly all the wall space devoted to brilliant stained glass. The essential ribbing on the ceiling is decorated with extra "tracery," or purely ornamental riblets. You can see why this is called "fan vaulting."

The Gothic style was very competitive. Architects, sculptors, and painters traveled all over Europe to compare and study new churches, causing Gothic churches to be remarkably consistent.

Italy tempered the tense verticality inherent in Gothic architecture to make it more compatible with the horizontal stability that came with her classic roots. This is particularly evident in the great Italian Gothic cathedrals of Florence (capped by a Renaissance dome), Siena, and Orvieto—not so tall, no flying buttresses, and more likely to please a Caesar.

Throughout Europe, these largest economic enterprises of the Middle Ages represented an unprecedented technical accomplishment and tremendous spiritual dedication. The building of a Gothic

Gothic Sculpture
Romanesque sculpture is "low relief," cluttered, telling a story and embedded deep in church walls and niches. Gothic steps farther out from the wall and shows a sense of calm, orderly composure. Still, these figures from Notre-Dame Cathedral in Paris are symbolic rather than realistic, and sculpture remains supportive of the architecture—far from the bold freestanding works of the Renaissance.

church dominated the rich and poor alike of an entire area for generations. Paris' Notre-Dame took 200 years to complete.

Gothic cathedrals are monuments of human devotion to something greater than any individual, even any generation. Not only did people commit their whole lives to it but they also committed their children and their children's children. Nowhere is the religious devotion of the medieval world more evident.

Sculpture took a giant leap forward in Gothic times. No longer just pillars with faces, as Romanesque statues tended to be, Gothic sculpture was more natural and freestanding. Many classical techniques were used, especially in making clothing appear to drape naturally over the body. Sculpted faces reflected personality and emotions. But art was still considered to be a religious tool, and like the stained glass of the time, every piece of sculpture had a symbolic message to those who came to worship.

A Gothic church was carefully designed to be—and usually still is—a place of worship, not a museum. If you think of it as just a dead building to wander through and photograph, you'll see the nave but miss the boat. To best experience a Gothic church, see it in action. Go to a service.

Gothic cathedrals are especially exciting when filled with music. Attend a concert or enjoy an "evensong" service. Meditate, cup your hands behind your ears, and catch every echo as the music rinses the medieval magic into your head. Follow with your eyes the praying hands of the arches; the fingers point upward to heaven. Be dazzled by the warm light of the sun shining through the glistening treasure chest that was melted down and painted onto the timeless windows. Wind up your emotions and let them go. A Gothic church can be as alive as you are.

Gothic Cathedrals:

Ste.-Chapelle, Paris	Salisbury, England
Notre-Dame, Paris	Toledo, Spain
Reims, France	Orvieto, Italy
Chartres, France	Milan, Italy
Köln, Germany	Mont-St. Michel, France
Kings College Chapel,	York Minster, York
Cambridge, England	

Europe's Medieval Masterpiece—The Gothic Church

Many great Gothic cathedrals adorn Europe. Chartres (an hour south of Paris) is considered by many to be the greatest Gothic building. Take one of Malcolm Miller's Gothic appreciation tours. Twice a day Europe's most famous lover of Gothic gives tourists a great lesson in how to enjoy the architectural triumph of the High Middle Ages. The Cologne Cathedral (Köln, Germany), one of Europe's tallest, is just across the street from the train station. Paris' famed Notre-Dame offers a great look at flying buttresses.

Pre-Renaissance Troubles—The Black Death

"When was such a disaster ever seen? Even heard of? Houses were emptied, cities abandoned, countrysides untilled, fields heaped with corpses, and a vast, dreadful silence settled over all the world." (Petrarch, Italian writer of the fourteenth century)

Nuclear holocaust? No, the medieval equivalent—the bubonic plague, or "Black Death," which killed a fourth of Europe in three long years (1347-1350). The disease spread quickly, killed horribly, and then moved on, leaving whole cities devastated in its wake. The economic, physical, and emotional shock is unsurpassed in European history. Most saw the plague as not just a disease but a heavenly curse "sent down upon mankind for our correction by the just wrath of God." Whatever the cause, it killed with such power and swiftness that "the living could scarcely bury the dead."

The Disease and Its Symptoms

The plague came out of Central Asia, passing to Marseilles on an infested Genovese ship. The disease is caused by a bacteria carried by fleas (which travel on rats). Humans get it when bitten by the fleas and then spread it by coughing. The unsanitary conditions in medieval Europe allowed the disease to move rapidly northward. London, Vienna, Florence, and Avignon (the papal city at the time) were particularly hard hit. In Florence alone, 100,000 died within four months. In some cities, 90 percent of the population was wiped out.

The symptoms were quick and harsh: The first sign was sneezing (hence, "bless you"), followed by the appearance of lumps, or "buboes" (hence, "bubonic"), in the groin or armpits, fever, constant vomiting (often blood), diarrhea, pneumonia, and, almost inevitably, death within three days.

So many died so quickly that there was no place to bury them. The survivors resorted to mass graves. "After the churchyards were full, they made vast trenches where bodies were laid by the hundreds, heaped therein by layers, like goods are stored aboard ship, then covered with a little earth," wrote one eyewitness.

The disease was so infectious that it seemed impossible to avoid. The most frightening part was that nothing could be done to help the afflicted, and they were abandoned by the healthy to avoid contagion. "Brother forsook brother; uncle forsook nephew; sister, brother; and often wife, husband; nay, what is more incredible still, fathers and mothers refused to visit or tend their very children, as if they had not been theirs," wrote Boccaccio, whose father succumbed to the plague in Italy.

And here is an eyewitness account of events in Piacenza, Italy: "I do not know where I can begin. Everywhere wailing and lamenting arose. The bodies of the dead without number to be buried. . . . They made ditches by the piazza and the courtyards where never tombs existed. The great and noble were hurled into the same grave with the vile and abject because the dead were all alike. . . . Husband and wife who placidly shared the marriage bed now separated. . . . And when the spirit left, the mother often refused to touch the child, the husband the wife—the victim lay sick alone at home—the physician did not enter; the thunderstruck priest administered the ecclesiastical sacraments timidly. What are we to do, oh good Jesus?"

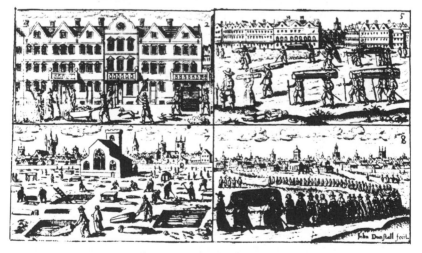

Plague Scenes, London—1665
Wheelbarrows of corpses, not enough coffins, and overcrowded graveyards. "Bring out your dead." Plagues were common throughout Europe's history, but the worst was in 1347-1350, when one out of every four Europeans died.

Europe Goes into Shock

How does one react to such a mysterious, deadly affliction? Many tried to flee from infested areas, but "the disease clung to the fugitives, who fell down by the roadside and dragged themselves into the fields and bushes to expire."

Those with the money withdrew to country houses and locked themselves in where they "abode with music and such other diversions, never suffering themselves to speak with any outsiders, or choosing to hear any news from without of death or sick folks." Boccaccio's *The Decameron* is a collection of stories told by such people to pass the time while hiding from the plague.

"Others, inclining to the contrary opinion," writes Boccaccio, "maintained that the best remedy was to carouse and make merry and go about singing and frolicking and satisfy the appetite in everything possible and laugh and scoff at whatever might happen. They

The Dance Macabre
The troubled fourteenth century gave Europeans many reasons to think they were victims of God's wrath. ONE two three ONE two three . . .

went about day and night, now to this tavern, now to that, drinking without stint or measure and breaking into abandoned houses, the laws having no effect due to the lack of ministers and executors."

The Aftereffects

The "fallout" from the devastation was felt for a century. First was the economic hardship. Thomas Walsingham, a fourteenth-century English historian, wrote, "A disease among cattle followed closely on the pestilence; then the crops died; then the land remained untilled on account of the scarcity of farmers, who were wiped out. And such misery followed these disasters that the world never afterward had an opportunity of returning to its former state."

Europe's emotional scars took even longer to heal. As one historian put it, "The mental shock sustained by all nations during the Black Plague is without parallel and beyond description." The survivors were left without hope for the future. They "closed their accounts with the world" and waited for death and the afterlife.

Convinced the plague was a punishment from God, certain fanatics thought worldwide repentance was necessary. The "Brotherhood of the Flagellants" tried to take the sins of Europe upon themselves. They marched through the cities, calling on the citizens to join them as they scourged themselves with whips. They became more popular in some areas than the priests, whose rituals had been powerless before the plague.

Jews were persecuted and blamed for poisoning wells and thus causing the pestilence. In Basel, Switzerland, the city's Jews were rounded up, locked in a specially built wooden structure, and burned alive.

Europe Recovers

Strange as it may sound, some good came out of all the loss of life, creating the economy that would support the Renaissance more than a century later. With fewer people, labor was scarce, and the common man could demand a better wage for his work. Technology itself had not been affected by the plague, and there were now fewer people to divide the fruits of that technology.

Europeans went on a buying spree, trying to forget the horrors they'd seen. Luxury goods—gay clothes, good food and drink, lavish houses, entertainment—were in high demand. For the first time, the lower classes enjoyed "luxury items" such as chairs, dishes, and fireplaces.

The plague eventually became just a lingering memory in Europe's collective subconscious. The words of Petrarch, who witnessed the horror of the plague years, might be prophetic: "Posterity, will you believe what we who lived through it can hardly accept?...Oh how happy will be future times, unacquainted with such miseries, perhaps counting our testimony as a mere fable!"

More Pre-Renaissance Troubles

Europe suffered other labor pains in the century before the Renaissance. Besides the plague, Europe was rocked by wars: Germany bashed itself about in a lengthy civil war, while England and France fought the bloody "Hundred Years' War" (1337-1453). (Wait a minute. 1453 minus 1337, that's...)

The super-success of the papacy led to corruption and extravagance within the church. Its giant bureaucracy had become flabby and self-perpetuating, and the popes lived in a grander style than any king. At one point there were two popes, one in Avignon and one in Rome. (Plan to explore Avignon's Papal Palace.) The popes excommunicated each other. No one knew whose ring to kiss. Reform was badly needed.

It was a strange and troubled time; social neurosis swept across Europe. People figured it had to be the wrath of God. The popularity of witchcraft soared; devil appeasement and death cults had much of Europe doing the "dance macabre." Some figured, "What the heck, the end is near" and dove headlong into one last hedonistic fling.

Actually, the wars and the plague that tore Europe to shreds served to thin out and vitalize society. The dead were mostly Europe's poor. For the first time, demand for laborers exceeded the supply. Society had to treat its bottom rung with a little more respect. A lean Europe was primed and ready to ride the waves of the future. Serfs up.

Relax...

You've just covered 1,000 medieval years. Before you leave the Dark Ages and enter the bright glow of the Renaissance, let your eyes adjust and take a break.

The Middle Ages—the bridge between the ancient and modern world—are often misunderstood. Review the time line on page 99. Overlay your travel dreams on the map of medieval and Renaissance Europe.

Time Line of the Medieval World

Several realms carried civilization through the Dark Ages after the Fall of Rome—the Christian and barbarian Europe of the Early Middle Ages, Byzantium (the Eastern Roman Empire), and the Islamic nations. At first, Europe had little contact with the two non-European realms and little cultural activity, as shown by the blank lower half of the chart.

Then, in the pivotal year 1000, great changes began. The Crusades sparked cultural exchange between East and West and a new spiritual awakening. Increased agricultural production, industry, and trade brought new prosperity.

Looking at vertical history, we see the fruits of these High Middle Ages in the rise in building and art (see the lower half of the time line). The spiritual awakening and prosperity inspired the construction of many churches in Romanesque and, later, Gothic style, beginning in France and moving to Italy, England, and Germany—each with its own type of Gothic, becoming increasingly more decorative. The Crusaders brought back Eastern knowledge of castle building, and soon every feudal lord had his own stone home.

As the European economy became more productive, centered in towns and relying more on trade and industry than on subsistence farming, feudalism was replaced by larger political and economic units. The Black Plague and costly wars further destroyed the old order. But all that blood and chaos fertilized the fallow soils of European civilization. The modern world was about to blossom.

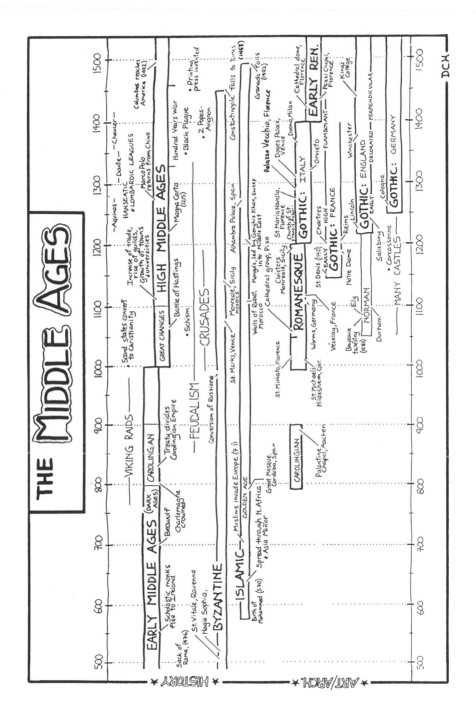

THE MIDDLE AGES

HISTORY

EARLY MIDDLE AGES (DARK AGES)

- Scholastic monks flee to Ireland
- St. Vitale, Ravenna
- Hagia Sophia
- Sack of Rome, (476)

BYZANTINE

ISLAMIC — Muslims invade Europe (?)
- Birth of Mohammed (570)
- Spread through N. Africa & Asia Minor
- GOLDEN AGE

VIKING RAIDS

CAROLINGIAN
- Beowulf
- Charlemagne Crowned

Treaty divides Carolingian Empire

FEUDALISM

Conversion of Russians

Scand. states convert to Christianity

GREAT CHANGES
- Increase of trade, rise of guilds, growth of towns & universities
- HANSEATIC & LOMBARDIC LEAGUES
- Marco Polo returns from China
- Aquinas —
- Dante —
- Chaucer —

HIGH MIDDLE AGES

- Battle of Hastings
- Schism:
- Magna Carta (1215)
- Hundred Years War
- Black Plague
- 2 Popes Avignon

CRUSADES

Constantinople Falls to Turks (1453)

Columbus reaches America (1492)
- Printing press invented

ART/ARCH.

St. Marks, Venice

Monreale, Sicily mosaics

Alhambra Palace, Spain

Walls of Rabat, Morocco

Cathedral group, Pisa

Cloisters, Monreale, Sicily

St. Maria Novella, Florence

Church of St. Francis, Assisi

Mongols, led by Genghis Khan, sweep into Middle East

St. Minato, Florence

CAROLINGIAN
- Palatine Chapel, Aachen

St. Michaelis, Hildesheim, Ger.

Worms, Germany

Vézelay, France

Bayeux Tapestry (1080)

ROMANESQUE

Durham

Ely

NORMAN

Carcassonne

GOTHIC: ITALY

St. Denis (1140)

Chartres

EARLY HIGH

GOTHIC: FRANCE

Notre Dame

Reims

Lincoln

EARLY

GOTHIC: ENGLAND

Salisbury

DECORATED

Orvieto

FLAMBOYANT

Winchester

PERPENDICULAR

Doges Palace, Venice

Duomo, Milan

Palazzo Vecchio, Florence

Granada Falls (1492)

Cathedral dome, Florence

EARLY REN.

Pazzi Chapel, Florence

Kings College

Cologne

GOTHIC: GERMANY

MANY CASTLES

Great Mosque Cordoba, Spain

500   600   700   800   900   1000   1100   1200   1300   1400   1500

DCX

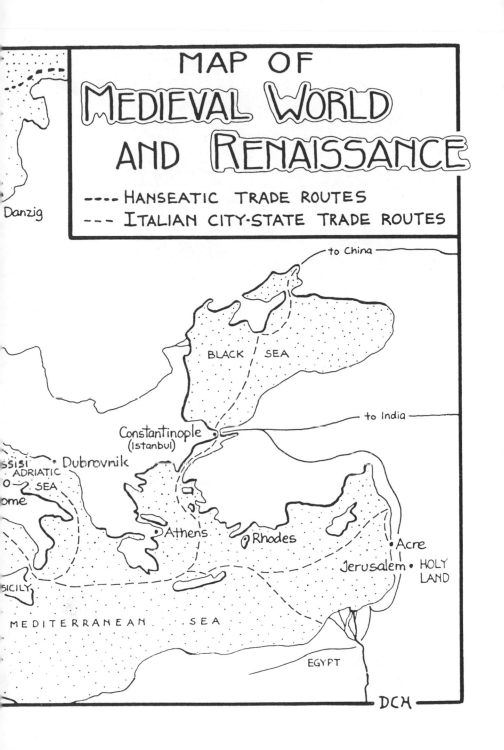

MAP OF
MEDIEVAL WORLD
AND RENAISSANCE

---- HANSEATIC TRADE ROUTES
--- ITALIAN CITY-STATE TRADE ROUTES

Danzig

to China

BLACK SEA

to India

Constantinople
(Istanbul)

·Dubrovnik
SSISI
ADRIATIC
O SEA
ome

·Athens

Rhodes

·Acre
Jerusalem · HOLY
LAND

SICILY

MEDITERRANEAN SEA

EGYPT

DCH

Michelangelo, *David* (Accademia, Florence)
The face of the Renaissance. Man was the shaper of his destiny—no longer merely
a plaything of the supernatural.

The Renaissance
A.D. 1400-1600

The Renaissance was the rebirth of the classical values of ancient Greece and Rome. ("Renaissance" means rebirth.) Northern Italians, taking a fresh, new, secular view of life, considered themselves citizens of a new Rome.

The new Renaissance man was the shaper of his destiny and no longer merely a plaything of the supernatural. Individualism and humanism skyrocketed, and life became much more than a preparation for the hereafter. People were optimistic and confident in their basic goodness and in their power to solve problems. This new attitude freed an avalanche of original thinking and creativity that gave our civilization its most exciting and fertile period of art since that great Greek streak 2,000 years earlier.

The Renaissance also did more for tourism than any other period in history. All over Europe, but especially in Italy, today's visitors set their touristic sights on the accomplishments of the creative geniuses of the Renaissance.

The Renaissance was more than simply a return to the ancient days and ways. It was a period of new birth as well as rebirth which laid the foundation of the modern world. Politically, the modern nation-state was born. Economically, as capitalism replaced feudalism, the middle class was born. Intellectually, this period spawned the Protestant Reformation, humanism, modern science, and secular thought.

Italy was the perfect launch pad for this cultural explosion. As the natural trading center and intermediary between the East and its luxury goods and the merchants of the West, its cities were rich. Venice was a thriving trading center of 100,000 people and 3,000 ships in 1400. The East-West trade shuttled many classical ideas, which had fled eastward with the fall of Rome a thousand years earlier, back to Italy. Italy never completely forgot her classical heritage, and she welcomed its return.

Northern Italy was the most urban corner of Europe. In 1400, 26 percent of the people there were city dwellers compared with the mere 10 percent of the English who lived in cities. The Italian cities were generally independent, not having to cope with a pope or worry about a king. They did their own thing, and that required participation in government, more literacy, and better communication. This urban metabolism stimulated commerce and industry. The cities actively recruited skilled craftsmen, and the social structure became more flexible, offering the working class hope for improvement.

Florence led the Renaissance parade. A leader in banking and wool manufacturing, it prospered after the Crusades. It had a large middle class and strong guilds (labor unions for skilled craftsmen); their success was a matter of civic pride. Florentines considered themselves cousins of the highly cultured people of the Roman Empire. They showed their pride in the mountains of money they spent to rebuild and beautify the city. Other Italian cities followed suit.

New ways of thinking brought prosperity (or, for you Marxists, prosperity brought new ways of thinking). The most talented and ambitious men of the Middle Ages had served in the church. Now an active life of business and politics was considered just as meaningful and respectable as the passive, contemplative life of the monastery. Chasing money was no longer considered shameful, as long as the wealth was used properly.

Such values were found in the writings, letters, and speeches of the ancient Romans, and, despite their pagan flavor, they were accepted by devout Christians. Scientific and religious beliefs merged.

Out of this secular orientation came the non-Christian school, training young people for the new world of business and politics. Schools and private tutors based on Roman models popped up all over. Throughout Europe, educated upper-class people had a common cultural base: they all spoke Latin, appreciated classical literature, and shared a common secular morality. There was a new international network besides the church to cut across borders and spread new ideas.

The Renaissance was not the repudiation of God; it was the assertion of humankind. In 1450, a Florentine author summed it up: "The world was created not for God who had no need of it but for man. Man is the most perfect work of God, the true marvel of his genius. Man has his end not in God but in a knowledge of himself and his own creativity."

Renaissance Florence

In many ways, Florence is the cradle of the modern world. Florence's contributions to Western culture are immense: the whole revival of the arts, humanism, and science; the seeds of democracy; the modern Italian language (which grew out of the popular Florentine dialect); the artworks of Michelangelo, Leonardo, and Botticelli; the writings of Machiavelli, Boccaccio, and Dante; and Amerigo Vespucci, who gave his name to a fledgling continent. But Florence, even in its golden age, was always a mixture of lustiness and refinement. The streets were filled with tough-talking, hardened, illiterate merchants who strode about singing verses from Dante's _Divine Comedy._

Florence's money—and hence her culture—came from wool and silk factories and from banking. The bankers soon broke the farm-based feudal lords by being pawnbrokers for them—loaning money at exorbitant rates and then taking their lands when they couldn't pay up.

Technically, Florence was a republic, ruled by elected citizens rather than a nobility. There was a relatively large middle class and some opportunity for upward mobility. The Florentines took great pride in this system. But in fact, power lay in the hands of a few wealthy banking families, the most powerful being the Medicis. The Medici bank had branches in ten sites in Europe, including London, Bruges (Belgium), and Lyon. The pope kept his checking account in the Rome branch. The Florentine florin was the monetary standard of the Continent.

Florence dominated Italy economically and culturally but not militarily. There was a loose "Italian League" alliance of city-states, but Italy was to remain scattered until the nationalist movement four centuries later. (When someone suggested to the Renaissance Florentine Niccolo Machiavelli that the Italian city-states might unite against their common enemy, France, he wrote back, "Don't make me laugh.")

Lorenzo de Medici (1449-1492), inheritor of the family's wealth and power, was the central figure of the golden age. He was young (20 when he took power), athletic and intelligent, a poet, horseman, musician, and leader. He wrote love songs and humorous, dirty songs to be sung loudly and badly at carnival time. His marathon drinking bouts and illicit love affairs were legendary. He learned Greek and Latin and read the classics, yet his great passion was hunting. He was the Renaissance Man—the man of knowledge and action, the scholar and man of the world, the patron of the arts, and the shrewd business-man. He was Lorenzo the Magnificent.

Lorenzo epitomized the Florentine spirit of optimism. Born on New Year's Day and raised in the lap of luxury (Donatello's *David* stood in the family courtyard) by loving parents, he grew up feeling that there was nothing he couldn't do. Florentines saw themselves as part of a "new age," a great undertaking of discovery and progress in man's history. They boasted that within the city walls there were more "nobly gifted souls than the world has seen in the entire thousand years before." These people invented the term "Dark Ages" for the era that preceded theirs.

Lorenzo surrounded himself with Florence's best and brightest. They formed an informal "Platonic Academy," based on that of ancient Greece, to meet over a glass of wine under the stars at the Medici villa and discuss literature, art, music, and politics; witty conversation was considered an art in itself. Their "neo-Platonic" philosophy stressed the goodness of man and the created world; they believed in a common truth behind all religion. The Academy was more than just an excuse to go out with the guys: the members were convinced that their discussions were changing the world and improving their souls.

Arts and Artists

Botticelli was a member of the Academy. He painted scenes from the classical myths that the group read, weaving contemporary figures and events into the ancient subjects. He gloried in the nude body, which he considered God's greatest creation. In Botticelli's art we see the lightness, gaiety, and optimism of Lorenzo's "court."

Botticelli, *Allegory of Spring* (Uffizi, Florence)
Pagan innocence. Botticelli was part of a youthful band of Florentines who saw beautiful things as an expression of the divine.

Another of Lorenzo's protégés was the young Michelangelo. Impressed with his work, Lorenzo took the poor, unlearned 14-year-old boy into the Medici household and treated him like a son.

Michelangelo's playmates were the Medici children, later to become Popes Leo X and Clement VII, who would give him important commissions. For all the encouragement, education, and contacts Michelangelo received, the most important gift from Lorenzo was simply his place at the dinner table, where he could absorb the words of the great men of the time and their love of art for art's sake.

Artists thrived on the patronage of wealthy individuals, government, church groups, and guilds. Botticelli commanded as much as 100 florins for one work, enough to live for a year in high style, which he did for many years. Artists mingled with scholars and men of wealth—a far cry from earlier generations, when artists were anonymous craftsmen.

Although artists were sought after in high society, some were rather odd ducks. Leonardo da Vinci, though very learned and witty, was considered something of a flake who never finished his projects. His claim to fame as a youth was his fine lute playing. Michelangelo put people off by acting superior to them. Piero di Cosimo shunned society, hiding in his room, subsisting on hard-boiled eggs, and living "the life of a wild beast rather than that of a man." The image of the artist as the lone genius—solitary, strange, melancholy, and poor—was forming.

The great masters were friends and rivals. When the established Leonardo and the young genius Michelangelo competed for the commission to paint a battle mural in the town hall, all eyes were on them. (Raphael even interrupted his studies to visit Florence for the event.) Both submitted much-admired "cartoons," or rough sketches. Competition between their fans was fierce—Michelangelo's cartoon was ripped up in jealousy by one of Leonardo's pupils—but the artists treated one another with respect.

Competition and jealousy showed itself in other ways, however. Vasari, the painter and biographer, insulted Leonardo's slow working pace and bragged that he himself had done the painting in the entire Roman chancellor's palace in 100 days. Michelangelo responded, "It's obvious."

Savonarola—A Return to the Middle Ages

Even with all the art and philosophy of the Renaissance, violence, disease, and warfare were present in medieval proportions. For the lower classes, life was as harsh as it had always been. Many artists and scholars wore swords and daggers as part of everyday dress. This was the time of the ruthless tactics of the Borgia and other families battling for power. Lorenzo himself barely escaped assassination during Mass.

Fifteenth-century Florence was decaying. The Medici banks began to fold due to mismanagement and political troubles. The city's wealth had brought decadence and corruption. Even Lorenzo got caught with his hand in the till. Many longed for a "renaissance" of good, old-fashioned medieval values.

Into Florence rode a Dominican monk named Savonarola preaching fire and brimstone and the sinfulness of wealth, worldly art, and secular humanism. He was a magnetic speaker, drawing huge crowds, whipping them into a frenzy with sharp images of the corruption of the world and the horror of hell it promised. "Down, down with all gold and decoration," he roared, "down where the body is food for the worms." He presided over huge bonfires where his believers burned "vanities"—clothes, cosmetics, jewelry, and wigs as well as classical books and paintings.

When Lorenzo died, the worldly Medicis were thrown out, replaced by a theocracy with Jesus Christ at its head—and Savonarola ruling in His absence. The theocracy (1494-1498) was a grim part of the Renaissance. Many leading scholars and artists followed Savonarola's call and gave up their worldly pursuits. "Vice squads" of boys and girls roamed the streets chastising drinkers, gamblers, and over-dressed women. Even so, governmental and church reforms promised by Savonarola were never accomplished.

Botticelli, *Slander* (Uffizi, Florence)
The Florentine Renaissance passed. Savonarola turned the city into a theocracy. High thinking is clubbed and dragged ingloriously past Renaissance statues that look down with shock and disbelief.

As the atmosphere of general fanaticism faded, so did Savonarola's popularity. In April 1498, to prove his saintliness and regain public support, he offered to undergo ordeal by fire—to be burned at the stake and escape unharmed. At the last minute he got cold feet, backed out, and was arrested. Then he had no choice: he was hanged and burned at the stake in the town square. (A plaque on Florence's main square marks the spot.) The Medicis returned.

Florence in 1500 was a more somber place than it had been during the gay days of Lorenzo. Botticelli, under Savonarola's spell, had given up painting his nudes and pagan scenes, letting the melancholy side of his personality come out.

Rome gradually became the center of the Renaissance center, but her artists were mostly Florentine. In the fifteenth century, the Holy City of Rome was a dirty, decaying, crime-infested place, unfit for the hordes of pilgrims that visited each year. The once-glorious Forum was a cow pasture. Then a series of popes, including Lorenzo's son and nephew, launched a building and beautification campaign. They used fat commissions (and outright orders) to lure Michelangelo, Raphael, and others to Rome. The Florentine Renaissance—far from over—moved southward.

Renaissance Art

The accomplishments of the Renaissance most obvious to the tourist are those in art and architecture. The art of the fifteenth and sixteenth centuries is a triumph of order and harmony and the technical remastery of the secrets of the classical artists, which had been lost during the Middle Ages. This period also saw the discovery and exploration of many new artistic techniques.

Like Greece's Golden Age, the Renaissance was a time of balance between stiff formality and wild naturalism. Later, in the baroque period (as in Greece's Hellenistic era), the artists went overboard in their naturalism—losing the sense of order in their works.

Renaissance art has many classical characteristics—realism, glorification of the human body and the individual, nonreligious themes, and an appreciation of beauty for its own sake. Overriding all these is the importance of balance—between emotion and calm and between motion and rest as well as among the various figures in the composition.

Acquiring beautiful art was a rich man's hobby. The new secular patronage stimulated art—giving it more pizzazz. The artist was hired to please his viewer sensually and to satisfy his patron. Wealthy merchants of the Italian city-states commissioned art for their personal collections and for public display as a show of civic pride. They wanted art to reflect the power of man, his dignity, and his vitality.

The medieval church's monopoly on art was broken. Secular patronage opened new realms for artists previously confined to religious subjects. Pagan themes were very popular.

Many Renaissance artists were very devout, however, and created more emotional and moving works than anything created in the Middle Ages. They glorified God by glorifying humanity, His greatest creation. Religious themes were portrayed more realistically, emphasizing the human aspect. In Michelangelo's Pietà, for example, the suffering of Jesus and his grieving mother are shown not symbolically but graphically. Michelangelo intentionally elongated Jesus' dead body to exaggerate its weight and the burden of sadness borne by Mary.

Michelangelo, Pietà (St. Peter's Cathedral, Rome)
Sculpted when Michelangelo was 22. The dead Christ is held by the eternally youthful Virgin Mary.

The artist was no longer an anonymous laborer, ranking socially with a bricklayer. He was well paid and accepted as a part of society's elite. Raphael and Leonardo were wealthy and famous. Their presence at a party made the evening.

In the past, artists had groveled for a prince's commission. During the Renaissance, when every town and court was competing for a famous artist's work, the tables turned and the artist could nearly dictate his terms and create what he wanted for whichever lucky prince landed him. At last, the artist could freely create.

Artists of the Renaissance deserved the respect they got. They merged art and science; their apprenticeship required mastery of the mathematical laws of perspective. They studied nature as a biologist would. They studied human anatomy as avidly as a doctor, learning not just how the body looks but also how it works, so that they could catch it in motion. They were well-rounded Renaissance men.

Technical expertise, combined with secular patronage and the classical love of sheer beauty, raised Europe to an unprecedented level of artistic excellence.

Architecture

The proud people of the Renaissance looked down on the "Middle Ages" that separated the glorious ancient world from their own glorious time. They labeled the art "Gothic" after the barbarians who looted Rome. To them, Gothic cathedrals looked tense, strained, and unstable. The Renaissance architect turned to his ancient Roman forefathers and developed, or rediscovered, a style that was round, geometrical, stout, symmetrical, domed, and balanced.

Filippo Brunelleschi fathered Renaissance architecture. Brunelleschi traveled to Rome to carefully measure and study the classical buildings and monuments. Back in his hometown he conscientiously copied Roman styles, building with columns, arches, pediments, and domes.

Brunelleschi, Cathedral Dome (Florence)—1420-1436
Inspired by the ancient Pantheon, this dome in turn inspired later ones, from Michelangelo's down to the present.

His masterpiece was the huge dome of Florence's cathedral, a triumph of beauty and science, demonstrating that Renaissance man was the equal of the great builders of Rome. It was the model for many domes to follow, including Michelangelo's St. Peter's in Rome. The classical order and the harmony of his design caused great excitement, inspiring other artists to mix Roman forms with original designs.

Italian architects and artists, in demand throughout Europe, had no shortage of commissions to build secular palaces, homes, and public buildings in the Renaissance style. The pope hired Michelangelo to travel to Rome and design the dome of St. Peter's, Christendom's greatest cathedral. French kings built Renaissance chateaus on the Loire, and even the Russian tsar imported Italian expertise to remodel Moscow's Kremlin in the new style.

Renaissance church design echoed the upbeat optimism and confidence of the time by trading the medieval Latin cross floor plan (symbolic of the Crucifixion) for the Greek cross floor plan (four equal arms symbolizing the perfection of God and the goodness of man, who was made in His image).

Courtyard of a Medici Palace by Michelozzo, Florence, 1450
Typical Renaissance architecture—balance, symmetry, arches, Corinthian columns, circles, and squares.

Renaissance Architecture:

San Miniato al Monte, Florence
Cathedral dome, Florence
Hospital of the Innocents (Brunelleschi), Florence
St. Peter's dome, Rome
Uffizi Gallery (the building), Florence
Tempietto, Rome
Pazzi Chapel, Florence
Urbino Palace, Urbino, Italy
Chambord, Chenonceaux, and several other Loire Valley chateaus, France
Campidoglio, Rome
Many palaces in Venice
Palmanova, a planned town in Italy

Brunelleschi, Pazzi Chapel (Florence)—1450
The ideal Renaissance church, Pazzi chapel is built symmetrically, perfectly proportional around a central point. Located next to the Sta. Croce church.

Sculpture

Like the ancients, Renaissance sculptors concentrated on portraying realistic, three-dimensional, natural, and preferably naked human bodies. They posed their statues classically, catching their subject balanced between motion and rest.

Donatello (1386-1466) was the first true Renaissance sculptor, combining the skill of creating classical sculpture and the personality of the Renaissance artist. His statues for the church of Or San Michele in Florence reveal his classical attitude toward the human body. St. Mark, although fully clothed, has the posture of a classical nude—with his weight resting on one leg. The clothing drapes naturally, formed not by the artist but by the body beneath. You almost feel that if you lifted Mark's robe, you'd get punched.

To see how far Donatello had progressed from Gothic sculpture, compare it with Nanni di Banco's *Four Saints*, done at the same time for the same church. Donatello's *Mark* stands boldly on the edge of his niche, but just around the corner, Nanni's *Four Saints* hide within

Chartres Cathedral Sculpture—1140   Nanni di Banco, *Four Saints* (Or San Michele Church, Florence)—1413

Sculpture gradually emerged from the shadows of church architecture. At Chartres, the stiff columnlike figures are embedded in the Gothic wall—entirely supportive of the architecture. Nanni's *Four Saints* has Renaissance solidity but is still niched deep within the wall. Nanni was on the cusp of the revolution. (Opposite page) Donatello's confident *St. George* steps right up to the edge of his niche and looks boldly into the future. Renaissance Man is stepping out. A few years later, Donatello's *David* stood on his own in the light of day—proud, naked, and bold.

a deep Gothic niche, attached to half-columns, afraid to step from the safe support of the church into the light of day. Donatello freed sculpture from its 1,000-year subservience to architecture.

While you're at Or San Michele, check out Donatello's famous *St. George*. It stands like a symbol of the Renaissance man—alert yet relaxed, strong yet refined, aggressive yet Christian. The serene beauty of medieval art was being replaced by the defiant and determined new outlook.

Donatello, *St. George* (Or San Michele, Florence)—1416

These works were commissioned by the church and by civic organizations. But another Donatello work, *David*, paid for by a private citizen for private display, is an example of how secular patronage freed the artist from medieval constraints.

Donatello, *David* (Bargello, Florence)—
c. 1430
The first freestanding male nude sculpted in a thousand years, this Early Renaissance masterpiece is blatant art for the sake of art.

Donatello's *David* was the first freestanding male nude sculpted since ancient times. During the Middle Ages it would have been condemned as a pagan idol. Although the subject matter—the boy David killing the giant Goliath—comes from the Bible, it's just an excuse for a classical study of a male nude. The focus is on the curves of the body (no longer a "dirty" thing), not the action or the facial expression. The statue serves no religious or civic purpose. It is a simple appreciation of beauty. Art for art's sake.

Works of Donatello:

David, John the Baptist, St. George (the original) and others in the Bargello, Florence

Mary Magdalene and other sculpture, Museum of the Duomo, Florence

St. John the Baptist, Frari Church, Venice

St. Mark and *St. George* (copy), outside Or San Michele, Florence

---

Painting

The great Florentine painters were sculptors with brushes. They painted the same way the ancient Greeks had sculpted, making solid figures that had great weight, solemnity, and presence. Many of them, such as Michelangelo, were equally famous for sculpture and painting. Both sculpture and painting evolved from flat, symbolic, medieval art to the full realism and three-dimensionality of the Renaissance.

Giotto (pronounced "ZHOTT-o," 1267-1337), who preceded the High Renaissance by 200 years, made the first radical break with the medieval past. He is the father of modern painting. Nothing like his astonishing paintings had been seen in a thousand years. Medieval artists painted stiff, two-dimensional figures with no sense of movement. Medieval artists didn't bother to paint backgrounds to give the illusion of depth. They were happy to tell the religious story with symbols, ignoring realism.

But Giotto takes us right to the scene of the action. He places his figures on a three-dimensional landscape, giving them depth, weight, and individuality. It's as though he has created small theater vignettes, designed the stage scenery, and then peopled it with actors.

Much of his art reflects the Byzantine and Gothic styles of his age—pointed arches, gold-leaf backgrounds, halos, no visible light source, and unrealistic scale—but he made great strides toward real-

Giotto, *Return of Joachim to the Sheepfold* (Padua)—1305
There's a background (the cliff) and a foreground (the sheep) to give the scene a realistic 3-D depth.

ism. The Byzantine influence gave Giotto the classical techniques of light and shading (which the East had stored in an artistic time capsule since the fall of Rome) and foreshortening, which gives the illusion of depth. His style excited the West and stimulated a renewed interest in the classics.

Giotto, *Madonna and Child* (Uffizi, Florence)
Singlehandedly, Giotto nearly started the Renaissance a century before its time. Pioneering the illusion of 3-D, he painted sculptural people in realistic settings.

Giotto was famous and in demand throughout Italy. This popularity for a painter was as revolutionary as his work. Until now, no one had cared about artists. But Giotto made it into all the gossip columns. Anecdotes were told about his social wit as well as his skill as a painter.

A century later, Masaccio carried Giotto's techniques further. He used light and shadow to depict depth and drama. Brunelleschi had discovered the mathematical laws of perspective, and Masaccio employed them to portray objects receding into the distance (a tree-lined road, for example). Masaccio, another Florentine (who died at the age of 27), was more influential than he was famous. The anatomical realism and dramatic power of paintings such as *The Expulsion from Eden*, which you can see in Florence, inspired many masters who followed.

Medieval church of St. Michael, Hildesheim, Germany, c. 1015

Masaccio (Florence)—1425

Michelangelo (Sistine Chapel, Vatican) —1510

Three looks at the Expulsion from Eden

The same scene in medieval, early Renaissance, and high Renaissance style. Notice the artistic differences, as well as how man's view of himself in relation to God changes. On the bronze doors of St. Michael's church, Adam and Eve are puny and twisted, ashamed of their nakedness. Humans are helpless creatures cowering before the supernatural. Masaccio shows more human drama and respect for the body. (The fig leaves were added later.) Michelangelo shows a strong Adam with a gesture that almost says, "All right, already, we're going!" Adam knows he and Eve will survive.

Masaccio, *Tribute Money* (Detail), (Florence)—1425
Here we see realism and "sculptural" figures developed further. Masaccio was the
first painter to fully master the newly discovered laws of perspective.

After Masaccio, lesser painters grappled with the new problems
of perspective. Paolo Uccello's *Battle of San Romano* looks like a
crowded, colorful, two-dimensional work in the medieval style. It's
only when we look closer that we see it as a study in perspective—

Uccello, *Battle of San Romano* (Louvre)—1455
This early attempt at 3-D gets lost in the crowd. Versions also in London's National
Gallery and Florence's Uffizi.

all the fallen weapons form a three-dimensional grid superimposed on the background. The fallen soldier at left is scarcely larger than the fallen helmet at right in Uccello's awkward attempt at foreshortening. All in all, it's a fascinating but weak transition from two-dimensional Gothic to three-dimensional Renaissance realism.

Perspective was mastered by relief artists of the period such as Donatello and Lorenzo Ghiberti. Donatello achieved the effect of infinite background in his low-relief St. George and the Dragon, beneath his statue of St. George at Or San Michele. In Ghiberti's famed bronze doors of Florence's Cathedral baptistry we see

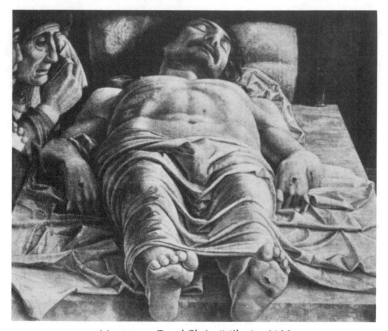

Mantegna, *Dead Christ* (Milan)—1466
A Renaissance experiment in extreme foreshortening that succeeds in bringing the viewer right to the scene of the action. The psychological effect of seeing the body from this intimate viewpoint is exciting.

Brunelleschi's influence. "The Story of Jacob and Esau" (one of 10 Bible scenes on the door) includes imaginary Brunelleschian architectural forms in the background receding into the distance according to mathematical perspective.

Ghiberti, _Story of Jacob and Esau_ (Baptistry, Florence)—c. 1430
The contest to decorate the bronze doors of Florence's Baptistry excited and encouraged artists throughout the city. Here, the winning artist shows mastery of depth and perspective.

You be the judge. Here are the two finalists for the Baptistry door competition—Ghiberti's and Brunelleschi's. Which do you like the best? The originals stand side by side in Florence's Bargello Museum.

(Ghiberti's, on the left, won.)

Botticelli, *The Birth of Venus* (Uffizi, Florence)—c. 1480
Botticelli's Venus is more graceful, thinner, and more flowing than the massive figures of Masaccio and Michelangelo. The long neck and smooth skin are almost medieval looking.

Botticelli (pronounced "bott-i-CHELL-ee," 1445-1510) excelled in his mastery of color, detail, and line. Not as sculptural as Masaccio, Michelangelo, and other Renaissance artists, Botticelli's figures have a pure, elegant, yet dreamlike quality. He mixes Gothic grace and fleshy classicism in his popular and wonderfully restored masterpieces *La Primavera* and *The Birth of Venus* (in Florence's Uffizi Gallery). Botticelli was a master in the Renaissance skill of diplomacy; he did justice to the "pagan" classical scenes he loved while not offending the religious powers with too much flesh.

Artists throughout the ages have struggled with spiritual problems. When Renaissance Florence fell into the grips of Savonarola, legions of Florentines became his fanatical followers. Even Botticelli tossed some of his more "pagan" artworks onto the righteous bonfires.

Major Collections of Renaissance Painting:
Uffizi, Florence
Louvre, Paris, France
National Gallery, London, England
Kunsthistorisches, Vienna, Austria
Alte Pinakothek, Munich, Germany
Prado, Madrid, Spain
Vatican Museum (Pinacoteca), the Vatican
Accademia, Venice

Leonardo, Michelangelo, and Raphael

The artworks of Leonardo, Michelangelo, and Raphael were the culmination of the Renaissance. The tremendous output of "the big three" sprang from their personal genius spurred on by a huge demand for quality art. Never before had artists been asked to do so much and been given so much money and freedom to do it. Cities wanted monuments and public buildings. Wealthy individuals wanted palaces and decorations. Popes wanted churches. And all of them wanted to hire Leonardo, Michelangelo, or Raphael.

Leonardo da Vinci

Leonardo da Vinci (1452-1519) typified the well-rounded Renaissance man. He was a painter, sculptor, engineer, musician, and scientist. He learned from nature, not books, which made his observations often more accurate than those of contemporary scholars. From his notebooks—written backward and inside out, so you need a mirror to decode them—we know that he dissected corpses, investigated the growth of children in the womb, formulated laws of waves and currents, diagrammed the flight of birds and insects, and followed the

Leonardo da Vinci, _Virgin and Child with St. John the Baptist and St. Anne_ (National Gallery, London)
Leonardo surrounds baby Jesus with a pyramid of maternal security.

growth of plants. He also designed military fortifications and sketched many inventions, foreshadowing the development of the airplane and submarine.

Leonardo was best known for his painting and sculpting. Princes and church authorities from all over Italy sought his work. However, he was temperamental and often left works unfinished. He insisted

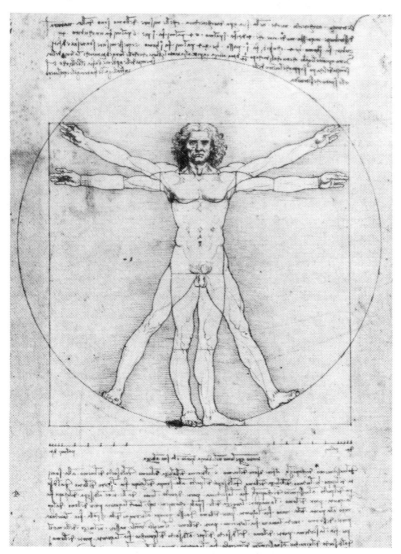

Page from Leonardo da Vinci's *Notebook*.
Leonardo invents the jumping jack.

Leonardo da Vinci, _Self-Portrait_

on working at his own pace, not the pace dictated by the clink of coins. None of his sculptures and only about twenty of his paintings survive.

The Last Supper demonstrates Leonardo's mastery of balance, realism, and drama. Depicting Christ and his twelve disciples, it is painted on the wall of a church—positioned in a manner so it looks like just another chapel extending off the aisle. The lines of the walls recede toward the horizon (following the laws of perspective) and come together at Christ's head. All the motion of the picture flows toward that serene center. Leonardo composed the Twelve in groups of three, each group contributing a dramatic movement in a wavelike effect toward the central figure of Jesus. (Groups of three symbolize the Trinity; four, the Gospels.)

Leonardo da Vinci, Last Supper (with schematic lines), (Milan)—1498
Leonardo combines human drama with geometrical perspective. All the receding lines (the upper edge of the tapestries, the ceiling tiles) point to the center—Christ's head. The twelve disciples, each with a unique personal expression, are grouped in threes. Even without a T-square, we feel the method in the artist's madness. Unfortunately, this "fresco" has not survived the centuries well.

Despite this complex composition, the picture is highly emotional, not forced or sterile. The Lord has just said that one of the disciples will betray him. Leonardo paints a psychological portrait of each of them at the very moment they ask, "Lord, is it I?"

It's said that Leonardo went whole days without painting a stroke—just staring at the work. Then he'd grab a brush, rush up, flick a dab of paint on. . . and go back to staring. (When you visit this or any artistic sight in Italy, be sure to dial the neighboring tourist-information box to English, put in a few coins, and listen to the gossipy story of the masterpiece.)

Every painting takes on life when you see it "in person." This is especially true of the Mona Lisa, thanks to a technique Leonardo used called *sfumato*. He blurred the outlines and mellowed the colors around the borders of his subject, making the edge blend with the background. This makes Lisa appear lifelike and her smile appear mysterious. Try as you will, you can't actually see the corners of her mouth.

Leonardo's Mona Lisa, found in tourist shops throughout Paris. (Oh, yes, she's also in the Louvre—just follow the crowds.)

When you finally see this most famous painting you might wonder, Why is she so famous? Mona Lisa was a people's favorite from the start because the woman portrayed is a very low-ranking noblewoman. The painting was Leonardo's personal favorite, one he never sold, keeping it in his possession until he died. (Leonardo spent his last years living in Amboise on the Loire, in the service of the French king, Francis I. So Mona Lisa wound up in the French collection.) The portrait of Mona was kidnapped early in the twentieth century. Her safe recovery made headlines, boosting her fame even higher. Artistically, she epitomizes the art of the Renaissance—balanced, subtle, and true.

Works of Leonardo da Vinci:

Mona Lisa, Madonna of the Rocks, John the Baptist, the Louvre, Paris

His home and models of inventions, Amboise (Loire), France

Last Supper, Santa Maria delle Grazie, Milan, Italy

St. Jerome, Pinacoteca Gallery, the Vatican

Annunciation and Adoration, Uffizi Gallery, Florence

Holy Family sketch; National Gallery, London

Madonna and Child, Alte Pinakothek, Munich, Germany

Michelangelo

Michelangelo Buonarroti (1475-1564), perhaps the greatest painter and sculptor of all time, had mastered nature; he strived to master himself. Michelangelo's art reflects the inner turmoil of his emotional and spiritual life. His biography is as important as his work; the two are intertwined, one influencing the other.

At the age of 15, Michelangelo was a prodigy, a favorite of Florence's leading citizen, Lorenzo de Medici. After serving his apprenticeship, he became dissatisfied with book knowledge and set out to study nature firsthand.

He had the curiosity and quick mind of Leonardo, but he applied them to only one subject—the human body. Mastering the techniques of the ancient Greeks and Romans, he added to them by dissecting corpses to learn anatomy. Dissection, which was strictly illegal, was key to understanding the body and portraying it realistically.

Throughout his life, Michelangelo's talents were in great demand. Popes and princes vied to commission him to paint, sculpt, or design churches and monuments. But even more than Leonardo, Michel-

Michelangelo, *Creation of Adam* (Sistine Chapel, Vatican Museum)

angelo struggled to remain independent of his patrons' demands. He did what he wanted the way he wanted. The remarkable thing is that patrons put up with this: the artist/patron relationship was turned upside down, with the artist on top.

Despite his great technical skill, Michelangelo thought that true creative genius came not from the rational planning of the artist but from divine inspiration. He was one of the first "mad geniuses" — working only when he felt inspired and then going at it with the intensity of a maniac.

He was influenced by the popular neo-Platonist movement, which stressed Plato's division between the physical body and the divine spirit. Michelangelo took Plato's words to heart: "If anyone tries to be a poet [artist] without the madness of the Muses, persuaded that skill alone will make him good, then shall both he and his works of sanity be brought to nothing by the poetry of madness."

Michelangelo's statues show us this divine genius trapped within the body, struggling to get out. The works are outwardly calm, stable, and balanced but seem to be charged with pent-up energy. They convey the inner restlessness and turmoil that marked Michelangelo's own life.

David, which he sculpted when he was 26, displays this blend of vibrant energy and calm. His posture is relaxed, but his alert, intense stare reminds us of Donatello's Christian warrior, *St. George*. Like the earlier work, Michelangelo's *David* became a symbol of the ready-for-anything confidence of the Florentine Renaissance. It is a

Michelangelo, David (Accademia, Florence)—c. 1504
Michelangelo's version of the giant-slayer shows the Renaissance Man in full bloom—alert, poised, cultured, ready to conquer his foe. Man has asserted himself. Compare this with Donatello's earlier David—a graceful, playful Renaissance "boy" (p. 115).

monumental work (13'5" tall), designed to stand on top of the cathedral until the city fathers elected to put it in a more visible spot outside the town hall (the Palazzo Vecchio) as a symbol of civic pride. Today a copy stands in the square and the original is in the Accademia, a fifteen-minute walk away.

When we compare Michelangelo's *David* with Donatello's earlier version, we see the Renaissance style of the artwork of Michelangelo. (See the illustration on page 115.) Donatello's David is young and graceful, coyly gloating over the head of Goliath, almost Gothic in its

Michelangelo, *Moses* (Rome)—1515
Powerful, ready to leap up and smash the tablets on the rocks. You'll find Moses in Rome, in the church of St. Peter in Chains, a short walk from the Colosseum.

elegance and smooth lines. Michelangelo's David is more massive, heroic in size and superhuman in strength and power. The tensed right hand, which grips stones in readiness to hurl at Goliath, is much larger and more powerful than any human hand; it's symbolic of divine strength. The concentrated gaze is that of the reserved but intense Renaissance man.

The inner power takes on a wrathful quality in _Moses,_ the depiction of an Old Testament prophet, whose calm but fierce expression demands attention. He seems capable at any moment of angrily destroying the stone tablets of the Ten Commandments he holds in his hands.

Michelangelo must at times have felt cursed by the "divine genius" within him and the responsibility to create that went with it. His _Prisoners,_ two works that struggle to "free" themselves from the uncut stone around them, symbolize the neo-Platonic struggle of the divine soul to free itself from the prison of the body.

Michelangelo had a unique view of art. Many painters, including Leonardo, thought of themselves as almost divine creators who could take a blank canvas and make a beautiful picture. Michelangelo, the sculptor, thought of himself as a tool of God, gifted with an ability not to create but to reveal what God had put into the stone.

Michelangelo, _Holy Family_ (Uffizi, Florence)
Michelangelo insisted he was a sculptor, not a painter, and this painting shows it—solid, statue-esque people posed in sculpture groups.

Artists such as Leonardo and Raphael took great pride in their high-class profession—they painted while wearing fine clothes, nibbling fresh fruit, sipping wine, and maybe even being entertained with live music, washing up before dinner and enjoying a high society ball that evening. But Michelangelo worked in a frenzy. In his sweaty work clothes, covered with marble dust, he'd often work doggedly, deep into the night—wearing a candle on his cap.

For Michelangelo, history's greatest bodybuilder, sculpture, not painting, was the most noble art form. He always insisted that he was a sculptor, not a painter. Fortunately for us, his patrons thought other-

Michelangelo, Sistine Chapel (Vatican)
The pictorial culmination of the Renaissance, Michelangelo's Sistine ceiling tells the entire history of the Christian world, from Creation to Christ. In the *Last Judgment*, on the wall behind the altar, painted 25 years after the original work on the ceiling, Michelangelo is less optimistic.

wise. Pope Julius II, as part of a massive effort to return Rome and the papacy to its former splendor and prestige, bribed and pressured a hesitant Michelangelo into painting an enormous fresco (a painting on wet plaster) on the ceiling of the Sistine Chapel. Michelangelo worked furiously for four years, producing a masterpiece of incredible proportion, unity, and emotional power.

The Sistine Chapel is the pictorial culmination of the Renaissance. It chronicles the entire Christian history of the world, from the Creation to the Coming of Christ to the Last Judgment. The several hundred figures not only tell the story but also add up to a unified, rhythmically pleasing composition. Their bodies are, as we would expect, dramatic, expressive, and statuelike, in the tradition of Giotto and Masaccio.

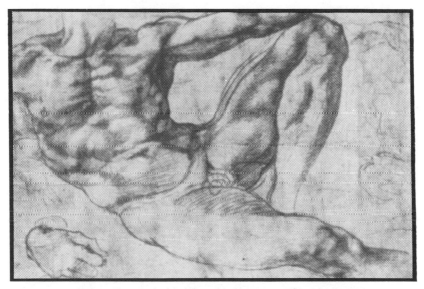

Michelangelo, Study for Adam for the Sistine Chapel—c. 1510
The Florentines were sculptors at heart. Here Michelangelo's sculptural orientation shows through. Compare this with the finished product, shown on p. 132.

The central scene shows the Creation of Man; Adam reaches out to receive the divine spark of life from God. (See page 132.) We can see the tenderness between a fatherly God and his creation, but the most striking thing about the relationship is its equality. Man is not cowering before a terrible God. He is strong and confident. Michelangelo shows us the essential goodness of man, who was created in the image of God, an important Renaissance idea.

Michelangelo, *The Last Judgment* (detail), (Sistine Chapel, Vatican)
A disillusioned and self-doubting Michelangelo paints his own face in the flayed, wretched skin in St. Bartholomew's hand.

Michelangelo, *The Last Judgment* (detail), (Sistine Chapel, Vatican)
Twenty-five years after painting the Sistine ceiling, Michelangelo portrayed Christ as a powerful, wrathful, and terrifying deity poised to strike down the wicked. Renaissance optimism had ended.

Michelangelo, Apse and Dome of St. Peter's Cathedral (Rome)—begun 1547
When asked to build the dome of St. Peter's, Michelangelo said, "I can build one bigger but not more beautiful than the dome of my hometown, Florence." Climb to the top—100 winding, sweaty yards up—and judge for yourself. Matching (but not outdoing) the grandeur of ancient Rome, the builders of St. Peter's proudly "put the dome of the Pantheon atop the Basilica Maxentius."

Michelangelo was also a great architect. He designed the dome of St. Peter's in Rome, influenced by Brunelleschi's dome in Florence.

The Campidoglio (the square a short but hot hike above the Forum at the top of Rome's Capitol Hill) was restructured by Michelangelo. The central feature was the ancient Roman statue of the Emperor Marcus Aurelius on horseback. (When the Christians gained power in ancient Rome, they destroyed many "pagan" images. This one was spared because they mistook Aurelius for Constantine, the first Christian emperor.) Around the statue, on three sides of the square, Michelangelo designed buildings to create the effect of an "outdoor room." The side buildings are not quite parallel, directing energy forward as they intersect at the Senator's Palace. Today these buildings house two fine history and ancient-art museums and a rare public rest room.

Michelangelo, Campidoglio (Capitol Hill, Rome)—c. 1550
Michelangelo, typical of the Renaissance genius, was expected to sculpt, paint, and be a world-class architect on command. No problema.

Michelangelo was something of a contradiction—forceful and self-confident (almost arrogant), yet tormented by self-doubt and a feeling of unworthiness. The contradiction, which blends so well in his early works, becomes more pronounced toward the end of his life. The inner turmoil rises to the surface; the bodies look more agonized. This is best seen in several later Pietàs (sculptures of the dead Jesus with his mother, Mary) in Florence and Milan.

Whether he died satisfied with his life's work we don't know. But he lived almost 90 years and was productive until the end. As a final show of independence and artistic devotion, when he designed the great dome of St. Peter's, he refused payment for his services.

Works of Michelangelo:

Pietà (the famous one), St. Peter's, the Vatican
David, Pietà, and *Prisoners*, Accademia, Florence
Dome of St. Peter's, the Vatican
Sistine Chapel ceiling and *Last Judgment*, Vatican
Pietà Robello, Milan
Pietà, Museo del Duomo, Florence
Moses, St. Peter in Chains church, Rome
Bacchus, Bruto, and a minor David, Bargello, Florence
Madonna and Child, Brugge, Belgium
Slaves, Louvre, Paris
Holy Family easel painting, Uffizi, Florence
Entombment (unfinished painting), National Gallery, London
Christ and Cross, Santa Maria Sopra Minerva church, Rome
Campidoglio, Rome
Night, Day, and others, Medici Chapel, Florence

Michelangelo, Pietà

Raphael

Raphael (1483-1520) is the best single embodiment of the harmony and pure beauty of the Renaissance style—a synthesis of the grace of Leonardo and the force of Michelangelo. He managed to achieve what had eluded painters before him: the realistic and harmonious composition of freely moving figures.

Raphael, *School of Athens* (Raphael Rooms, Vatican)—1510 Renaissance thought brought together the church and the great classical philosophers. Notice the fantastic Renaissance architecture, the unfinished St. Peter's church. As in Leonardo's *Last Supper,* the receding lines of perspective meet at the heads of the central figures, Plato and Aristotle.

Raphael's fresco *The School of Athens* embodies the spirit of the High Renaissance. Its subject is classical—Plato and Aristotle surrounded by other Greek philosophers engaged in highbrow jawing. The architecture of the school, unlike anything found in ancient Greece, demonstrates pure Renaissance use of classical forms.

The composition is like Leonardo's *Last Supper,* with figures grouped rhythmically around a center of calm. The lines of sight meet at the "haloed" figures of the two "saints" of knowledge, just as they did at Leonardo's Jesus. Each figure makes a specific gesture that reveals his inner personality. The bearded figure of Plato is none other than Leonardo—Raphael's tribute to the aging master. Michelangelo is shown meditating, sitting with his head in his hand in the foreground.

The fresco shows Michelangelo's influence in the solid, sculptural bodies and the dramatic power reminiscent of the Sistine Chapel. In fact, Raphael was working on this in the Vatican Palace while Michelangelo was climbing the walls of the Sistine Chapel next door. *The School of Athens* is one of many Raphael masterpieces that adorn the rooms through which you walk immediately before you enter the Sistine Chapel. (If you didn't buy our book, *Mona Winks,* all's not lost. You and your partner can spend the $14.95 you saved on rental radio headphones to guide you through these rooms and the Sistine Chapel.)

Raphael's fame was equal to Michelangelo's, and his influence on subsequent generations was perhaps even greater. Periodically through the centuries, artists returned to the vision of ideal beauty depicted by Raphael, who was known as the "Master of Grace." However, these imitators often ignored the realism and power of Raphael, turning out pretty pictures with little substance. It's tempting to blame Raphael for all those boring, sickly sweet, dainty pictures by

Raphael, *La Belle Jardiniere* (Louvre)—1507
A typical pyramid, or triangle, composition by the "Master of Grace." Most tourists burn out on the very common "Madonna and Child" scene long before they get to Raphael. Be sure to save time and interest for Raphael, the master of this form. See the composition diagram on page 307.

lesser painters you'll see in countless museums, but Raphael never flattered his subjects. He created a world that was idealized yet very real.

Raphael was the most loved Renaissance painter until this century. Only in our generation have Michelangelo and Leonardo passed him in postcards and calendars sold.

When Raphael died in 1520, the center of Renaissance painting shifted once again—this time northward, to Venice.

Raphael, *The Transfiguration* (detail), (Pinacoteca, Vatican)
As he was dying, Raphael set his sights on heaven and painted possibly his most beautiful work—the heavenly face of Jesus.

Raphael's Works:

School of Athens, Deliverance of St. Peter, and others, Vatican
Transfiguration, Pinacoteca Gallery, Vatican
Most major art galleries, including Uffizi, Prado, Louvre, Alte Pinakothek, Kunsthistorisches
Borghese Palace, Rome
Chateau Chantilly, France

Renaissance Venice—Europe's Rich Middleman

In Venice, Renaissance art and architecture was financed by its lucrative overseas trading empire. For 500 years, Venice was known as "the Bride of the Sea" and the envy of all of Europe. The economy, glorious buildings, art, and gay way of life all depended on sea trading. Every year the leader of Venice, after pronouncing a solemn promise, tossed an elegant ring into the Adriatic. This act symbolized the marriage between the sea and its bride.

Doge's Palace (Venice)—1340 The multinational corporation known as the Venetian Empire was ruled from this palace—the home of its C.E.O., the Doge, or Duke. A good example of Venetian Gothic, this building (often called the tablecloth) was the political center of the most prosperous city in Europe for several centuries. Today it's packed with art masterpieces, history, and tourists.

Venice had been founded as a kind of refugee camp around the year A.D. 400 by Italian mainlanders. After suffering one too many barbarian rape-pillage-and-plunders, the Venetians got together and decided to move out into the lagoon, hoping the barbarians didn't like water. They built on muddy islands, pounding in literally millions of tree trunks for support. They dredged canals for passageways rather than trying to build solid roads.

Farming was impossible in the mud, so the Venetians quickly learned to trade fish and salt (for preserving meat) with their neighbors for grain and other agricultural products. Gradually, their trading took them to more and more distant lands. They were situated perfectly to link Europe with the wealthy Byzantine Empire and the treasures of the East. When the Crusades created a demand in Europe for Eastern luxury goods, Venice became the go-between.

Venice went between so well that by A.D. 1200, she was Europe's economic superpower. Products from as far away as Scotland and India passed through Venetian warehouses. The Rialto Bridge area became the world's busiest trading center. The wares traded included iron, copper, and woven textiles from Northern Europe and raisins, pepper, wines, lemons, silk, Persian rugs, leathers, precious stones, perfumes, and spices from the East.

Venetians did no overland trading. Instead, they used a chain of ports and friendly cities in the eastern Mediterranean. Goods arrived (sometimes by camel caravan) and the Venetians shipped them westward to where European land traders picked them up.

Venice, with 150,000 citizens, was the most populous city in Europe in 1500. (Paris had 100,000.) The ducat, because of its stability and high gold content, became the monetary standard for the Eastern world. (The Florentine florin was the West's.) The "gross national product" of this city was 50 percent greater than that of the entire country of France.

Her sea trading spawned other industries including shipbuilding, warehousing, insurance, and accounting. The Arsenal, the largest single factory in Europe, employed 16,000 people at its peak and could crank out a warship a day.

Besides expanding its commercial empire, Venice hired generals to conquer many of the cities in northern Italy and profited greatly from the Crusades.

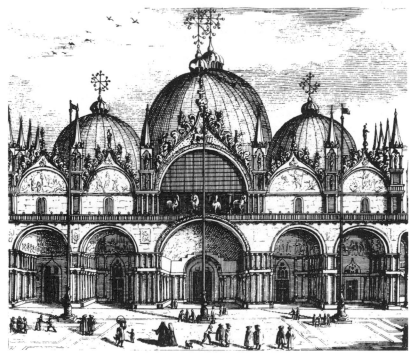

St. Mark's Cathedral, Venice
Mark Twain called it "a warty bug taking a walk."

All this wealth did not go to waste. The fifteenth century was a time of massive building and rebuilding. The earliest structures of this century show a Byzantine influence. The most distinctive, however, are "Venetian Gothic" in style, such as the Doge's Palace. They have Gothic pointed arches, but they're much gayer and more fanciful than the Gothic churches of Northern Europe. Later structures are Renaissance style, with rounded Roman arches.

St. Mark's Cathedral, one of the world's most famous, is the best example of "Venetian Byzantine" architecture with its onion-shaped Eastern domes, Greek cross floor plan, and interior mosaics. But the style might better be called "Early Ransack": the cathedral is a treasure chest of artifacts looted from other cities during Venice's heyday.

Even the bones of Venice's patron saint, Mark, which reposed there, were booty. Middle Age Europe was into relic worship. In 829, the young but powerful city-state of Venice was really nothing on the religious map. It needed some relics to give it some clout. A band of merchants trading in Alexandria, Egypt, stole the bones of the Evangelist (a writer of one of the New Testament Gospels) from Alexandria's Moslem rulers, put them in their church, and, bam, Venice became an important religious destination. St. Mark is housed in the basilica that bears his name, and his symbol, the winged lion, replaced Theodore's dragon as the symbol of the Venetian Republic.

Tintoretto, *Paradise* (Doge's Palace, Venice)
Tintoretto's monsterpiece has more square footage than my apartment. Over 500 (count 'em) figures.

With its newfound sanctity, Venice grew rapidly. The Rialto Bridge spanning the Grand Canal, originally a covered wooden drawbridge, was rebuilt in an arched style. The straight, wooden planks of Venice's drawbridges had allowed horses and mules to pass over. When builders installed the new, arched bridges, horses were banned from the city—just as cars are today.

The Venetian empire was controlled by an oligarchy of wealthy families, who comprised about 5 percent of the population. They elected a council of rulers led by a duke who served for life, known as the "Doge" (pronounced "dozh," not "doggie").

The rest of the population had no political rights, but they were treated well and prospered. Until 1423 the people had final veto power over election of the Doge. The council would present him in St. Mark's Square, saying, "This is your Doge, if it please you." They invariably approved the election by cheering—until one Doge-elect, an unpopular man, feared he might not please them. From then on, the council said only, "This is your Doge." (Throughout history, democracy has been a bonsai tree in the house of the powerful—it looks nice, and when it grows too big you simply cut it back.)

Venetian society was rigidly structured, but it was also quite tolerant. It was a cosmopolitan city where traders from all over the world rubbed elbows. Some foreigners were even allowed to settle there— Turks, Dalmations, Arabs. (The bell at St. Mark's is rung by two statues of Moors.) There was a Jewish community—giving us our word "ghetto," meaning a neighborhood set aside for minorities. The largest foreign group was the Greek population, especially after the disastrous sack of Constantinople by the European Crusaders (in 1204) and the city's fall to the Turks (in 1453). There were about 5,000 Greeks, one of whom was Domenico Theotocopoulis, who became a famous painter in Spain only after he agreed to shorten his name to El Greco ("The Greek").

The Catholic church was often at odds with Venice, partly because of her close ties with the rival Greek Orthodox Christians. The proud Venetians thought of themselves as Catholics. . . but not Rome-an Catholics.

Elegant Decay—Venice's Cinquecento

The year 1450 marked the height of Venice's economic power. Following that year, a series of world events set in motion three centuries of slow decline. In 1453, the Moslem Turks captured and looted Constantinople. Uninterested in trading with the West, they began attacking Venice's foreign ports. Venice not only lost its links with the East but it was also forced to fight costly wars with the Turks.

The next blows came from the West, when explorers from Spain and Portugal discovered America and new sea trade routes to the East. By 1500, Portugal was using Vasco da Gama's route around South Africa to trade with the Moluccas and India. Venice's Eastern monopoly was broken. Her trade plummeted.

The period of decline was perhaps Venice's most glorious, however. Like so many cultures past their peak of economic expansion, Venice turned from business to the arts, from war to diplomacy, from sternness to partying, from buying gold to selling tacky souvenirs. The "Cinquecento" (pronounced "CHINK-kwa-CHEN-to"), as the Italians call the century of the 1500s, was a time for merrymaking and festivity that was legendary in Europe.

Veronese, *Feast of the House of Levi* (Accademia, Venice)
This was originally titled *The Last Supper* until Veronese was hauled before the Inquisition for painting Christ and His holy apostles in a Venetian orgy. Veronese didn't change a thing, except the title.

Venice's economic decline went hand in hand with political corruption and repression. Venice had never been a democracy, though it had been ruled in the past by an elected Doge and council members known as "The Ten." In later years, those Ten were whittled down to "The Three," who shared sweeping powers. The people had a saying: "The Ten send you to the torture chamber; The Three to your grave." Venice had some of Europe's most convincing torture chambers.

Casanova, the renowned rogue, spent time in a Venetian prison, which he described as follows: "Those subterranean prisons are precisely like tombs, but they call them 'Wells' because they contain about two feet of filthy water which penetrates from the sea. Condemned to live in these sewers, they are given every morning some thin soup and a ration of bread which they have to eat immediately or it becomes the prey of enormous rats. A villain who died while I was there had spent 37 years in the Wells."

The famous Bridge of Sighs (rebuilt in 1600 and open today to visitors) connected the lawyers' offices in the Doge's Palace with the prisons. Prisoners could be brought from the prisons, tried in closed court, and sentenced without the public knowing about it. As they passed over the bridge to their deaths, they got one last look at their beloved city—hence, the "Bridge of Sighs."

The long, glorious decline was hastened by two brutal plagues that devastated the population. When Napoleon arrived in 1797, the city was defenseless. He ended the Republic, throwing the city into even worse chaos. It became a possession of various European powers until 1866, when it joined the newly united Italian nation.

The city today is older, crumbling and sinking, but it looks much the same as it did during the grand days of the Renaissance. For that we can thank Venice's economic decline: the inhabitants were simply too poor to rebuild. Venice is Europe's best-preserved big city. It is the toast of the High Middle Ages and Renaissance—in an elegant state of decay.

Many people actually avoid Venice because of its famous "smelly canals." So that you'll know how serious this problem is, we've recreated the Venetian stench here so you can scratch 'n' sniff—and decide for yourself.

Scratch 'n' sniff
—Venice—

Art of the Venetian Renaissance

The Cinquecento produced some of the greatest Renaissance art. Bellini, Titian, Giorgione, Tintoretto, and Veronese—whose works embellish churches, palaces, and museums throughout the city—forged a distinct Venetian style that emphasized color over outline. While Florentine painters drew massive sculptural figures with a strong outline, Venetians used gradations of color to blend figures into the background. The result was a lighter, more refined, and more graceful look—understandable in an elegant city of lavish palaces and glittering canals.

The same delicate, atmospheric haze that often hangs over the city of Venice also characterizes Venetian art. It's like a picture taken with a soft-focus lens on the camera, making everything glow and blend together, bathing it in light. This is Leonardo's sfumato taken one step farther.

Giorgione, _The Tempest_ (detail), (Accademia, Venice) —c. 1505
While Florentine art tended to be sculptural with strong outlines, the Renaissance art of Venice was colorful and romantically atmospheric—like its hometown.

Giorgione's _The Tempest,_ with bright colors and a hazy quality, marks a trend new to Italian painting—the landscape. Like painters from the North, Venetians enjoyed painting pleasantly detailed scenes that show a love of the natural world. This painting experiments with composition, using color, not just the figures, to balance and unify. In contrast with Florentine art that puts the human form at the center of every work, the soldier on the left and the woman and child on the right are almost secondary to the true subject of the painting—the slash of lightning in the center that's about to shatter their serene scene.

Titian the Venetian was one of the most prolific painters ever, cranking out a painting a month for almost 80 years. Like it or not, you'll see plenty of Titians on your trip (especially in Venice). His canvases have richness of color and brilliance of light burning through the night. He used color and light rather than the drawn line to balance his work and direct the viewer's eyes. (When Michelangelo met the great Titian, whose fame rivaled his own, he praised his work and then said, "But it's a pity you Venetians cannot draw.")

Titian, *Danae* (Kunsthistorisches Museum, Vienna)
Luxurious and fleshy Venetian art reflected the values of the merchant city.

When Raphael died, Titian (c. 1490-1576) became the most sought after portrait artist, and Venice was Italy's art capital. Titian could capture a personality and endow it with a calm, meditative, serene air—a mood that pervades all Venetian painting (as well as many of its back streets). A famous example of Titian's prestige: once, when he dropped a brush during a sitting, his subject, Emperor Charles V of Spain, picked it up for him. Whether this actually happened is unimportant. This

Titian, *Venus with the Organ Player* (Prado, Madrid)
Rich Venetians dealt with the conflict between sacred artistic pursuits (for example, music) and worldly, sensual pursuits (for example, the naked lady). Here, the torn musician leers at Venus while keeping both hands at work on his organ.

often-repeated anecdote represented to future generations the triumph of artistic genius.

The happy-go-lucky Venetian attitude can be seen in Paolo Veronese's huge, colorful scenes of the Venetian high-life. He once painted the "Last Supper" scene as if it were a typical Venetian dinner party. We see drunks, buffoons, dwarfs, a German mercenary soldier, dogs, a cat, and a parrot. The authorities were so shocked that they demanded he repaint it to reflect a more somber mood. Instead, he simply retitled it. We know the work as *Feast of the House of Levi* (in Venice's Accademia).

The bright colors of the Venetian style take on an almost surrealistic tint with Tintoretto (1518-1594). His works glow like black velvet paintings. He also experimented with new techniques of composition showing his main subjects at odd angles and in twisted poses, whipping up the excitement. Tintoretto's dramatic style went beyond serene Renaissance balance, pointing toward the next phase in art—baroque.

Venetian Art:

Accademia, Venice
Doge's Palace, Venice
Basilica dei Frari, Venice
Scuola San Rocco (works of Tintoretto), Venice
The city of Venice herself, including most churches
Prado, Madrid, Spain
Kunsthistorisches Museum, Vienna, Austria
City of Dubrovnik, Yugoslavia

The Northern Renaissance

The Renaissance in the north countries was more an improvement on medieval art than a return to classical forms. Northern artists used Italian discoveries of perspective, anatomy, and knowledge of classical forms but kept their style distinctly Northern.

Late Gothic art is characterized by grace and lightness, delicate flowing lines, and an appreciation for things that are just plain beautiful. Human bodies are slender and gently curved, with smooth, unmuscled skin. Colors are bright and pleasant.

Northern artists loved detail. Like craftsmen working on a fine Swiss watch or German cuckoo clock, they thought nothing of spending hours on end slaving over, say, the hairs on a dog's head to get them just right—even when the dog was just a minor figure in a large canvas. Their appreciation of the many wonders of nature shows in their work.

Medieval paintings often look crowded. Details abound—the more, the better. Crammed with objects and minute details, Northern Renaissance works are best viewed as they were painted, slowly and carefully.

Van Eyck, *Arnolfini Wedding* (detail), (National Gallery, London)—1434
This early masterpiece from the Northern Renaissance shows the characteristic medieval attention to detail and the down-to-earth personal style typical of Belgian and Dutch art. You can even see the couple's reflection in the round mirror in the rear. "Wedding?" Well, maybe she's just fat. Actually, there was a time when women would wear a pillow to their wedding—to improve their chances of becoming pregnant.

Albrecht Dürer (1471-1528), a German working at about the same time as Michelangelo, finished his apprenticeship and traveled to Venice to learn the techniques he'd heard so much about. When he returned home and achieved fame, he helped "Italianize" the North. He has been called the "Leonardo of the North."

Dürer combined the Italian painters' laws of perspective and human anatomy with the Germans' attention to detail. Although he never mastered Michelangelo's ability to make a solid, statuelike body, his paintings are astonishingly realistic. With the patience formed from his mastery of the grueling process of woodcuts and engraving, he painted with incredible detail. Dürer was Europe's first top-selling artist. His popular works were reproduced and sold in large quantities.

A woodcut is made by sketching black lines on a white-painted block, then chipping off the white so only the desired lines remain standing. This woodcut is then dipped into ink and used the way we use a rubber stamp today. An engraving, the opposite of a woodcut, cuts the "lines" into the plate and, when mastered, allows for even more detail than a woodcut. An etching, which is an improved version of engraving and was used by later artists such as Rembrandt, is made by coating a copperplate with wax and scratching an image into the wax which is then burned with acid. Prints are then made from the plate in the same manner as engravings.

Dürer was impressed by the respect Italian artists enjoyed. Northern artists had always been anonymous craftsmen, laboring in guilds. Dürer helped change that. He kept journals and wrote books, convinced

Dürer, *Self-Portrait* (Prado, Madrid)—1497
In this first full self-portrait by an artist, the German painter Dürer declares that artists deserve and will get respect.

that his personal life and thoughts were as important as his handiwork. His famous self-portraits (a first) portray him as an elegant, confident, even arrogant, man of the world.

Matthias Grünewald (pronounced "GROON-uh-vald," 1470-1528) was a great but mysterious Northern Renaissance artist. (We're not even sure that's his real name.) Like Northern Renaissance art in general, his

Dürer, *Four Horsemen of the Apocalypse* (British Museum)—1498
Dürer's woodcuts were the first mass-produced art Europe had seen. His mastery of lines and detail went well with this painstaking medium. Notice his famous A.D. monogram (D inside A) at the bottom.

style grew out of the Gothic stage. His anonymity is medieval, as is his gripping religious devotion. Grunewald often ignored realism (so important to Dürer and the Italians) to make a religious point.

His famous *Isenheim Altarpiece* in Colmar, France, is one of Europe's most exciting and powerful masterpieces. In this set of scenes from Jesus' life, Grünewald uses distorted shapes and dazzling, unreal colors to grab the emotions. You feel the agony of Christ twisted stiffly and heavily on the cross, the humility of Mary, and the exuberance of the resurrected Christ springing psychedelically from the tomb as if shot out of a Roman candle.

Hieronymous Bosch (rhymes with "gosh", 1450-1516) was another interesting artist of this era. We know almost nothing about him except

Grünewald, _Isenheim Altarpiece_ (Colmar, France)—1515
The mysterious, late Gothic master painted one of the most gripping crucifixions ever. Notice the weight of Christ's body bending the cross bar, his stiff fingers, mashed feet, dislocated elbows—and the grief on Mary's face (kneeling). Though Renaissance in its technique, there is still medieval symbolism—the lamb with a cross and cup, John the Baptist holding a book, and so on. Turn to p. 308 for a closer look at this masterpiece.

what we learn through his fantastic paintings. "Hieronymous the Anonymous" painted medieval fears with modern skill. His huge canvases are crowded with grotesque, humorous, and all-around bizarre people and creatures. Most of his themes are intriguing and were very meaningful to the medieval mind. He painted strange-looking plants and animals in many of his works. Doing so was common among artists who painted during the years when Columbus and other explorers were bringing fascinating creatures back from the New World.

Today, although much of the meaning of his art is lost, the intrigue remains.

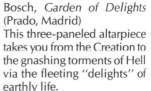

Bosch, _Garden of Delights_ (Prado, Madrid)
This three-paneled altarpiece takes you from the Creation to the gnashing torments of Hell via the fleeting "delights" of earthly life.

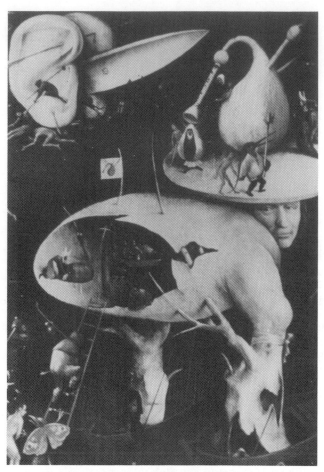

Bosch, *Garden of Delights* (detail from Hell), (Prado, Madrid)—1510
In just a tiny bit of this monumental three-paneled altarpiece we see a self-portrait of
Bosch with a broken-eggshell body, tree trunk legs, crashed-through wooden dinghies
in a frozen lake with giant birds leading naked people around the brim of his hat. Nothing
unusual—for Bosch.

Dürer, *Adam and Eve* (engraving)—1504

Northern Renaissance Art:

Alte Pinakothek, Munich, Germany
Kunsthistorisches Museum, Vienna
Prado, Madrid
Isenheim Altarpiece, Colmar, France
Rijksmuseum, Amsterdam
Ancient Art Museum, Brussels
Dahlem Museum, Berlin, Germany
Last Judgment, Beaune, France
Adoration of the Mystic Lamb, St. Bavo's Church, Ghent, Belgium

Time Line of the Renaissance

The Renaissance spread as countries reached an economic affluence that could support the arts. It began in Florence and then spread to Venice, Rome, Spain, Portugal, and finally the northern countries, Flanders, France, and England.

The earliest Renaissance artists, Brunelleschi, Masaccio, Donatello, and Botticelli, lived in Florence at the time the powerful banking family, the Medicis, ruled the city. The High Renaissance shifted to Rome (Michelangelo and Raphael) and Venice (Titian).

Meanwhile, the rest of Europe was discovering new lands with which to trade. Spain and Portugal broke Venice's monopoly on Eastern trade by finding new routes to the East. England, Holland, and France built large merchant fleets and banking houses to expand their trade with the rest of Europe and the New World. With the invention of the printing press, ideas were exchanged as quickly as goods.

Each of these countries was touched by its own Renaissance. Portugal flowered with the Manueline architectural style; Spain inspired the art of El Greco (he arrived via Venice); and the northern countries spawned the masterpieces of Dürer, Bosch, and Brueghel.

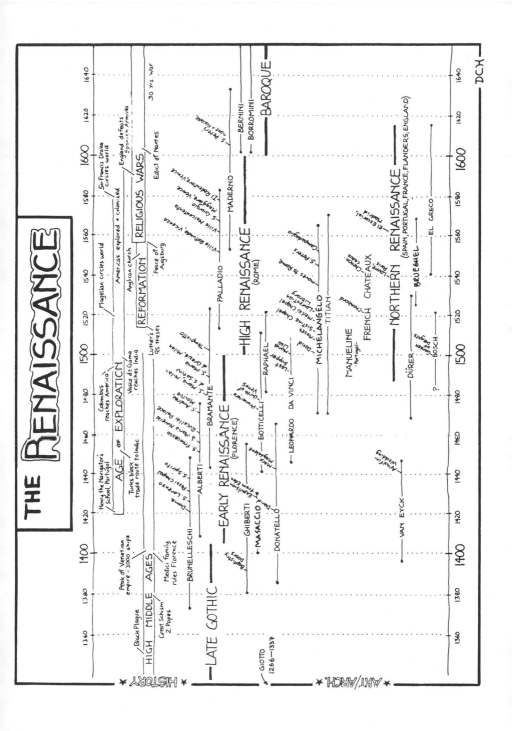

THE RENAISSANCE

HISTORY

1360 — 1380 — 1400 — 1420 — 1440 — 1460 — 1480 — 1500 — 1520 — 1540 — 1560 — 1580 — 1600 — 1620 — 1640

Black Plague
Great Schism 2 Popes
HIGH MIDDLE AGES
Peak of Venetian empire - 3000 ships
Medici family rules Florence
Henry the Navigator's School, Portugal
Turks block trade route to India
AGE OF EXPLORATION
Columbus reaches America
Vasco da Gama reaches India
Magellan circles world
Americas explored & colonized
Anglican church
Sir Francis Drake circles world
England defeats Spanish Armada
30 yrs War
Luther's 95 theses
REFORMATION
Peace of Augsburg
RELIGIOUS WARS
Edict of Nantes

ART/ARCH.

GIOTTO 1266-1337
LATE GOTHIC
BRUNELLESCHI
Baptistry Doors
S. Lorenzo
Pazzi Chapel
S. Spirito
ALBERTI
Duomo
S. Francesco
Rucellai Palace
S. Maria Novella
EARLY RENAISSANCE (FLORENCE)
GHIBERTI
MASACCIO
DONATELLO
David
BRAMANTE
S. Maria delle Grazie, Milan
S. Satiro
Tempietto
PALLADIO
Villa Rotonda, Vicenza
S. Giorgio, Venice
Il Redentore, Venice
Villa Malcontenta
MADERNO
S. Peter's façade
BERNINI
BORROMINI
BAROQUE
BOTTICELLI
Birth of Venus
Primavera
RAPHAEL
School of Athens
LEONARDO DA VINCI
HIGH RENAISSANCE (ROME)
MICHELANGELO
David
Sistine Chapel
Pietà
Moses
Laurentian Library
Medici Chapel
Campidoglio
Moses to Rome
S. Peter's
TITIAN
MANUELINE Portugal
FRENCH CHATEAUX
Château Chambord
Louvre, Paris
NORTHERN RENAISSANCE (SPAIN, PORTUGAL, FRANCE, FLANDERS, ENGLAND)
VAN EYCK
Arnolfini Wedding
DÜRER
BOSCH
Garden of Earthly Delights
BRUEGHEL
EL GRECO
El Escorial, Madrid

DCM

After the Renaissance: Mannerism

Looking at the ceiling of the Sistine Chapel might make you think, How could there be anything more beautiful? Well, that's what artists after Michelangelo thought—and worried about, too. How could art advance beyond the works of the great Renaissance masters? They had explored and conquered every facet of painting and sculpture—the human body, the laws of perspective—showing nature on the canvas flawlessly. It seemed as though the future of art would be little more than copying the forms and techniques of Michelangelo, Leonardo, Raphael, and Titian.

The Renaissance was a hard act to follow, and for a while many artists were stuck in the rut (but what a beautiful rut!) of Raphael's style. We call the style of this period (1530-1600) Mannerism because the art followed only the "manner" of the Renaissance masters—often neglecting the spirit of their work.

Many artists made bold, occasionally ridiculous, attempts to be original, to do something new. Using Renaissance techniques of portraying nature, they experimented with more complex composition, more striking colors, the contrast of light and shadow, and a greater display of emotion—elements that would later be exhibited in the baroque style.

Relax . . .

You've just absorbed a direct hit from the most powerful cultural explosion in Europe's history.

Take a break.

While you're sorting out the accomplishments of Leonardo, Michelangelo, and company, you might want to flip to the back of the book and browse through the articles on art appreciation, art patronage, and common subjects and symbols in art.

The Early Modern World
A.D. 1500-1815

The Reformation

Before the Renaissance, the church was the richest, most powerful, and best organized institution in Europe. Like a monastic mafia, it was Europe's greatest landowner, collected taxes through tithes, patronized great art, and influenced political decisions. Kings and princes needed papal support to maintain their political power. Average Europeans identified themselves by their bishopric, not by citizenship in a particular country. A crime was a sin, and a sin was a crime.

Nevertheless, the church's rich and worldly position caused corruption, and a reforming spirit grew. When political rivalries and jealousies were added, reforming changed to splitting. New churches were formed, and because religion and politics were intertwined, Europe experienced a chaotic period of political upheaval. This period of religious and political turmoil is called the Reformation. Much of the Europe you see today was shaped to some extent by this period.

Church Corruption

The church certainly needed reform. Many priests were illiterate and immoral. Bishops meddled in politics, governing like petty tyrants. The clergy sold important church offices and dispensations (exemptions from church laws) to the highest bidder. The medieval church showed not a hint of the voluntary poverty of the early Christians. In addition, the church had lost touch with ordinary folk. Mass was celebrated in Latin, a language spoken only by the educated.

To pay for Rome's face lift, the pope sold indulgences. (Renaissance artists such as Michelangelo didn't come cheap.) To anyone who paid the price, the pope promised "forgiveness for all thy sins, transgressions and excesses, how enormous so ever they may be so that when you die the gates of Hell shall be shut and the gates of Paradise shall open with delight"—a bargain at twice the price.

"I'd like two adulteries and a small order of lies to go."

Tickets to heaven, the sale of indulgences, Germany, woodcut
People actually bought letters of forgiveness in the marketplace. A scene that bothered Martin Luther.

Church corruption was one reason for the Reformation, and the sale of indulgences might have been the final straw. But there were deeper causes: the decline of papal prestige, a new secularism, and stronger, more assertive national governments.

The pope had lost prestige among both kings and commoners. During their medieval heyday, popes could make or break kings. But after the popes moved to Avignon, France (they resided there from 1309 through 1372), to enjoy the protection of the strong French kings, they were seen as French popes, and their international influence suffered. When a second pope popped up back in Rome and each pope excommunicated the other, papal prestige sank to mud-wrestling depths. Even after the papacy returned, united, to Rome, it never quite recovered from what was called the "Babylonian Captivity."

New Secular Forces

The church had to cope with a new secularism bolstered by the rise of capitalism and many new Renaissance ideas. The newly invented printing press sped the spread of new scientific discoveries and secular ideas. Reformers risked death to print local-language versions of one especially radical book—the Bible. After Copernicus and Galileo disproved the church's traditional explanation of the earth-centered universe, nothing was accepted blindly. A new, more independent, scientific, economic, and political world confronted the church.

Kings jumped on the reforming bandwagon out of political greed. They saw the church as a rival power within their borders. Tithes sent to Rome were taxes lost. The church was Europe's number one landowner. Clergy was exempt from taxes and could ignore local laws. Many kings wanted not only to reform the church but also to break with it for good. The political rewards were obvious. Kings and princes encouraged spiritual people to challenge church authority.

Martin Luther

At first, Martin Luther (1483-1546) was merely an ordinary German monk trying to reform church abuses from within. He believed that the word of God lay not in the doctrine of the church but in the Bible. The Bible talked of salvation by simple faith in God. Salvation was a free gift to believers, not something anyone could earn or buy. Elaborate church rituals and the granting of dispensations and indulgences made no sense to him and his followers.

Martin Luther's birthday was commemorated on an American stamp.

Luther nailed to the door of the Wittenberg cathedral a list of ninety-five ideas for debate. Not interested in debating, the church called Luther a heretic and sent him a "papal bull" of excommunication. Luther, not cowed, burned the pope's letter—the Renaissance equivalent to burning your draft card, only much more serious.

Now a criminal as well as a heretic, Luther took refuge in a German prince's castle. From behind those walls he established the German church, translated the Bible into German (giving birth to the modern German language), and led the rebellion against the pope. Local kings confiscated church lands, established their own "protestant" (protesting) state churches, and geared up to face the armies of the nations loyal to the church.

The wars came. Lucky for the German Protestants, the pope's strongest defenders (the southern countries that remained Catholic) were preoccupied with internal problems and with fighting the Turks who were invading Eastern Europe. The result of the wars (which culminated in the Treaty of Augsburg in 1555) was that each German prince could decide the religion of his territory.

CATHOLIC/PROTESTANT DIFFERENCES

The differences between Protestant and Catholic doctrines have divided Christians for centuries. Protestants emphasize a more direct relationship between the individual and God, rejecting church rituals and the necessity of ordained clergy for salvation. Bible study and personal prayer are seen as more valuable than sacraments presided over by a priest. Some of the Catholic practices rejected by Protestants are: celibate priests, veneration of saints and the Virgin Mary, use of Latin in church services, and holy orders (monks and nuns). The differences between Catholics and Protestants are not so great today, and a spirit of unity is growing.

Reformation and Religious Wars

The Reformation—and its violence—went beyond Germany. In Switzerland, Geneva was ruled by a theocratic government under the direction of John Calvin (c. 1550). Calvinism, which stresses belief in salvation by God's grace rather than by rituals and good deeds, spread from Switzerland through France, the Netherlands, and beyond to Scotland.

England's break with the church had political roots. King Henry VIII wanted the pope's permission to divorce Catherine of Aragon to marry Anne Boleyn. The pope refused to grant a divorce and so, to break all ties with Catherine, Henry broke all ties with Rome. He confiscated church lands, formed the Church of England, and married Anne. The Church of England, or Anglican church, was largely an English Catholic church without a pope. For the next hundred years, England struggled as her kings and queens tried to impose their various personal religions on the people.

The religious wars between Catholics and Protestants lasted for more than 100 years and were some of the bloodiest in European history. Kings generally fought for purely political reasons, but the fighters were fueled by religious fervor, convinced that God was on their side. The grand finale was the Thirty Years War, Europe's first "world war," with mercenary warriors from just about every country taking part. When the war ended in 1648, Europe was devastated, a third of Germany was dead, and Western civilization realized what it should have known from the start—that Catholics and Protestants would have to live together.

The Religious Wars, c. 1520-1648
Europe fought bloody religious wars for a hundred years after the Reformation. Often called "the First World War," these wars—Europe's biggest yet—involved nearly every nation.

The Peace of Westphalia (1648) ended the wars, decreeing that the leader of each country would decide the religion of his nation. Generally, the northern countries went Protestant and the southern ones stayed with Rome. The line dividing Catholic from Protestant Europe was (and remains) almost the same line that separated barbarian Europe from Roman Europe way back when the Christians were still hiding out. Roughly every country north of the Danube and Rhine rivers—Scandinavia, the Low Countries, northern Germany, and England—protested, while Spain, Portugal, Italy, France, and southern Germany remained loyal to Rome.

Counter-Reformation

The Vatican countered the Protestant revolution with the Counter-Reformation—an attempt to put the universal Catholic church back together by means of internal reform, propaganda, and war.

One of the church's weapons was the Inquisition, a network of church courts for trying and punishing heretics and sinners. The Inquisition, which dated back to medieval times, was set up to punish witches, devil worshipers, and adulterers as well as Jews, Moslems, and unorthodox Christians. Later, Protestants and heretic Catholics were hauled before the courts on the slightest evidence of guilt or nonconformity.

Torture, terror, imprisonment, and confiscation of property were often used to extract confessions—standard judicial practice of the day. Once the accused confessed, they were really punished. Punishments ranged from recitation of a certain number of prayers, fasting, and alms-giving to imprisonment and death.

Heretics, Protestants, Jews, and others could be punished quite thoroughly by the church.

Reformation Sights:

John Knox home, Edinburgh, Scotland
Reformers monument, Geneva
Cathcdral, Worms
El Escorial, near Madrid (Counter-Reformation)
Ruined abbeys of England
Various Bibles in the British Museum, London
Gutenberg Museum, Mainz, Germany
Rothenburg ob der Tauber and Dinkelsbühl (pawns of the Thirty
   Years War), Germany

Absolutism and Divine Monarchs

The Thirty Years War reshuffled Europe's political cards. The old-style baronies and dukedoms were replaced by new, more modern governments headed by strong kings. In the Middle Ages, the "nation" had been a weak entity. Popes, nobles, and petty kings bickered for power while the common man went about his business, ignoring the affairs of state.

Now government functions were specialized, bureaucrats ran things, and the state took over many jobs that had been carried out by the church. A strong "divine" monarch was all-powerful, claiming that his right to rule came directly from God. More than ever, the government was "mother-in-lawing" its people. And after 100 years of war, most Europeans didn't mind.

Growing Economy

The growing merchant class welcomed this strong central government. Traders needed stable governments, common currency, standard measures, and fewer tariffs. Early medieval trade had been stifled by the chaos of rural, feudal kingdoms. The trend toward unification begun in the High Middle Ages was paying off. Centralized governments and the wealthy urban middle class were natural allies.

Overseas trade gave these new governments wealth and strength. Newly discovered America and routes to the Far East opened a floodgate, bringing in waves of raw materials and luxury goods. The sale of captured Africans as slaves in the New World brought unprecedented wealth. Spain, England, France, and the Netherlands built large merchant fleets to exploit this wealth, which required naval protection, which required more taxes to maintain, which required more efficient governments to collect and administer the taxes. The state grew.

Louis XIV, the Sun King

"If Louis XIV had not existed, it would have been necessary to invent him."   —Voltaire

France's Louis XIV (who reigned from 1643 to 1715) was Europe's king of kings—the absolute example of an absolute monarch. Louis ruled

The Absolute Monarch—Ruling Like a God in Heaven
The 1600s and 1700s were a time of "divine" kings and absolutism. Many kings succeeded in convincing their people that they had been deputized by God to rule with complete and unquestioned power.

for seventy years, making France the political and cultural heartbeat of Europe. He strengthened the military, expanded France's borders, stimulated trade, and built a large and effective government.

The France Louis inherited was the strongest nation in Europe, with 18 million people. (England at this time had only 5.5 million.) The economy, directed by Minister Colbert (the first man to take a balance sheet seriously), was strong at home and spreading, thanks to a large merchant marine, to the luxurious East and the West Indies. Louis organized an efficient bureaucracy for gathering taxes, yet he himself remained at the controls. He was no scholar—in fact, he was "extraordinarily unlearned"—but as a ruler he was top-notch.

Although he was neither tall (he was 5'5") nor handsome, he seemed to strike people as both. He was charming, a great conversationalist, and a great horseman. He played the harpsichord and guitar (acoustic) and loved ballroom dancing. He was perhaps the most polite king ever: he always listened closely to his courtiers and tipped his hat to everyone on the street. Most of all, he was an outdoorsman, and that love made him want his palace in the countryside, not in stuffy Paris.

Louis XIV, portrait by Rigaud, in the Louvre
Louis XIV, the premier monarch of Europe, was every king's model of how to live and reign. He ruled the "Oz" and "Hollywood" of Europe for more than five decades and, even as an old man, had a fine set of gams.

Louis called himself the "Sun King." State medallions showed the light and warmth of the sun bouncing off his chest onto the people of France. To make their "divine authority" more believable, divine monarchs such as Louis went to great lengths to control nature. For instance, Louis had an orange grove on wheels that he had his servants roll out of his greenhouse on sunny days. His people would stroll through the finely manicured gardens of Versailles, proud to be ruled by such a wonderful king—a king deputized by God, and the only one who could sip an Orange Julius in the dead of winter.

Louis "domesticated" his nobles so they wouldn't threaten his absolute power. His trick was to reduce them to petty socialites more concerned with their position at court than with political issues. It worked so well that Louis had the high-and-mighty dukes and earls of France bickering over who would get to hold the candle while he slipped into his royal jammies. The tremendous expenses of court life weakened the nobility economically. Louis had them in a state of loyal servitude.

As Louis said, "L'etat, c'est moi!" ("The state? It's me!")

Versailles—Europe's Palace of Palaces

If you call yourself a divine monarch, you'd better get a big house. Louis moved his court to Versailles, 12 miles outside Paris. There he built Europe's greatest palace, at the cost of six months' worth of the entire income of France. Swamps were filled in, hills were moved, and a river was rerouted to give Louis a palace fit for a divine monarch. He established a magnificent court, the Oz and Hollywood of Europe, that attracted the leading artists, thinkers, and nobles of the day. Though it was France's capital for only a century (1682-1789), Versailles was the social, cultural, and intellectual capital of Europe.

Europe's Palace of Palaces, Versailles

Enormous palaces dwarfed by endless gardens. Great halls decorated in the "Grand Style" with chandeliers and mirrored walls. Tapestries, gold leaf and silver plating. Fountains, pools, and manicured shrubs. We can marvel at these today at Versailles, but they hardly give a full picture of the glory—and decadence—of everyday life under the Sun King, Louis XIV.

What we don't see: those thousand orange trees planted in silver tubs; the zoo with exotic animals in cages; the sedan-chair taxis for hire to shuttle nobles from chateau to chateau; the 1,500 fountains (only 300 remain); the Leonardos, Raphaels, Titians, Rubenses, and Caravaggios (now in the Louvre) that hung in halls and bedrooms; the gondolas from Venice poling along the canals at night, accompanied by barges with musicians; the grand halls lit by thousands of candles for a ball. Most of all, we don't see the thousands of finely dressed nobles and their servants—and the center of all the gaiety, Louis himself.

Louis lived his life as though it was a work of art to be admired by all. He rose late and was dressed not by servants but by nobles and barons. Around noon he ate breakfast, and then he attended Mass. In the afternoon Louis worked—and worked hard—meeting advisers, generals, and bishops. At 5:00 p.m. he ate dinner, either alone or with the queen, though he wasn't ever really alone—every action was a public ritual attended by nobles of the court.

The Hall of Mirrors, Versailles
This is where France's beautiful people partied. Pass the Fromage-Whiz.

Louis had an enormous appetite. His typical dinner might have included four different soups, two whole fowl stuffed with truffles, a huge salad, mutton, ham slices, fruit, pastry, compotes, and preserves.

Nighttime was spent playing royal games, gambling, or socializing. Louis then had a late supper (near midnight) and retired.

Louis' life of leisure was nothing compared with that of the nobility who had absolutely nothing to do day after day except play. They had no government function in France's "modern" bureaucracy except to attend to Louis' daily rituals. They survived on favors from the King—pensions, military and church appointments, and arranged marriages with wealthy nobles. It was essential to be liked by the king or you were lost. If Louis didn't look at you for weeks on end, you knew you had to seek an audience with him and apologize—with many tears and much hugging of the royal knees. Compare the position of France's weakened nobility with that of England's at the same time: the lords in Parliament had just beheaded one king and thrown out a second.

Versailles in its heyday had 5,000 of these domesticated nobles (with at least as many dependents) buzzing about the grounds seeking favors. Business was conducted while at play—at billiards, dances, concerts, receptions, and the most common pastime, gambling. (They usually played a version of 21.) Large gambling debts made many nobles still more dependent on Louis.

Dressing properly was part of the favor-seeking game. Men shaved their rough beards and put on stockings and silk clothes. Big, curly wigs became the rage when Louis started to go bald. A contemporary wrote, "It was possible to tell the women from the men only when it was time to go to bed."

French fashions from the days of Louis XIV

One of the "fashions" was adultery, an accepted—almost obligatory—social ritual. Louis' succession of mistresses has become legend. Still, he remained faithful to the institution of marriage itself and fulfilled his obligation to the queen, Marie-Therese of Spain, by sleeping with her every night (after a rendezvous with one of his lovers).

Versailles allowed the perfect escape from life's harsh realities. Even in his choice of art, Louis preferred grandeur and idealized beauty to simplicity and realism. He detested the naturalism of the Dutch and Flemish masters and encouraged baroque opulence.

Still, on his deathbed, he advised his five-year-old great-grandson Louis XV, "Don't imitate my extravagance. Alleviate the suffering of your people and do all the things I was unfortunate enough not to do." Perhaps little Louis was too young to understand, for he, too, succumbed to the lure of wealth. The Sun King's words went unheeded, and his successors in the Old Regime at Versailles continued in their gambling, fashion shows, and playing—oblivious to the world changing around them—right up until the French Revolution.

Le Nain, *Peasant Family* (Louvre)
When the queen said to France's grumbling poor, "Let them eat cake," this was the look she got.

Surviving Versailles

If you visit only one palace in Europe, make it Versailles. Europe's palace of palaces is an easy, $2, twelve-mile train ride from downtown Paris.

Some background in Greek mythology will help you appreciate the palace art because much of it tells symbolic stories of Zeus and his Olympian family. Louis XIV, like Apollo, called himself the Sun King. Versailles' ceilings are covered with magnificent paintings, most of which deal with mythological subjects.

Versailles can have horrifying crowd problems—waking nightmares of tour bus crowds crushing in, hysteria breaking out, people, separated forcibly from their children, screaming and not enjoying Versailles. It makes a Rolling Stones concert crowd look like monks in a lunch line.

The palace is packed on Tuesdays, when most Parisian museums are closed. Versailles is closed on Mondays. Beat the crowds by arriving before the 9:45 a.m. opening time. Take the train from Les Invalides or St. Michel stations in Paris to Versailles R.G., the end of the line. The palace is a ten-minute walk from the station. Bring a picnic.

Because there are no guided tours of the palace, you will find the self-guided tour of Versailles in our *Mona Winks* guidebook (Santa Fe, N.M.: John Muir Publications) particularly helpful.

Tourist crowds at Versailles

The grounds surrounding Versailles are a sculptured forest, a king's playground. Explore the backyard. Marie Antoinette's little Hamlet (le Hameau) gives any historian or romantic goosebumps. This is where the queen (who eventually laid her neck under the "national razor" during the Revolution) escaped the rigors of palace life by pretending she was a peasant girl, tending her manicured garden and perfumed sheep.

Other Absolute Monarchs

Louis was every king's model. Every nation in Europe had its "Louis" and its own "Versailles." As you travel, you'll notice that most palaces, from La Granja in Spain to Peter the Great's Summer Palace outside of Leningrad, are modeled after Versailles, with sculpted gardens and Halls of Mirrors—all trying, but none succeeding, to match the splendor of Louis' place.

In Vienna the Hapsburg king, Leopold, built the impressive Schonbrunn Palace. A musician at heart, he established Vienna as the music capital of Europe. Vienna later produced Haydn, Mozart, Beethoven, and many of the classical superstars, who lived, worked, taught—and occasionally jammed together—in the city.

King Frederick William of Prussia (eastern Germany) copied France's centralized government and turned his loose collection of baronies into a monolithic European power. The "goose step" and Germany's strong military tradition came from Prussia.

England also had strong monarchs, but her people insisted on constitutional limits. Henry VIII's daughter, Elizabeth I, made England the world's top naval power and enjoyed the loyalty and support of nobles and commoners alike. However, her successors, the Scottish Stuart family, alienated the English with their "divine right" style. The English Parliament rebelled against King Charles (Stuart), and a Civil War broke out in the mid-1600s. In the end, the king was beheaded, and a member of Parliament, Oliver Cromwell, took power. When Cromwell died, the monarchy was restored, but the ruler's power came from Parliament, not from God.

(You'll find much more about England's bloody and glorious history in the special chapters on Britain in Part II.)

Spain and Portugal—A Capsule History

Louis XIV's great rivals for European superiority were his neighbors to the southwest, Spain and Portugal. During their Golden Age (1500-1650), Spain and Portugal dominated the economy of Europe. Gold and raw materials poured in from their colonial possessions in the New World, Asia, and Africa, making the Iberian Peninsula the most powerful corner of Europe.

The story of Spain and Portugal's rise as Europe's first colonial powers is a fascinating one, weaving strands from different cultures. To explain it, we'll need to backtrack a bit in time. Switch your orientation from chronological to geographical and prepare yourself for a slight jolt. Here goes.

The Moors (711-1492)

The Moors, North Africans of the Moslem faith who occupied Spain, had a great cultural influence on Spanish and Portuguese history. They arrived on the Rock of Gibraltar in 711 and moved north. In the incredibly short period of seven years, the Moors conquered virtually the entire peninsula, leaving only small pockets of Christian culture.

They established their power and Moslem culture—but in a subtle way. Non-Moslems (both Christans and Jews) were tolerated and often rose to positions of wealth and power. Instead of blindly suppressing the natives by force, the Moors used their superior power and knowledge to develop whatever they found. For example, they encouraged the growing of grapes for wine even though, for religious reasons, they themselves weren't allowed to drink alcohol.

Throughout the Moors' seven-century reign, pockets of Christianity remained. Local Christian kings fought against the Moors whenever they could, whittling away at the Moslem empire, gaining more and more land. After a sustained push, the last Moorish stronghold, Granada, fell to the Christians in 1492.

The slow process of the Reconquista (reconquest) resulted in the formation of the two independent states of Portugal and Spain. In 1139, Alfonso Henriques conquered the Moors near present-day Beja in southern Portugal and proclaimed himself the king of the region. In 1200, the state of Portugal had the same borders it has today (making it the oldest unchanged state in Europe). The rest of the peninsula was a loosely knit collection of smaller kingdoms until 1469, when Ferdinand II of Aragon married Isabella of Castile. Known as the "Catholic Monarchs," they united all the kingdoms on the peninsula under their rule.

The Golden Age

The expulsion of the Moors set the stage for the rise of Portugal and Spain as naval powers and colonial superpowers—the Golden Age. It was Ferdinand and Isabella who financed Columbus's expedition to seek a new, western trade route to Asia.

Through exploration (and exploitation) of the colonies, tremendous amounts of gold were stockpiled in Portugal and Spain. The aristocracy and the clergy swam in money. Art and courtly life developed fast in this Golden Age.

The Spaniards, fueled by the religious fervor of their Reconquista of the Moslems, were interested in spreading Christianity to the newly discovered New World. Wherever they landed, they Christianized the natives—with the cross when possible, with the sword when necessary.

The Portuguese expansion was motivated more by economic concerns. Their excursions overseas were planned, cool, and rational. They colonized the nearby coasts of Africa first, progressing slowly to Asia and South America.

Monument to the Discoverers (Belem, near Lisbon)
With Henry the Navigator at the lead, these explorers expanded Europe's horizons and made Portugal a superpower 500 years ago.

When Vasco da Gama sailed around the southern tip of Africa, he opened a profitable new trade route with the East, breaking Italy's monopoly on trade with the Orient. The states on the Atlantic seaboard—Portugal, Spain, Holland, and England—emerged as the superpowers of trade.

From that point on Italy stagnated, becoming an economic backwater and a political pawn of the stronger nations that took the lead economically as well as culturally. The Prado collection, chockful of Italian masterpieces bought with New World gold, testifies to Spain's wealth. The focus of European civilization shifted west.

Iberian Art and Architecture

The two most fertile periods of architectural innovation in Spain and Portugal were the Moorish occupation and the Golden Age. Otherwise, Spanish architecture follows many of the same trends as the rest of Europe.

The Moors brought with them many Middle Eastern design elements, such as the horseshoe arch, minarets, and floor plans designed for mosques. The Islamic religion forbids the sculpting or painting of human or animal figures ("graven images"), so artists expressed their creativity with elaborate geometric patterns. The ornate stucco of the Alhambra in Granada, the striped arches of Cordoba's mosque, and decorative colored tiles are evidence of the Moorish sense of beauty. Mozarabic (Christians under Moslem rule) and Mudejar (Moslem) styles blended Eastern and Western elements.

As Christians slowly reconquered the peninsula, they turned their fervor into stone, building huge churches in the heavy, fortress-of-God Romanesque style (as seen at Santiago de Compostela) and in the lighter, heaven-reaching, stained-glass Gothic style (as seen in Barcelona, Toledo, and Sevilla). Gothic was an import from France, trickling into conservative Spain long after it swept through Europe.

The money reaped and raped from Spain's colonies in the Golden Age (1500-1650) spurred new construction. Churches and palaces were built in both the solid, geometric style of the Italian Renaissance (such as the severe El Escorial palace) and the more ornamental baroque. Ornamentation reached unprecedented heights of frilliness in Spain, culminating in the Plateresque style of stonework, so called because it resembles intricate silver filigree work.

Portugal's economic boom also triggered a cultural boom. The sixteenth-century Manueline style in art and architecture is an exuberant combination of Gothic and Renaissance forms— decorated with shells, anchors, ropes, and exotic nautical motifs— a tribute to its "patron," the lucrative sea trade. You can see fine examples of this "Portuguese Renaissance" style in the Lisbon suburb of Belem. The regional highlight is the cloisters of the Jeronimos Monastery.

After the Golden Age, innovation in both countries died out, and most buildings from the eighteenth and nineteenth centuries follow predictable European trends.

In painting during the Golden Age, Italian Renaissance style was the rage. The Prado's vast collection of Titians makes this clear. Local Spanish painters, caught in the grip of the medievel Inquisition and the holy war against the Moors, concentrated on religious scenes. Secular art had to be imported.

El Greco (1541-1614) fused Italian Renaissance technique with the Spanish religious sense. Born in Greece (his nickname means "The Greek"), trained in Venice, and caught up in the devout fervor of Spanish mysticism, El Greco combined all of these influences—

El Greco, Pentecost scene
From El Greco's time on, artists were free to go beyond naturalism.

Greek iconography, Venetian color, and Spanish Catholicism—to create an individual style.

El Greco's people have unnaturally elongated, slightly curved bodies, like flickering flames. The serene faces look like those of saints on a Byzantine icon. Yet it is obvious from the natural, personal details of his portraits that El Greco learned Renaissance realism. His splashy color schemes are Venetian in character.

El Greco is often called the first "modern" painter because he deliberately chose to tamper with realism to emotionalize a painting. Nature and realism had been mastered, so he and other artists set about busily exploring new realms.

If you fall in love with El Greco at the Prado, then you must visit his hometown, Toledo, which is dotted with his works. Toledo, the historical and cultural capital of Spain, is a great place to gain an appreciation of the "Spanish Renaissance." A tour of Toledo's cathedral, with masterpieces from the greatest Spanish artists of each era from Gothic to baroque, will open your eyes to the fact that Italy didn't have a monopoly on artistic genius. Local pride shines through as your guide shows you what was going on in Spain while Michelangelo was busy painting the Sistine Chapel.

Slow Decline

The dazzling, fast money from the colonies blinded Portugal and Spain to the dangers at home. Great Britain and the Netherlands, which had become strong naval powers, defeated the Spanish Armada in 1588.

During the centuries when science and technology in all other European countries developed as never before, Spain and Portugal were occupied with their failed colonial politics. The Portuguese imported everything, stopped growing their own wheat, and neglected their fields.

Endless battles, wars of succession, revolutions, and counterrevolutions weakened Spain and Portugal.

In the eighteenth century, Spain was ruled by the French Bourbon family, as is evidenced by the French style of the major sights of the era: Madrid's Royal Palace and the nearby La Granja Palace. In the chaos, there was no chance to develop democratic forms of government. Dictators in both countries made the rich richer and stifled the underprivileged masses.

(Democracy is a recent phenomenon in Spain and Portugal. In the 1930s, Spain suffered a bloody and bitter civil war between fascist and democratic forces. The fascist dictator Franco won, ruling the country until his death in the 1970s, when democratic elections were finally held. Portugal, following an unbloody revolution, also held democratic elections in 1975. Today, moderate Socialists are in power in both countries, trying to fight the problems of unemployment and foreign debts—with moderate success. Spain, a latecomer to the

Bernini, *Louis XIV* (Versailles), 1665

European Economic Community, is now enjoying a boomtime. Hordes of visitors will travel to Spain in 1992 to celebrate the World's Fair, the Olympic Games, and the 500th anniversary of Columbus's "discovery of America." Viva España is sung _con gusto._)

Palaces of the Divine and Absolute Monarchs:

Versailles, France
Schönbrunn, Vienna, Austria
Royal Palace, Madrid, Spain
Residenz of the Prince Bishop, Würzburg, Germany
Hofburg (Imperial Palace), Vienna, Austria
Frederiksborg Slot, north of Copenhagen, Denmark
Drottingholm, Stockholm, Sweden
Residenz, Munich, Germany
La Granja, outside Madrid, Spain

Baroque Art

After 100 years of religious wars and squabbles over who would rule whom and who would worship which way, Europe chose religious toleration, stability, strong "absolute" monarchs, and a pro-status-quo art called baroque. (Like Gothic, baroque was an insulting term, meaning "irregular." It was coined by the people of the following era.) Baroque contrasts with the simplicity and balance of Renaissance art.

It is propaganda art. It was meant to wow the masses into compliance with authority. Artists demonstrated their respect for the church and king by using the most complex, dazzling, and moving effects ever. Ornamentation abounds. Abundance abounds. Church decoration became a cooperative adventure, with painters, sculptors, stucco workers, and metalworkers all teaming up to portray Heaven itself. The common man could step into a world of glittering gold, precious stones, and a ceiling painted as if it opened up to the sky, with angels, saints, babies that looked like clouds, and clouds that looked like babies—all of them (in better baroque) balanced into a unified whole.

Baroque architecture uses Renaissance symmetry decorated with lots of ornamental curlicues, stucco work, ovals, and elliptical shapes. The interiors are bright, with clear windows, whitewashed

St. Peter's Basilica (Rome)
The baroque movement was born here, in the grandest church in Christendom.

walls, colored marble, and gold leaf. Many darker medieval buildings were given an update as centuries-old frescoes were whitewashed and fine old sets of stained glass were replaced by clear windows. Subtlety was out, as straight lines were interrupted whenever possible with medallions and statues.

Bernini — Father of Baroque

Baroque was born in Rome. Its father was Lorenzo Bernini (1598-1680), its mother, the wealthy Catholic church. Rome bubbles with Bernini fountains and sculpture. His masterpiece is his work on, in, and outside of St. Peter's church, including the canopy over the altar and the very unsquare St. Peter's Square. Bernini was a master of all the Renaissance techniques but wasn't chained by its classical rules of simplicity.

His art maximizes emotion — in the subject as well as the viewer. His famous statue of the mystic nun, St. Theresa, is a perfect example of a complex but unified composition, expressive portraiture, and details suggesting movement and passion — all adding up to a very theatrical and emotional work. Bernini shows her with a heart pierced by an angel's arrow. Theresa described the feeling as "a pain so great that I screamed aloud; but simultaneously I felt such infinite sweetness that I wished the pain would last forever." As we gaze at the statue, Bernini makes us feel the same ecstasy, the same "sweet pain."

Bernini, *Apollo and Daphne* (Rome)—
c. 1624
Bernini, the father of the baroque movement, captures the exciting moment
when Apollo thinks he's got the nymph
Daphne. But just when he's ready to
jump on her, she turns into a tree—
her fingers sprout leaves, her feet
sprout roots, and Apollo is in for
one rude shock.

Bernini, *St. Theresa in Ecstasy* (detail), (Rome)—1650

Rubens—"The Fury of the Brush"

In painting, baroque meant big canvases of bright colors, classical subjects, optical illusions, and swirling action.

Bernini's painting counterpart was Peter Paul Rubens (1577-1640) from Catholic Flanders (Belgium). Rubens studied in Rome, where he picked up the Italian fad of painting giant compositions on huge canvases.

He could arrange a "pigpile" of many figures into a harmonious unit. Each painting was powered with an energy and gaiety people called his "fury of the brush."

Rubens, *The Rape of the Daughters of Leucippus* (Alte Pinakothek, Munich)—c. 1617
Rubens's typically robust, energetic style: fleshy women and "fury of the brush" were his trademarks. Compare this baroque vibrancy to the Renaissance composure of the Raphael on page 138 or Mona Lisa on page 127.

Rubens's work, while very colorful, intricate, and lighthearted, was always robust, strong, and solid. Like Bernini, Rubens draped clothing on his subjects in a manner that suggested rippling motion and energy—a popular trick.

A famous scholar and diplomat, Rubens was welcomed at every royal court in Catholic Europe. His Antwerp house (now a fine museum) was an art factory, designed to mass-produce masterpieces. After he laid out a painting, his apprentices painted the background and filled in the minor details. Rubens orchestrated the production from a balcony, and before a painting was carried outside his tall, narrow door, he would put on the finishing touches—whipping each figure to life with a flick of his furious brush.

Caravaggio

Caravaggio (pronounced "carra-VAW-jee-o," 1573-1610) set out to shock people with his paintings. He depicted subjects realistically, no matter how ugly or unpleasant. He set sacred Bible scenes in the context of the seedy, seamy side of his Roman neighborhood. Caravaggio lived much of his life on the edge of society. Quick-tempered and very opinionated, he killed a man over a dispute in a tennis match and spent years as an outlaw.

Caravaggio, *David with the Head of Goliath* (Kunsthistorisches Museum, Vienna)—c. 1605
Using harsh, exaggerated light/dark contrasts, Caravaggio powers his early baroque paintings with emotion. The severed head is Caravaggio's self-portrait.

Caravaggio painted with a profound psychological realism that captures the inner feelings of the common people he used as subjects. It brings to mind the style of his contemporary, Shakespeare, who acquainted himself with English low-life and incorporated it into his plays.

You'll recognize Caravaggio's works by the strong contrast between light and dark. Whole sections of canvas are in shadow with details obscured. If light does shine on a subject, it's a harsh, unflattering, "third-degree interrogation" light that pierces through anything glorified or idealized, exposing the real person underneath.

Caravaggio wanted to paint events of the Bible to be real and tangible—like today, next door. His saints have dirty feet. In Caravaggio's style, Doubting Thomas would be painted as an old common laborer. To depict the scene when Jesus said, "Reach hither thy hand and thrust it into my side," Caravaggio would paint Thomas with his grubby finger actually inside Jesus' wound.

Royal Art—Court Painters

You'll see plenty of royal portraits in European museums. The court painter was the "official photographer" of the day. To keep the royal egos happy, most court paintings were unrealistic, melodramatic, and flattering. Two royal portraitists, Van Dyck and Velázquez, were unusually realistic, and their works offer a rare, real peek at royal Europe.

Velázquez, *The Maids of Honor* (Prado, Madrid)—1656
The Spanish court and the painter himself (at left), shown in a realistic way, without emotion.

Sir Anthony Van Dyck (1599-1644), a follower of Rubens, set the standard for portraits of the absolute monarchs. The court painter for Catholic King Charles I of England, he portrayed him for what he was—elegant, scholarly, and aristocratic. Lesser painters of this period unnaturally flattered and exaggerated the elegance of their subjects. (See the pantyhose portrait of Louis XIV on page 165.)

Diego Velázquez (pronounced "vel-LOSS-kess," 1599-1660) the Spanish royal court painter, was particularly realistic—influenced by Caravaggio's hypernaturalism. He painted without showy emotion or unnecessary ornamentation. His work appears intricately detailed, but if you look closely, you see a new technique in brushwork. Velázquez suggested details with a quick stroke of the brush—a bit like Rubens but also a peek at the future style, impressionism.

Christopher Wren

England never really liked baroque elegance but nevertheless built its share of impressive architecture. The chance to make a radical break with the medieval past came when London was toasted by the Great Fire of 1666. Almost before the ashes had cooled, a young architect named Christopher Wren was in the mayor's office with exciting plans to rebuild the city. He got the job and set out to decorate the new downtown with more than fifty of his churches.

Wren, St. Paul's Cathedral, London
Wren's tomb inside the church has the epitaph: "If you seek a monument. . . look around you."

Wren's style shows baroque and Gothic influences (Gothic remained popular in England long after the Middle Ages) as well as many classical features.

Although better examples of Wren's architectural genius are found in smaller churches nearby, his most famous work is St. Paul's Cathedral. In studying St. Paul's, you'll notice a central baroque cupola lined with classical columns and flanked by Gothic towers. The overall effect, however, is one not of baroque movement, tension, or exuberance but of classical restraint and stability.

Rococo—Uncontrolled Exuberance

The baroque movement spread from Rome throughout Catholic Europe by way of the court of Louis XIV at Versailles. Louis' great-grandson, Louis XV, championed a new style related to baroque but even more ornamental and less symmetrical. It is called rococo (pronounced "ro-KO-ko").

Baroque and Rococo Architecture:

Versailles
St. Peter's church, the Vatican
Residenz and Chapel of the Prince Bishop, Würzburg, Germany
Schönbrunn, Vienna
St. Paul's, London
Il Gesù church (the scroll-shaped facade was the model for Jesuit churches throughout Latin America), Rome
Piazzas of Rome, especially St. Peter's Square
Benedictine monastery, Melk on Danube, Austria
Charles Bridge, Prague, Czechoslovakia
St. Stephan's Cathedral, Passau, Germany
Rococo Bavarian churches (Wies, Oberammergau, Ettal, Asam in Munich)

Other Baroque Art:

Paintings by Rubens in the Prado (Madrid), Louvre (Paris), National Gallery (London), and most major museums
Rubens's home, Antwerp, Belgium
Bernini fountains, Rome
Bernini's altar canopy, dove window, and statues at St. Peter's, Vatican, Rome
Museo Borghese, Rome
Music of Bach, Vivaldi, Scarlatti

Die Wies, Church in Bavaria, Rococo
This beautiful example of Bavarian rococo is near Oberammergau and Füssen
in southern Germany.

Rococo is lighter and daintier, without the Renaissance-like robustness and balance of baroque. Light pastel colors, ivory, gold, mirrors, and slender columns with curvy frills characterize rococo interior decoration. This giddy style, using decoration almost to the obliteration of form, spread quickly from Paris to Germany and Austria during the 1700s.

Northern Protestant Art

The art in Protestant Northern Europe is entirely different from the flashy art that filled the churches and palaces of the Catholic world. Protestant artists had to manage without the rich and powerful Catholic church's patronage. Depiction of elaborate ritual and anything with even a hint of idolatry was out. Religious art fell out of favor, and Protestant artists specialized in subjects that had nothing to do with the church.

During this period many northern European churches channeled their artistic energy into music, with orchestras and elaborate church organs. Choirmaster/composer/organists (such as J. S. Bach) enjoyed a new, loftier status.

New Patronage, New Art

The wealthy merchants of the prosperous middle class became the new patrons of northern art. These city burghers were playing catch-up with the ruling class, and a great way to rise above society's small fries was to have a distinguished portrait of yourself painted.

Rembrandt, *The Dutch Masters* (Rijksmuseum, Amsterdam) Even in his later years Rembrandt could paint better portraits than anyone. He shows us not just faces but personalities as well.

The commissioned portrait was the artist's bread and butter. Northern artists made portraits come alive without employing the artificial or flattering poses of baroque portraiture. From Hans Holbein (see his portrait of Henry VIII on p. 280) to Frans Hals to Rembrandt, portraitists got better and better at capturing the real character of their subjects in a relaxed, "unposed" pose.

Sadly, many of those who paid and posed were tight-fisted—more interested in value for their money than in encouraging good art. Great artists often wasted their talents on unimaginative works simply to earn a meager living from the fickle patronage of a nouveau riche whose taste was mostly in its mouth.

The only alternative for artists was to to sell their work on the open market—an art history first. Art was sold in marketplaces and fairs as well as through art dealers.

Without a king or the Catholic church to buy their art, Dutch artists worked for the urban middle class painting fun, unpreachy, and affordable art.

This new "patronage" pointed art in new directions. Along with portraits, artists painted scenes the average person would like—and buy—such as landscapes, seascapes, slices of daily life, and fun looks at human folly. Paintings were generally small and affordable.

Slice-of-Life Art

Peter Brueghel (1564-1638) used Italian techniques to depict Flemish peasant life. A townsman himself, painting for fellow townspeople, he depicted peasants as peasants, simple and happy, but also as hicks worth laughing at. His crowded and brightly colored scenes of people are fun and entertaining. At the same time, we can sympathize with his characters, seeing a bit of ourselves in their actions. Brueghel's paintings were very popular and often imitated. (The Museum of Ancient Art in Brussels and the Kunsthistorisches museum in Vienna have two of Europe's best collections of Brueghels and Brueghel-style art.) They give travelers a great glimpse of old peasant life-styles.

Brueghel, *Peasant Wedding* (Kunsthistorisches, Vienna)—c. 1565
Crowded, colorful, detailed look at everyday peasant life. These scenes were popular with the urban middle class who bought art.

In a more serious style, Jan Vermeer (1632-1675) perfected the art of showing the natural beauty of common people and simple, everyday objects. His tiny domestic scenes and tranquil landscapes are a far cry from the huge, colorful, fleshy, and exciting baroque scenes of Greek gods.

Vermeer, *Milk Maid* (Rijksmuseum, Amsterdam)

Vermeer, *The Little Street* (Rijksmuseum, Amsterdam)
Vermeer creates a quiet little world where we can see the beauty in everyday things. This was the view from his house in Delft.

Rembrandt

The plight of the creative artist at the mercy of unenlightened patrons is epitomized by the life of Dutch genius Rembrandt van Rijn (1606-1669). Young, successful, and famous as a portrait painter for wealthy merchants, he fell out of favor, probably because he had a mind of his own and refused to compromise in his portraits. If his painting's composition required it (or if he didn't like someone), he might depict his patron in a shadow or even with an arm in front of his face. Few would invest in a wonderful—but risky—Rembrandt portrait. He spent his last years painting himself and poor street people, and he died in poverty.

Rembrandt, _Self-Portrait_ (National Gallery, London)—1669

The silver lining to this story is that by rejecting commissions, Rembrandt was free to paint subjects he found interesting and challenging. His Bible scenes come alive before your eyes. Like Caravaggio, he refused to idealize or beautify his subjects. His religious scenes are group portraits of the common people of Amsterdam.

Also like Caravaggio, Rembrandt can be recognized by his experimentation with contrasting light and shade. He played around with the source of light and the illumination of his figures, generally painting a dark-brown background. When he does shine a light on his subject, the effect is powerful and dramatic.

Rembrandt, *Supper at Emmaus* (Louvre)—1648
Christ's face shining brightly out of the dark-brown surroundings. Rembrandt often chose the commoners of Amsterdam as models for religious subjects.

Northern Art Museums:

Rijksmuseum (Dutch art, especially Rembrandt and Vermeer), Amsterdam
Alte Pinakothek (German art), Munich, Germany
Kunsthistorisches Museum, Vienna

Rembrandt, *The Night Watch* (Rijksmuseum, Amsterdam)
Rembrandt makes this much more than a group portrait. It's an action scene, capturing the can-do spirit of the Dutch Golden Age.

Van Der Helst, *Schuttersmaaltijd* (Rijksmuseum, Amsterdam)
Everyone got his money's worth in this colorful group portrait. Every face is flash-
bulb perfect. Compare it with Rembrandt's rowdy *Night Watch*.

The Age of Enlightenment

The scientific experimentation begun in the Middle Ages and the Renaissance finally bloomed in the 1600s. Galileo, Copernicus, Kepler, and Newton explained the solar system, disproving the church's view that the earth was the center of the universe. The "scientific method" was seen as a way to solve all problems: if humanity could figure out through science the motion of the planets and explain the circulation of blood through the body, this enlightened thinking should be useful in answering moral and political questions as well.

The philosophers of the Enlightenment (1700s) thought that nature obeyed laws and that all of those laws could be understood by reason. Every institution and every established school of thought was given the "test of reason." Superstition and ignorance were attacked. The "Old Regime" (the era of divine monarchs, feudalism, serfdom, and so on) was picked to pieces. Thinkers and writers proposed a complete reorganization of society determined by reason, not by accident of birth.

England and France produced the social philosophies that laid the foundation of modern thought. Adam Smith established the basis for laissez faire, the free economy of capitalism. Rousseau wrote about the "Social Contract," saying that the government is the servant of the people and that a people's revolution is justified when their government screws up. A kind of "religion of reason" was created, and for the first time, many people—respected people—said Christianity was stupid.

John Locke and Voltaire wrote of "natural laws" and "self-evident truths" in human relationships that make necessary a more democratic form of government. Many of Locke's phrases are used in the U.S. Declaration of Independence, a document based on the ideals of the Enlightenment. Thomas Jefferson prided himself on being a part of this enlightened movement.

The kings of this period are called "enlightened despots." They ruled efficient, modern states and supported many ideas of the Enlightenment. But while royal parlor talk might have been "enlightened," the kings of this period were still despots, refusing to share power with the lower classes. The growing urban middle class, often as wealthy and educated as the nobility, wanted a bigger slice of the governmental pie. But the Old Regime lived on, and people were divided into the rulers and the ruled by birth—not by ability or wealth.

In the Enlightenment, a new world was conceived. Europe was fast outgrowing its archaic shell. Enlightened thoughts were about to become violent actions.

Rococo Madam Pompadour (left) and the neoclassical gal (right) could well have been mother and daughter. But in the age of Revolution, Europe dumped its curls and ribbons for pure classical truth. Talk about a generation gap.

The French Revolution

In France, the decay of the Old Regime made especially fertile conditions for the seeds planted by the Enlightenment to blossom—metaphorically speaking.

With the rise of the cities and strong monarchs, the Old Regime became the dying regime. The three-part feudal order of nobility, clergy, and peasantry had to deal with two new social forces: the merchant class and Europe's national monarchs.

Nationalism

Basic loyalties had shifted, over the centuries, from tribe to church to monarch to nation. Nationalism was the "ism" of the nineteenth century.

Nationalism and the democratic ideas of the Enlightenment were tested and proven practical and possible by the American Revolution. The United States was the first truly modern nation to have a constitution based on the protection of individual rights, freedom of religion, and democracy. In 1776, Europe's eager revolutionaries were taking careful notes.

France—the home of the Enlightenment, ruled by a very unenlightened government—was ripe for revolt. Two percent of the country—the nobles and clergy—owned a third of the land and paid no taxes. The ambitious middle class, or bourgeoisie, was strong economically but weak politically. They were unhappy with a society based on a divinely ordained division of people into rulers and the ruled led by corrupt political and religious organizations.

France's National Assembly, the First Step to Revolution

The restless middle class got its chance when King Louis XVI (the Sun King's great-great-great-grandson) called an assembly of representatives to raise taxes. (Ironically, part of this money raised was for French aid to the American Revolution.)

The parliament (1789) met as three "estates," or classes—nobility, clergy, and peasants. The merchant class, newcomers to the social scene, were lumped in with the peasants as part of the "Third Estate." Historically, the estates voted as a unit, and the nobility and the clergy always outvoted the peasantry two to one. The middle class demanded that the assembly be restructured so that the vote would be general rather than by estate. Because the peasant estate had more representatives, this would break the Old Regime's monopoly on power. After a six-week deadlock on this issue, the Third Estate declared itself the National Assembly—whether the other two liked it or not—and vowed not to go home until a modern constitution had been created.

This was a revolutionary step. The king called out 18,000 troops —an act that the commoners perceived as the king's loyalty to the nobles. Traditionally, the king was anti-feudal and pro-people. The masses felt betrayed. Sides were drawn and royal orders were boldly defied.

The National Assembly became a forum for all kinds of democratic ideas. The privileged classes protested feebly as the slogan "Liberté, Egalité, Fraternité"—Liberty, Equality, Brotherhood— was born.

Mass Revolution

Like most revolutions, the French one started moderately and then took off. The masses had been awakened, and before they knew it, the rich and liberal middle-class leaders of the Third Estate were riding out of control on a lower-class revolutionary stallion.

The masses were hungry and restless, having suffered several bad harvests. The rulers had ignored the first rule in keeping the people docile by allowing the price of bread to climb to record heights. (Even today, authoritarian governments subsidize the price of bread to pacify the masses.) When the mad mobs of Paris demanded cheaper bread, Queen Marie Antoinette (so the story goes) enraged them with her famous solution, "Let them eat cake." The hungry masses said, "No."

On July 14, 1789, angry Parisians stormed the Bastille, a fortress that symbolized the Old Regime. (Today it's a famous nonsight. Don't look for it.) The revolution escalated when prisoners were released. The mayor of Paris was beheaded with a dagger, and the mob paraded through the streets with his head on a pole. (Bastille Day, the French "Fourth of July," is celebrated today with comparable pageantry and local color.)

Angered by a lavish and well-publicized party at Versailles, the hungry women of Paris marched on the palace. The king returned to Paris, where the government had come under the control of the radical city elements.

Revolutionary government of France at work, accusing each other of insufficient revolutionary zeal.

Throughout the countryside that summer, the peasants went on a mysteriously spontaneous rampage, sacking chateaus, rousting the nobility, and burning the feudal documents that tied them to the land. Overnight the manorial system (serfdom) was physically destroyed. The National Assembly followed by legally abolishing serfdom, manorialism, tithes, and tax loopholes.

Feudalism was dead in France and shock waves rippled through Europe. Royalty quivered, nobility shivered, and the middle classes and peasantry drooled with excitement as the French created the "Declaration of the Rights of Man and of the Citizen."

Much of France's ruling class took refuge in foreign palaces. They pushed for war, telling their European counterparts that they would be the next to go if they didn't do something quickly.

The revolutionaries running France also wanted a war—both to establish and solidify their new republic by banding against a common enemy and to spread their enlightened revolutionary gospel.

By 1793, it was France against the rest of Europe. A "levee en masse," or complete mobilization of the society, fueled by tremendous national patriotism and led by brash young risk-taking generals, enabled France to keep the Old Regime at bay.

Reign of Terror

On the home front, pressures of the war and economic problems drove the revolution to wild extremes. During this "Reign of Terror" (1793-1794), the king and queen were beheaded and wave after wave of people went to the guillotine. Political factions accused each other of halting the progress of the revolution. Enemies of the current ruling party were executed in public demonstrations in Paris' Place de la Concorde. People were sent to the "national razor" if they were even suspected of insufficient patriotism. Flags waved furiously as the blade dropped on over 17,000 necks.

The head (right) of King Louis XVI (left)
Thousands of heads rolled in the early 1790s. The guillotine was set up on Paris' Place de la Concorde.

The revolution snowballed until even the raging fanatic liberal, Robespierre, was made a foot shorter at the top by the guillotine. Paris cooled off when it realized that the revolution was out of control and actually eating itself up. This reaction even caused some people to consider reinstating the monarchy.

The revolution struggled along for five years. At the same time the French heir to the throne was calling for revenge, from his Italian refuge. To keep the revolution alive, the revolutionary leaders decided to give the army control rather than lose everything to an Old Regime king. They needed a revolutionary hero—an enlightened, charismatic, dashing general, a short guy who kept his feet on the ground, his eyes on the horizon, and his hand in his shirt. In 1799, a 30-year-old general named Napoleon took power. He promised to govern according to the principles of the revolution.

Napoleon

Although Napoleon was basically a dictator (who later proclaimed himself emperor) and many civil liberties were suspended during his reign, he was true to his promise to carry out what the revolution was all about. Church lands were confiscated and sold, privileged classes were abolished, and feudalism was finally buried.

Napoleon Bonaparte

During his rule (1799-1814), Napoleon carried the revolution—by war—to the rest of Europe. France, Europe's richest, most populous, and best-educated state, was his arsenal. With the barriers of class and privilege smashed, he was able to tap the wealth and talent of France. The French army had grown strong and tough during the wars of the revolution, and Napoleon had no trouble conquering Europe. A grand Napoleonic Empire covering the entire Continent was created, and many people spoke of Paris as the "New Rome."

To some Europeans, Napoleon was a genius, a hero, a friend of the common man, and an enemy of oppression. (Beethoven had originally planned to dedicate his third "Heroic" Symphony to him.) To others, he was the Hitler of his century—pompous, tyrannical, vain, and egotistical, suppressing a desire to be like the royalty he opposed.

The Complex Corsican

Born on the Mediterranean isle of Corsica (the year after it became French) of Italian parents, Napoleon was educated in French military schools. Originally an outsider, he quickly lost his accent and rose through the ranks of the army during the chaotic French Revolution.

Napoleon, Emperor of France
"We must not leave this world without leaving traces which remind posterity of us."

He was brash, daring, and always successful at a time when the old order was being turned upside down.

Napoleon's personality was as complex as his place in history. He was actually of average height and thin (until age and high living put on the pounds), with brown hair and eyes and a classic, intense profile. He was well read, a good writer, and a charming conversationalist who could win friends and influence people with ease. He had few of the vices that plague world conquerors: he cared little for good food and drink or fancy clothes, and he worked himself as hard as he worked others. Nevertheless, he could be cold, distant, and ruthless with his enemies.

Above all else, he was egotistical and power hungry, convinced of his inherent right to rule others. Yet he was a genius of military and political administration. Although he was easily flattered, he never let flattery cloud his judgment. His letters and diaries are sprinkled with objective self-criticisms such as, "In the last analysis, I blame myself."

Russia, Waterloo, and the Revolution Ends

Napoleon's empire didn't last long. In 1812, he led half a million soldiers into Russia. The vastness of Russia, the Russians' "scorched earth" policy, and the nation's special ally, the horribly cold winter, spelled disaster for the Grand Army. Only 10,000 Frenchmen returned to France. The nightmares of that ill-fated invasion haunted soldiers' minds for generations. (Europe's best military museum, Les Invalides, is in Paris, next to Napoleon's tomb.)

With Napoleon reeling, all of Europe called for a pigpile on France, vowing to fight for 20 years, if necessary, until France was defeated. The French people took the hint, toppling Napoleon's government and sending him on a permanent vacation on the island of Elba, off the Italian coast.

As evidence of Napoleon's personal charisma, he soon returned from his exile-in-disgrace, bared his breast to the French people, and said, "Strike me down or follow me." They followed him into one last military fling. It was only after the crushing defeat at Waterloo in 1815 that Napoleon was finished. (The battle site is in Belgium, south of Brussels, but not worth a detour except to true Bonapartisans.)

Bonaparte was exiled again, this time to a tiny island in the south Atlantic, and France was ruled by a "modern" king. Napoleon was the last of the "enlightened despots" of the Old Regime and the first of the modern popular dictators. He was a rationalist and agnostic of the passing age of Voltaire and the Enlightenment and the model heroic individual of the future Romantic world. The French kings after Napoleon were limited by a constitution. They went to work every day like any businessman: in a suit, carrying a briefcase.

Neoclassicism

Baroque had been the art of the Old Regime—of divine-right monarchs, powerful clergy, and landed aristocracy. The French Revolution killed that regime and its art, replacing it with a style more in tune with the Enlightenment. This new art was modeled not on the aristocratic extravagance of Versailles but on the "democratic" simplicity of ancient Greece and Rome. It is called "neoclassical."

Archaeological discoveries had roused France's interest in the classical world. Pompeii, the Roman city buried by a volcano in A.D. 79, was unearthed, giving Europe its best look ever at Roman daily life, dress, customs, art, and architecture. Books on Roman and Greek life came into vogue. Parisian women wore Pompeiian hairdos. Artists studied ancient art; they found that the art of the Renaissance was not truly "classical," and they tried to capture the true Greek and Roman style. Ancient became modern, and classical was in.

Throughout Europe, but especially in Paris, tourists are fooled by classical-looking buildings that are actually neoclassical—only 200 years old.

French Art of the "New Rome"

In France, the official style of the Revolution and the Napoleonic era was neoclassical. The French thought of themselves as citizens of the new Rome and wanted art to match. In Paris, the Pantheon and the Arc de Triomphe were built to look like grand Roman monuments. Funded by the spoils of Napoleon's conquests in Europe, Paris was rebuilt and ornamented with gas lamps and new bridges.

Napoleon had himself crowned emperor in an elaborate ceremony in the style of the Caesars. Classical backdrops masked the Gothic columns of Notre Dame cathedral so the emperor could be crowned as "Romanly" as possible. Paris was the new Rome; Napoleon was the new Caesar.

The great painter Jacque-Louis David (pronounced "dah-VEED," 1748-1825) was France's virtual dictator of fashion during this period. Marriage ceremonies, clothing styles, hairdos, and giant government propaganda spectacles were designed according to David's interpretation of neoclassicism. David's painting style was realistic, dignified, and simple—like a classical statue.

David, *Coronation of Napoleon* (Louvre, Paris)
There's Napoleon with his wife Josephine (kneeling) and his proud mom (looking on from the balcony). The pope (seated behind Napoleon) came all the way from Rome to crown him. But no ordinary mortal was good enough for that job, so Napoleon did it himself.

Neoclassicism, like the Enlightenment, was international. Thomas Jefferson, a child of the Age of Reason, designed his residence, Monticello, in the neoclassical style. The Capitol of the United States and many state capitols are neoclassical. Napoleon's armies spread neoclassicism throughout Europe. "Enlightened" people everywhere rejected the gaudy ornamentation of baroque in favor of austere arches and pure columns.

New Patronage — The Academy

The French Revolution and the rise of democracy in Europe changed the economics of art just as the Reformation had changed the economics of art in the Protestant countries of the North. Art became less and less the domain of the elite class and the church and more the domain of the middle class. Commissions became rare, and the gap between the artist and his patron widened.

Previously, artists had studied as apprentices under a master who was employed by a wealthy patron. Now they went to "Académies" (pompously named after Plato's Academy of Philosophy in Athens) to study art history, theory, and technique. Here, artists were free to pursue and paint their own idea of beauty — not that of whomever was paying them.

As a result, art went beyond mere decoration. Art became an expression of individuality—not a craft but Art, with a capital "A."

Pantheon, Paris
Built during France's bold experiment in democracy and free-thinking, this was like a Greek Temple of Reason.

Neoclassical Art and Architecture:

Neoclassical room (Ingres, David), Louvre, Paris
British Museum (exterior), London
Arc de Triomphe, Paris
Pantheon, Paris
La Madeleine, Paris
Lutheran Cathedral and Senate Square, Helsinki, Finland
Royal Crescent and Circus, Bath, England
Georgian mansions in Bath, England, and Edinburgh, Scotland
Music of Mozart, Haydn, Beethoven

Musical Vienna

While France dealt with revolution and Napoleon, Vienna enjoyed Europe's greatest age of music. Vienna was to music what ancient Athens and Renaissance Florence were to painting and sculpting.

Never before or since have so many great composers and musicians worked and competed side by side—Haydn, Mozart, Beethoven, and Schubert all worked in Vienna at roughly the same time (1775-1825). Their works changed music forever, raising it from simple entertainment to High Art.

Why Vienna? A walk through the city explains part of it. The peaceful gardens, the architecture, and the surrounding countryside were inspiration for composers, many of whom wrote tunes in their head as they strolled through the streets. Beethoven was a familiar sight, striding quickly, his hands behind his back, staring straight ahead with a brooding look on his face. He claimed he did his best writing away from the piano.

Money Makes Music

But the true root of all musical inspiration in Vienna was (as is the case with most art) money. The aristocracy found music more interesting than politics. Concerts were the social hub of high society. Many leading families employed their own orchestras to play at their parties. Some nobles were excellent amateur musicians: The Emperor Joseph II played both violin and cello; Empress Maria Theresa was a noted soprano.

Professionals were needed to perform, conduct, compose, and give lessons. Musicians from all over Europe flocked to Vienna, where their talents were rewarded with money and honor.

Before 1750, music had been considered a common craft, like shoemaking, and musicians were treated accordingly. Composers wrote music to order, expecting it to be played once and thrown away like Kleenex. The new breed of composers, however, beginning with Haydn, saw music as a lasting art on par with painting and sculpture.

They began to demand equal treatment from their employers. Beethoven, it is said, considered himself to be superior to his employers—he was an artist, they were merely royalty. When Mozart became composer-in-residence for a Viennese prince, he was paid a princely sum and then told to eat his meals with the servants. Mozart turned on his heel and walked out, refusing from then on to accept an "official" position.

Unappreciated Geniuses

Vienna fawned over its composers but only as long as they cranked out pleasant tunes. The minute they tried something new, daring, or difficult, the public turned on them.

Mozart was adored as a cute, clever six-year-old who could play the harpsichord as well as anyone in Europe. He won the hearts of the

Portrait of the child prodigy, Mozart
It's said Wolfgang cuddled in the laps of more queens than anyone in history.

nobility by declaring that he wanted to marry the Princess Marie Antoinette. But as a grown man writing mature and difficult works he was neglected and often maligned. When he died, broke, at 35, his body was buried in an unmarked grave. Only later was his genius fully appreciated and a statue erected to honor him. As the saying goes, "To be popular in Vienna, it helps to be dead."

Beethoven, like Michelangelo before him, played the role of the temperamental genius to the hilt. His music and personality were uncompromising. A bachelor, he lived in rented rooms all his life—sixty-nine different ones at last count. He had some bad habits that explain his migratory existence—such as playing the piano at two in the morning and pouring buckets of water on himself to cool off. His rooms were always a mess, with music, uneaten meals, and atonal chamberpots strewn about.

Beethoven, Mozart, and Haydn might have known one another, despite their age differences. "Papa" Haydn (so called because of his way with younger musicians) encouraged Mozart and gave lessons to Beethoven. Beethoven also learned from Antonio Salieri, Mozart's composing rival, who (according to legend) poisoned Mozart. Music in Vienna flourished with so many talented people rubbing elbows and engaging in healthy competition.

Musical Renaissance II

The only music scene that can compare with the Vienna of 1775-1825 is . . . the Vienna of 1860-1910—the years of Brahms, Mahler, Bruckner, and Richard Strauss, as well as the young pioneers of twentieth-century music, Schönberg, Berg, and Webern. These were the late-romantic-era composers who wrote big, intense, passionate works that often as not were booed or laughed at. A riot nearly broke out at the debut of Mahler's Fourth Symphony, with the crowd taking sides over the piece's merit. Viennese crowds loved what was safe. The most popular works were those of the classical masters of the earlier period—works that had been derided as too daring in their own day. With such stress on tradition, it's easy to see why avant-garde composers often went unnoticed until after their death.

Strauss Waltzes

And then there was Strauss. And then there was Strauss, Jr. The waltz craze swept through Vienna in the early nineteenth century and has continued in three-quarter time to the present. The two leading composers and conductors of the waltz were father and son—Johann Strauss, Sr., and Johann Strauss, Jr.

The waltz was the Beatlemania of its time. Many considered it decadent because of the close contact of the partners and the passionate sound of the music. Dances lasted from dusk to dawn, night after night. Johann the Elder played the violin and conducted simultaneously with wild gestures, whipping the crowd to "bewildering heights of frenzy till they were frantic with delight and emitting groans of ecstasy," according to composer Richard Wagner.

Young Johann took the baton when his father died and raised the waltz to respectability. His "Tales from the Vienna Woods" and "Blue Danube" immortalized his beloved hometown.

Imagine the lavish balls where this music was played during the Golden Age of Emperor Franz Joseph. Chandeliers, carriages, mirrored halls, sumptuous costumes, ceremony, and white-gloved ritual were the heart and soul of the conservative aristocracy. Franz Joseph of the royal Hapsburg house was not merely a king but also the Emperor of the Holy Roman Empire—namely, Austria and Hungary.

The Vienna of today clings to the elegance of its past and maintains much of that musical tradition. The Ministry of Culture and Education is the new patron. The State Opera, the Philharmonic Orchestra, the Vienna Boys' Choir, and the Society of Friends of Music still thrive as they did in Beethoven's time. There are statues of all the famous composers who were neglected in their day. And if you dial 1509 on a telephone in Vienna, you will hear a perfect A-note (440 Hz) for tuning your instrument.

Congratulations . . .

You've survived the wars, despots, and revolutions of Europe's Early Modern Age. Next come the wars, despots, and revolutions of the Modern World. But first, see if you can make some sense of this time line.

Time Line of Early Modern Europe

The Reformation and religious wars split Europe into two camps: the Protestant North and the Catholic South. In general, the northern countries, relying on a strong middle (merchant) class, were democratic. The South tended toward rule by absolute (and occasionally Enlightened) despots. In succeeding centuries, the democratic ideals of the Enlightenment sank in and old regimes gave way to more-modern governments.

This historical journey from religious division to absolute monarchy to democracy is also apparent in art styles. (See the lower half of the time line.) The lavish baroque style, associated with the Catholic church and absolute monarchs such as France's Louis XIV, was centered in Italy and France. At the same time, the middle-class Northern Protestant countries (Holland and England) developed a less-grand style, as exemplified by the works of Rembrandt and Christopher Wren. As both North and South moved toward democracy, a new style appeared that reflected the ideals of the ancient world—neoclassicism. This was the dominant style of the French Revolution and the reign of Napoleon, the emperor of the "New Rome."

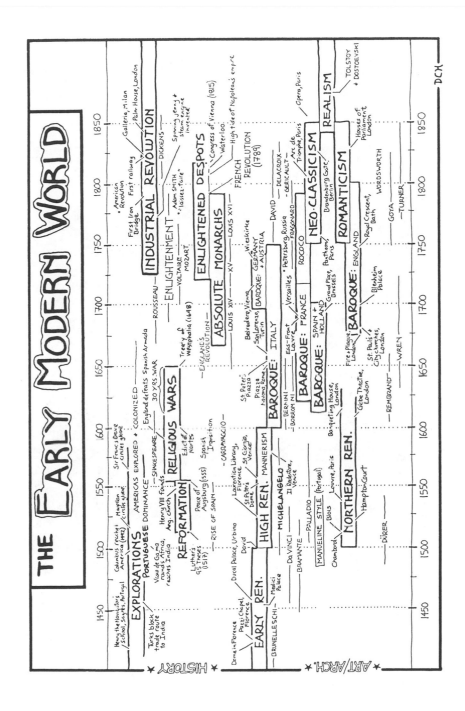

Delacroix, *Liberty on the Barricades* (Louvre)—1830
This dramatic scene captures the spirit of patriotism. "Liberty," in the form of a woman, carries a gun in one hand and a flag in the other—the winning combination for nineteenth-century nationalist movements.

The Modern World
A.D. 1815 – Today

The Age of Nationalism

Europe entered the modern world walking backwards. After the French Revolution and Napoleon had been crushed, European royalty did their best to return to the archaic world of feudalism and the Old Regime, ignoring the rights of individuals and nations. Beneath this conservative crust, however, Europe bubbled with new ideas and technology that were soon to erupt, cool, and harden into the Europe we know today.

Nationalism, a patriotic desire for national unity, was the dream and the political drive of the 1800s. When you travel in Europe, keep in mind that 140 years ago Germany, Italy, and Yugoslavia did not exist. They were patchwork quilts of feudal baronies, dukedoms, and small kingdoms—not places on the map. As you tour castles, treasuries, and palaces scattered across these nations, you're seeing the White Houses and crown jewels of such "countries" as Piedmont, Saxony, Slovenia, and Bavaria.

But as democratic ideals became popular among the middle class and intellectuals, the people were no longer satisfied to be ruled by a royal family that, in most cases, was from another country. In the previous century, most of Europe had been ruled by the Bourbon, Hapsburg, and Hohenzollern families. The king often spoke a language different from that of the people he ruled.

Now people insisted on a government that reflected their will, including their language, ethnic heritage, culture, and religion. People now identified themselves as citizens of a particular nation—even if their nation was not yet a political reality. The stove setting switched from simmer to high and Europe's nationalistic stew was ready to boil over.

Unification of Italy

In the mid-1800s, the petty kingdoms and city-states of the Italian peninsula began a move toward unity. The governments were content but the people weren't, and talk of the "Risorgimento" (resurgence) of national pride was everywhere. As national revolts were crushed by local governments, patriotism grew. The liberals of Europe supported the Italian cause, and a local writer, Mazzini, made unification

ITALIAN UNIFICATION

Four Italian leaders welded the Italian States into the Kingdom of Italy. Dates indicate year of annexation to the Kingdom of Sardinia (after 1861, the Kingdom of Italy).

Mazzini   Cavour

Garibaldi

Victor Emmanuel

almost a holy crusade. Several shrewd patriots organized a campaign for unification, channeling nationalistic fervor into the formation of Italy.

The logical first king of Italy was the only native monarch of the region, Victor Emmanuel II, King of Sardinia. His prime minister, Cavour, a cunning, liberal, yet realistic politician, orchestrated the unification of Italy. Guided by Cavour, Sardinia joined the Crimean War in order to get allies who would support Sardinia in a war with Austria (a war Sardinia couldn't win without allies). Sure enough, Cavour wrested Italian Lombardy (North Italy) from Austria. His cunning statesmanship, combined with many local revolutions that were legitimized by plebiscites (local votes of popular support), brought most of northern Italy together by 1860.

Meanwhile, a powerful revolutionary general, Garibaldi, sailed with 1,000 "red shirts" to Sicily, where his forces were joined by local revolutionaries in annexing the Kingdom of Two Sicilies into the New Italian State.

Remember the names of these Italian patriots. Throughout Italy you'll find squares and streets named after the "Washingtons" and "Jeffersons" of the Italian resurgence—Via Cavours, Piazza Garibaldis, and monuments to Victor Emmanuel, including the gaudy white mega-monument near the Roman Forum nicknamed "The Dentures."

National pride was fueled by the romantic movement in art. Artists returned to their ethnic roots, incorporating folklore into their novels and folk music into their symphonies. In Italy, Giuseppe Verdi used the opera to champion the unification movement. Opera houses rang with the sound of patriots singing along with anthem-like choruses. The letters in Verdi's name were used as a nationalistic slogan: Victor Emmanuel Roi (king) di Italia.

Unification of Germany

In 1850, Germany was thirty-nine little countries. Twenty years later it was united, and it was Europe's number one power.

During that period of growth, German iron and coal output multiplied sixfold, surpassing that of France. Cities, industries, and trade boomed. The stage was set for one of the German states, Prussia (a militaristic eastern German state), under Prime Minister Bismarck, to assert itself as the goose-stepping force behind German unity.

Otto von Bismarck, the original master of "realpolitik," was one of the greatest political geniuses of all time. He said, "Not by speeches and majority votes are the great questions of the day decided—but by blood and iron." For him, the great issue was German unification—under Prussia.

Bismarck united Germany as if he were reading from a great political recipe book. He used a logical, calculated, step-by-step approach, and when he finished he had created the dish nobody in Europe wanted—a united Germany.

Otto von Bismarck (1815-1898)
The great realistic politician of the 1800s, Bismarck created what no one outside his country wanted: a united Germany.

It's a long and complex recipe that is worth studying. Bismarck accomplished his objective of a united Germany by starting and winning three wars after carefully isolating each opponent.

The big question was, Which would Germany be united under: Prussia or Austria? Bismarck subdued Denmark with the help of Austria. Dividing the spoils gave Bismarck the excuse he sought to fight Austria. After he defeated Austria, Bismarck managed to drive all the little, independent (and anti-Prussian) German states into his camp by forcing them to choose between Prussia and France in the Franco-Prussian War.

He made alliances simply to break them, thereby creating a handy excuse to fight. After wiping out his opponent, he would make a fast and generous peace so he could "work with" that country in the future. He made concessions to the liberals of his parliament to become their hero. He levied and collected unconstitutional taxes to build up his armies. He winked at Europe's great leaders, gained their confidence, and proceeded to make them history's fools. He leaked inflammatory comments to the press to twist public opinion into just the political pretzel he needed.

He did whatever he had to, and in the end he got exactly what he set out to get. The fragmented Germany that Europe had enjoyed for centuries as a tromping ground became a Prussian-dominated conservative and militaristic German Empire. In 1871, after crushing France in a war, Germany emerged as Europe's most powerful nation. The leaders of Europe were concerned. The balance of power had been disturbed. They hoped the unification of Germany would not lead to a large war—or two.

Romanticism and Romantic Art

The artistic movement known as "romanticism" seemed to go hand in hand with nationalism; rules and authority were thrown out the window as individuals asserted their right of personal expression. And just as national groups could not be suppressed by Old Regime aristocratic rulers, romantic artists refused to conform their powerful inner feelings to society's code.

Romanticism—which has little to do with roses and chocolate hearts—was a reaction to the stern logic and reason of the neoclassical movement. Like neoclassicism (which carried on through much of the romantic period), it went beyond art. It was a way of living. It meant putting feeling over intellect and passion over restrained judgment. The rules of neoclassicism were replaced by a spirit that encouraged artists to be emotional and create not merely what the eyes saw but also what the heart felt.

Romantics made a religion of nature. They believed that taking a walk in the woods, communing with nature, taught man about his true self—the primitive, "noble savage" beneath the intellectual crust.

The cultural heartbeat of this movement came not from the lavish Medici palace in Florence or the elegant salons of Paris but from a humble log cabin in England's Windermere Lake District—William Wordsworth's "Dove Cottage." The English poets Blake, Coleridge, and Wordsworth rejected the urban, intellectual, scientific world for simple cottage life, soaking in the awesomeness of nature.

At Oxford and Cambridge, a walk in the woods was a part of every scholar's daily academic diet. Even today, the Lake District in northern England is a very popular retreat for nature lovers. It has more youth hostels per square mile than any place on earth, and they are perpetually booked up, filled with rucksack romantics worshiping the wonders of nature-walking.

Until the romantic era, mountains were seen only as troublesome obstacles. Now they attracted crowds of nature lovers drawn to their rugged power. High-class resorts, such as Interlaken in the Swiss Alps, were born. Why did people climb these mountains? Because they were there. Romanticism.

Turner, *Buttermere Lake* (Tate Gallery, London)—1798

Constable, Delacroix, Gericault, and Ludwig II

Romantic artists glorified nature. Landscapes illustrated nature's awesomeness and power. In the early 1800s, Englishman John Constable (1776-1837) painted honest, unidealized scenes, recognizing the beauty in "natural" nature. His contemporary, J. M. W. Turner, differed by charging his landscapes with his emotions, using bright super-"natural" colors and swirling brushwork. He personified nature, giving it the feelings and emotions of a romantic human being. (The Tate Gallery has a very good collection of Turner landscapes.)

Eugene Delacroix is a classic example of a romantic painter. (See page 208.) Solitary, moody, emotional, and endlessly imaginative, he broke all the neoclassical rules. His exotic and emotional scenes, wild color schemes, and complex, unrestrained compositions bubble with enough movement and excitement to ring any viewer's emotional bells.

Gericault, _Raft of the Medusa_ (Louvre)—1818
Gericault goes to great lengths to portray the death and suffering on this raft. At the same time a powerful pyramid of hope reaches up to flag down a distant ship. Romantics painted both ends of the emotional spectrum.

Theodore Gericault (1791-1824), in preparing to paint his gripping masterpiece _Raft of the Medusa_, visited an insane asylum and slept in a morgue so that he could better portray death and terror on the faces of his subjects. Nature was awesome, emotions were truth, and the romantic artists were the prophets of a new religion.

The fairy tale castle of Neuschwanstein is a perfect example of romantic emotion dominating over intellect. Its medieval style seemed to turn its back on the encroachment of science during the Industrial Age. Built on a hilltop, commissioned by King Ludwig II of Bavaria, it served no military purpose—but offered a grand view. The architect was a designer of theater sets. The king was a romantic. His best friends were artists, poets, and musicians. Scenes from Wagner's romantic operas decorate his castle. His dreams were not of empires and big armies but of fairy tale castles and candlelit concerts.

Ludwig II is known as "Mad" King Ludwig because of his romantic excesses. He drowned mysteriously before his Neuschwanstein castle, his dream about to come true, was completed.

Neuschwanstein Castle (Bavaria)—1886
The fairy tale castle of Bavaria's "Mad King" Ludwig II is typical of the romantic period. It was built on a hilltop in medieval style long after castles had lost their function as fortresses. Ludwig put it here for the view. The only knights in shining armor you'll find in this castle are on the wallpaper.

Ludwig almost bankrupted Bavaria building his Disneyesque castles, but the country is being paid back today with interest as huge crowds of tourists from all over the world pay to see Europe's most popular castle. Get there early or late or you might spend more time in line than in the castle.

Goya

Francisco de Goya (1746-1828) was a portraitist for the Spanish royal court. A romantic painter, he has been described as the first painter with a social conscience. His _Third of May_ is a gripping combination of nationalism and romanticism, showing a faceless government execution squad systematically gunning down very human victims with all the compassion of a lawn mower.

Goya, _The Third of May, 1808_ (Prado, Madrid)—1815
Romanticism expresses itself here in a powerful social statement against war and repression by faceless foreign invaders. The victims are Spaniards dying for the cause of liberty.

Artistically, Goya went through several stages. His last, after he lost his hearing and became bitter and disillusioned with life, was one of nightmarish fantasy. It's as if he let his innermost emotions fingerpaint in blood grotesque and awesome figures that mirrored the turmoil that racked his soul. (Romantic, huh?)

Goya, *Saturn Devouring His Son* (Prado, Madrid)
Here, Goya's gory message is that Time devours us all.

The Prado Museum in Madrid has a room dedicated entirely to the bizarre visions of Goya's "Dark Stage." One of the most gripping is the painting, *Saturn Devouring His Son*, detailing in ghastly, twisted lines and vivid, garish colors how time eventually "eats" us all. "Romantic" isn't only "mushy-kissy." This is romanticism at its emotional best. No matter how cheery you are when you enter, you'll leave Goya's Dark Stage in a gloomy funk. (Don't plan a picnic for right after.)

Blake

William Blake of England was another master at putting inner visions on canvas. A mystic, nonconformist poet, he refused to paint posies for his supper. He made a living only through the charity of fellow artists who recognized his genius. Blake's watercolors (wonderfully displayed in London's Tate Gallery), with their bizarre,

Blake, *Elohim Creating Adam* (Tate Gallery, London)—1795

unearthly subjects and composition, reveal how unschooled he was in classical technique. But his art grabs the viewer by the emotional lapel, and that's what romanticism is all about.

Romantic Art Highlights:

Paintings in the Louvre's romantic art room (Delacroix and Gericault), Paris
Tate Gallery (Blake and Turner), London
Poetry of Shelley, Keats, and Byron
The so-called Keats/Shelley House by the Spanish Steps, Rome
Music of Liszt, Chopin, Beethoven, Wagner, Schumann
Chopin's grave, Pere Lachaise Cemetery, Paris
Neuschwanstein and Linderhof castles, Bavaria
Neo-Gothic Halls of Parliament, London
The Alps
The Rhine

The Industrial Revolution

The Industrial Revolution, along with the rise of nationalism and democratic governments, shot Europe into the modern world. While the scientific achievements of the Enlightenment broadened human knowledge, practical inventions and applications didn't crank into motion until the 1800s.

This century of exciting technological advancement shifted nations from dependence on agriculture to dependence on industry. Britain's textile industry led the way as new, steam-powered factories lured people from the countryside to the cities.

The invention of the train shifted the revolution into high gear. More products could be shipped faster, and huge new trade markets opened up. Rails laced European nations together; a person could travel across a country in a day's journey or less. From 1830 through 1860 one-sixth of all the world's track was laid (and then came the Eurailpass).

Europe's business energy could not be contained. Before long, most of the world had been colonized by European nations. Europe collected raw materials and luxury goods from underdeveloped nations, processed them, and sold the resulting products at great profits. Although every European nation had a slice of the world economic quiche, Britain had the lion's share. At one point, her colonial empire included nearly a quarter of the world's land and people. Brits boasted, "The sun never sets on the British Empire." It was always daytime somewhere the British flag flew.

The riches of England's Industrial Revolution came with its problems. This nineteenth-century engraving shows poor, dirty, overcrowded slums housing masses of industrial workers under roaring smokestacks.

Technological progress made people optimistic. Seeing how quickly technology changed nature and life-styles, people figured it was the answer to the world's problems. Unfortunately, it was not. In fact, it created many new problems: poverty, slums, polluted and overcrowded cities, child labor, unemployment, overwork, and the alienation of workers from the fruits of their labor. (Today, technology poses a threat to the survival of the planet.)

Socialism and Communism

The Socialist movement tried to solve the social ills brought on by the industrial age. Socialists challenged the old laissez-faire policy of government nonintervention in business affairs. Socialists and trade unions worked to restrict the power of factory owners and distribute wealth more fairly. In his _Communist Manifesto_, Karl Marx took a more extreme approach, advocating a worker (proletarian) revolution that would overthrow the capitalist (bourgeois) establishment. Years later V. I. Lenin, using Marxist principles, led fellow Russian workers against the tsarist regime, giving birth to the Soviet Union.

The four giants of Soviet Marxism keep watch over a meeting of the Communist International, 1935
(Left to right) Karl Marx (1818-1883) and Friedrich Engels (1820-1895), both from Germany, co-wrote the influential _Communist Manifesto_ (1848), developing the theory that workers, not factory owners, should benefit most from industry. In the nineteenth century, Communist and Socialist organizations gained power throughout Europe. Though there was never a classic "workers' revolution," which Marx and Engels had predicted, their ideas spurred reforms to benefit the working class. Vladimir Lenin (1870-1924), a Russian, used Marxist ideas to plan the Bolshevik Revolution, overthrowing Russia's monarchy (1917).He had to adapt industrial Marxism to a country that, at the time, was still practicing medieval feudalism. Josef Stalin (1879-1953) succeeded Lenin as ruler of the Soviet Union, instituting the iron rule we associate with Russian totalitarianism. These figureheads of communism were commonplace in Eastern Europe and the USSR until the revolutions of 1989 and 1990.

The French Revolution had adjusted society to accommodate the urban merchant and business class. Now a new social group, the workers, used Socialist and Communist ideas to gain their rightful slice of the social pie.

The Industrial Revolution and Art

The Industrial Revolution put new tools and materials in artists' hands. Concrete, iron, and glass opened many new architectural doors. People were proud of their "modernity" and their ability to build like never before. More buildings were raised in the nineteenth century than in all previous centuries put together. It was the day after Christmas and Europe was a child with a colossal erector set.

Crystal Palace interior, London, 1850
This huge iron-and-glass structure was built on a strict schedule, marveled at, and taken down on a schedule. Europe was feeling its industrial oats, and similar structures were built all over. You'll see many Crystal Palace-type train stations in your travels.

At World's Fairs and Exhibitions, giant structures of iron ribs and glass walls were proudly assembled and promptly disassembled on rigid time schedules—just to prove it could be done. People traveled from all over Europe to marvel at London's marvelous but short-lived Crystal Palace. Paris, also feeling its industrial oats, built the Eiffel Tower to celebrate the 100th birthday of the French Revolution. The French planned to take down the tower, which they considered very

ugly, but it had become a symbol for Paris and so they decided to keep
it. ("Who knows? Maybe someday that ugly erection will attract
some tourists!")

As you travel around Europe, you'll see huge iron and glass train
stations—more products of Europe's early industrial muscle.

But the Industrial Revolution also threatened art. New building
techniques and materials made past architectural styles obsolete
except as decoration. Modern buildings such as the neo-Gothic British Houses of Parliament were built in a modern way and then decorated with "fake" Gothic arches or Renaissance columns. (Remember
the ancient Roman use of Greek styles? Solid Roman engineering
with Greek niceties for looks.)

Houses of Parliament, 1836-1860, London

Painters were threatened by the newly invented camera (developed around 1830), which could make portraits faster, cheaper, and
sometimes better than they could. (Sitting for a portrait had been a
real pain in the wallet for the "time-is-money" businessman of the
precamera age.) The challenge and incentive to portray nature was
gone. It seemed as though a simple camera could do it better. The
artist's traditional role as the preserver of a particular moment, person, or scene had become obsolete.

Technology widened the gulf between the artist and the public.
Modern man could get homes, furnishings, arts, and crafts from
engineers, technicians, and mass production. For their part, artists
grew to disdain those who put a price on art the same way they priced
pork, kerosene, or a day's work in the factory.

Struggling to come to terms with the modern industrial world,
Art left technology behind, focusing the artistic lens of the Western
world on hazy frontiers of the future.

Eiffel Tower, Paris, 1889

Industrial Revolution Sights:

Iron Bridge Gorge open-air museum (birthplace of Industrial
  Revolution), Coalport (north of Stratford), England
Iron and glass train stations (such as the Orsay Museum
  building)
Eiffel Tower, Paris
Blackpool Tower, England
Gallerias (grand iron-and-glass shopping arcades) in Milan and
  Naples, Italy, and Brussels, Belgium
Covent Garden, London

Art Nouveau

The art nouveau (pronounced "new-VOH") style was a reaction to the
mechanization and mass production of the Industrial Revolution.
Longing for the beauty of the preindustrial age, artists rebelled
against mass-produced goods. Their art emphasized uniqueness and
included the artists' personal touch.

Whereas industrial art and architecture were geometrical, with
rigid squares and rectangles, art nouveau, or "new art," used delicate,
flowing lines, like the curvy stems of plants. Iron grillwork became
a new art form.

Drawing by Aubrey Beardsley
Art nouveau's flowing lines in graphic design.

Art nouveau influenced architecture, painting, ironwork, furniture, graphic design, and even women's fashion. In America, Louis Tiffany's natural-looking "flower petal" lamps were the rage.

Antonio Gaudi, born near Barcelona, employed the art nouveau style in his distinctive architecture. Many architecture students

Gaudi, Casa Mila apartment house (Barcelona)—1905
This ice-cream castle of a building does everything possible to disrupt the rigid angles of the industrial world.

make a pilgrimage to Barcelona to see his most famous works. He's considered a pioneer, a prophet, and a dreamer who was lucky enough to see his dreams become concrete.

Art nouveau's intentional curviness eventually gave way to the straight lines and rigidity we see in modern "International Style" skyscrapers, but its influence has been seen throughout the twentieth century.

Metro station, Paris
Curviness for the sake
of curviness.

Art Nouveau Sights:

Green iron grillwork at old Metro stops, Paris
Orsay Museum (exhibits on mezzanine level), Paris
Jugendstil sights (the Germanic version of art nouveau), Vienna
Various buildings in Brussels, Belgium; Munich, Germany; Glasgow, Scotland; and Helsinki, Finland
Gaudi architecture (especially Sagrada Familia cathedral), Barcelona, Spain

Impressionism

Impressionism was the greatest revolution in European art since the Renaissance and the first real "modern" style of art. Realism, in the traditional sense, was thrown out. The artist was interested only in the "impression" made by the light, shadows, and atmosphere of a scene.

Although its name was originally coined as an insult (like "Gothic" and "baroque"), impressionism is actually one of the few appropriate art labels. Claude Monet (pronounced "mo-NAY,"

1840-1926) the movement's father, called the style "instantaneity." The artist, with a few quick brush strokes, captures a momentary "impression" of a subject.

The realistic and the impressionist styles can be illustrated by comparing what Leonardo da Vinci and Monet each see as they drive across the Nevada desert on a hot summer day. Ahead of his Ferrari, Leonardo, a realist, sees heat rising from the asphalt, making the black road look like a bright, shimmering patch of silver. In spite of the way it appears, he knows the road is really black and so he will paint it that way—disregarding the momentary impression of silver.

Monet, an impressionist, excitedly stops his Peugeot, sets up his easel, and captures the impression of the shimmering heat waves cutting a silver slice through the yellows and browns of the desert.

The realist paints what his mind knows is there; the impressionist paints what his eye sees.

Light and Color

Light plays endless games on the same subject and, to the impressionist, that same subject is different with each time of day and atmospheric condition. Monet, the most famous impressionist, often did a series of paintings of a single subject (for example, Rouen Cathedral) at different times of day.

Photo of Rouen Cathedral, impressionist painting of Rouen Cathedral by Monet
We can see the artist's fascination with the play of light on the building. Detail fades away and we are left with a blurry, yet recognizable, impression of the cathedral.

In capturing the moment, the impressionist sacrifices details and outlines to make the overall image more effective. In fact, the subject matter is actually the light and the bright and glowing colors. Paint often is laid on thickly, with heavy brush strokes.

Sometimes the painter doesn't even bother to mix the colors on his palette. He puts a dab of blue and a dab of red side by side to make a green that shimmers in the viewers' eye. This brush technique was taken to extremes in Georges Seurat's "pointillism," a "mosaic" of colored dots with no lines at all. (If you look carefully at a newspaper photo, you'll see that it is a mechanical form of pointillism.)

Seurat, *Bathers at Asnieres* (Tate Gallery, London)—1883
Here Seurat uses a technique called pointillism, a mosaic of colored dots with no lines. Pointillist motto: "Dot's all, folks!"

From Ridicule to Acceptance

Impressionism was born in the "Salon of the Rejected," sort of the "off-off Broadway" of struggling Parisian artists. Initially, people were outraged by this rough, messy style. One newspaper reported that after seeing an early Monet painting, "one visitor went mad, rushed out into the street and started biting innocent passersby." (Although it's much safer today, caution is still advised near Parisian modern art galleries.)

Renoir, *Dance at the Moulin de la Galette* (Orsay Museum, Paris)

The stuffy board of the Louvre Museum refused to display the new art even after the public accepted it. The nearby Jeu de Paume, a former indoor tennis court, was used to store the masterpieces of the movement. Later, impressionism was accepted by more of the artistic community (many impressionist artists—Manet, Degas, Renoir, Rodin—had first-class classical backgrounds), but it remained in its little museum. Today, impressionism is considered far from radical; it hangs in living rooms and corporate boardrooms, and people from all over the world tour Europe's great galleries of impressionism. The Jeu de Paume collection has been moved, and it is the major attraction in the wildly popular new Orsay Gallery, in Paris.

Degas, _Rehearsal at the Ballet_— 1885
Degas combined the impressionist "quick sketch" approach with more traditional outlines. He used his knowledge of photography in his paintings, giving us a candid view of the dancers.

Auguste Rodin (pronounced "ro-DAN," 1840-1917) blended impressionist ideas with his classical training to become the greatest sculptor since Michelangelo. He had the uncanny ability to capture

Rodin, _The Kiss_ (Tate Gallery, London)

the essence of a subject with his powerful yet sensitive technique. The rough "unfinished" surfaces of his works reflect light the same way the thick brush work of an impressionist painting does.

The Rodin Museum in Paris, near Les Invalides (where Napoleon is buried), is well worth an afternoon. It has one of Europe's finest collections of the work of a single artist.

Post-Impressionism

After impressionism, the modern artistic world splintered, never again to be contained by any one style. Within twenty years, impressionism had branched into two post-impressionist movements. One stressed form and order; the other demonstrated emotion and sensuousness.

Cézanne, *Still Life: Basket of Apples*—1894
Cézanne painted numerous still lifes in his experiments with form and composition. He once remarked that nature reveals itself in the geometric forms of cylinders, spheres, and cones. In this painting we see cylindrical biscuits, spherical apples, and a conical bottle.

Paul Cézanne (pronounced "say-ZAWN," 1839-1906) a man of independent means, ignored Paris, the critics, and the buying public. He accepted the impressionist approach of capturing what is seen, not what is there, but he balanced this with the order, outline, and solid forms of more traditional painting. Cézanne worked to create the best of both worlds—the instantaneity of impressionism and the realistic depth and solidity of earlier styles.

The sensual side of post-impressionism was led by Paul Gauguin ("pronounced go-GAN," 1848-1903) a stockbroker who chucked it all to become a painter. Like Cézanne, he left the artsy folk of proud Paris for inspiration in simple surroundings. He spent time with van Gogh in southern France—until Vincent attacked him in a fit of artistic rage—and then sailed for Tahiti. Gauguin's bright and bold paintings of native scenes hit Europe like a coconut. He used "primitive" techniques—simple outlines, sharply contrasting colors, and a flat, two-dimensional look—to create a naive and naturally expressive style that inspired many twentieth-century artists.

Gauguin, _Nave Nave Fenua_ (The Yummy Yummy Earth)—1894
In this woodcut we sense Gauguin's inner vision of a Tahitian paradise. The black-and-white simplicity emphasizes his passion for the primitive.

Van Gogh

The art of Vincent van Gogh (pronounced "van-GO," or "van-GOCK" by the Dutch and the snooty; 1853-1890) is an expression of his inner feeling. He used impressionist techniques powered with passion—painting not only what he saw but also what he felt. For this reason, his art truly reflects his life.

His early life was religious, not artistic. Disillusioned with the shallow values of the modern world, he served as a lay preacher for poor coal miners. In his late twenties, he channeled that religious vision and spiritual intensity into his art.

After learning from the impressionists in Paris, he moved to southern France to cloister himself in nature and his art. He did most of his great paintings there in the space of three years. They show the extreme loneliness, the emotional ecstasy, and the spiritual struggles he went through. Several times his work was interrupted by mental illness. Finally, believing that insanity was destroying his creative abilities, he killed himself.

Van Gogh, *Self-Portrait* (Orsay Museum, Paris)
With swirling brush strokes, Vincent charged impressionism with emotion. His canvases take you through the rapids of his life.

Van Gogh's art is an oil-on-canvas translation of his soul, his genius, and his emotions. The subjects were simple—common people and landscapes. His style was untrained and crude. But he could distort and exaggerate certain colors and details to give them spirit and emotions.

Van Gogh's love of the common man shines through in his painting. They seem to glow with, as he put it, "that something of the eternal which the halo used to symbolize."

In his landscape, *Road with Cypress Trees*, we see a simple, peaceful scene "van Gogh-ed" into a stormy sea of turbulence and emotion. He uses the strong, thick brush strokes and bright colors of the impressionist not to capture the light of the scene but to churn it up with emotion. Waves of wheat and flames of trees vibrate with an

Van Gogh, *The Potato Eaters* (Van Gogh Museum, Amsterdam)
Vincent worked with the poorest of the poor. He understood their dark, dreary world and painted it with dignity.

inner force that van Gogh believed inhabits all things.

Perhaps the best examples of van Gogh's art are his self-portraits. These show the man as well as his talent. Haunted and haunting, we see in his burning eyes the passionate love of all things and the desire to paint them onto canvas.

Europe's van Gogh treasure chest is the great van Gogh Museum in Amsterdam (next door to the Rijksmuseum). His art is well displayed, in chronological order, with each of his artistic stages related to events in his personal life. It's one of Europe's most enjoyable museums.

Van Gogh, _Sunflowers_ (National Gallery, London; other versions elsewhere)
Shortly after painting these sunflowers, the artist killed himself. Vincent van gone.

Van Gogh:

Rijksmuseum Van Gogh, Amsterdam
Kroller-Muller Museum near Arnhem, Netherlands
Orsay Museum, Paris
National Gallery, London

Impressionist and Post-Impressionist Sights:

Orsay Museum, Paris
Tate Gallery, London
National Gallery, London
Monet's garden, Giverny, near Paris
Rodin Museum, Paris
Marmotten Museum (Monet), Paris
L'Orangerie Museum (more Monet), Paris
Munch Museum, Oslo (Expressionism), Norway
Toulouse-Lautrec Museum, Albi, France
Van Gogh Museum, Amsterdam
Kroller-Muller Museum (Van Gogh), Arnhem, Netherlands

Europe in the Twentieth Century

Contemporary Europe is just as exciting as historic Europe and shouldn't take a back seat to Old Regime palaces and ancient ruins. Most of the sights tourists chase in Europe date back to before the twentieth century, but an understanding of our tumultuous age is important in understanding Europe's number one tourist attraction —its people.

The twentieth century began with the sort of easy happiness and nonchalance of a summer barbecue. The average European in 1910 felt very lucky to be living during those prosperous and peaceful times.

Behind the scenes, however, the tension in Europe was growing. Germany's late entry onto the European economic game board caused competitive rivalries. Tension mounted as Germany grabbed

EUROPE IN 1914

NORWAY · FINLAND · SWEDEN · NORTH SEA · DENMARK · GREAT BRITAIN · ATLANTIC OCEAN · NETH · BELG · GERMAN EMPIRE · POLAND · RUSSIA · FRANCE · AUSTRIA · SWITZ · HUNGARY · PORTUGAL · SPAIN · Sarajevo · SERBIA · RUM. · BULG. · BLACK SEA · ITALY · ALB. · GREECE · TURKEY (OTTOMAN EMPIRE) · MEDITERRANEAN SEA · SPANISH MOROCCO

⊞ ALLIES BASIS: TRIPLE ENTENTE (1907)
▤ CENTRAL POWERS BASIS: TRIPLE ALLIANCE (1882)
▨ ITALY (LEFT CENTRAL POWERS & JOINED ALLIES 1915)
☐ NEUTRAL

DCH

for its "place in the sun." It understood that capitalist economies need a colonial source of raw materials and a marketplace for finished products. By this time, most of the underdeveloped world was already controlled by other European powers.

Diplomatically, Europe was weaving a complex web of alliances. No one wanted to be left without an ally, so most countries dove headlong into an international game of "Let's Make a Deal." Alliances were secret, often conflicting, and no one knew for sure exactly where anyone else stood.

The modern nationalities of Europe were awakening, and particularly in the vast Hapsburg Empire, national groups were working aggressively for independence.

World War I

Beneath its placid exterior, Europe was ready to explode. The spark that set off World War I was the assassination of Archduke Ferdinand, heir to the Hapsburg throne, by a Serbian nationalist in 1914. The Hapsburg government, which ruled Austria, jumped at the opportunity to crush the troublesome Serbs (residents of modern-day Yugoslavia).

One by one, Europe's nations were drawn by alliance into this regional dispute. Each had a self-serving interest. Russia, slavic Serbia's big brother, aided Serbia, while Germany gave Austria a "blank check" of support. Germany knew that Russia was about to complete a new railroad mobilization plan that would give Russia first-strike capabilities. Many speculate that Germany thought a war at that time, while Russia was still slow to mobilize, was a safer bet than a war later, when Russia would be better prepared.

But when Austria attacked Serbia and the Russians mobilized, Germany invaded . . . France! France was allied to Russia, and Germany hoped to wipe out France by surprise rather than waging a two-front war. (Isn't it frightening how easily wars can start? History 101 should be required of all world leaders.)

Well, it didn't work out quite the way Germany had planned. Germany and France stalemated along their common border. Soldiers dug trenches to duck the machine-gun bullets. France and Germany settled into a battle of attrition, in which the political and military leaders of opposing nations decide to bash their heads against each other, each knowing it will suffer horrendous losses but calculating that the other will bleed white and drop first.

For four years, generals waved their swords and wave after wave of troops climbed out of their trenches and fell into their graves. On many occasions, France lost 65,000 people in one day. (That's more than the U.S. lost in the entire Vietnam War.) By 1918, half of all the men in France between the ages of 15 and 30 were dead.

Often, military leaders are the heroes of previous wars who underestimate new war technology. In World War I, that technology was the machine gun, a tool so awesome that a newspaper columnist of the day called it the "peacekeeper" because no civilized commander could send his boys into its fire.

Russia and Germany fought a very fluid and bloody war with the help of trains on the eastern front. Meanwhile, Austria had trouble with the stubborn Serbs.

Europe dove into the "War to End All Wars" expecting a quick finish. It took four bloody years for the Allies (France, England, Russia, and, ultimately, the United States) to defeat Germany and Austria. When the Treaty of Versailles was signed in 1919, nine million of the sixty-five million soldiers who fought were dead. Germany lay crushed and saddled with demoralizing war debts. Once-mighty Austria was reduced to a poor, tiny, landlocked country with a navy of three police boats on the Danube. France was finished as a superpower. Europe lay dazed and horrified at the unthinkable—which had just happened.

With a little study you could fill a whole tour with World War I and World War II "sights." In northern France and Alsace, you can tour bits of the Maginot Line and visit emotionally moving memorials at famous battle sights such as Verdun, near Reims.

After the war, the map of Europe was redrawn. The old ruling families of Germany, Russia, and Austria and the Ottoman rulers of present-day Turkey were finished. New, democratic nations drew borders along cultural and ethnic boundaries, defining Finland, Austria, Hungary, Czechoslovakia, Poland, Yugoslavia, Latvia, Estonia, and Lithuania. Germany handed over the provinces of Alsace and Lorraine to France.

Compared with war-ravaged Europe, the United States was a dominant, seemingly boundless superpower. By 1929, it boasted a whopping 42 percent of the entire world's industrial output.

Between the Wars—Totalitarianism

After World War I, the big question was, Would Germany be democratic or Communist? Russia had recently ended its Communist revolution and had become the Soviet Union. According to Marxist theory, industrial-based Germany was the perfect candidate to lead the world into communism. But the victorious Allies (the United

States, Great Britain, and France) managed to install the Western-style "Weimar" government, and the German Communist party was literally buried one night when the top 1,000 Communists, including leaders Rosa Luxembourg and Karl Liebknecht, were shot.

The German people associated their new Western government with the hated Treaty of Versailles. Although the Weimar government was technically a modern constitutional democracy, behind the scenes ticked the old ruling order—the army and industrialists —scheming to reverse the war's outcome and revive Germany as Europe's foremost power. Many people view World War II as the logical continuation and conclusion of World War I and its misguided Treaty of Versailles, which simply announced the intermission.

Meanwhile, in Italy, a violent, melodramatic nationalism and an anti-intellectual movement called fascism were born. Benito Mussolini led the Fascist party, stressing unity and authority. Capitalizing on Italy's corrupt government, miserable economy, and high unemployment, he rose easily to power. As in Germany a few years later, the rich and the businessmen believed fascism to be distasteful but supported it as the only alternative to Europe's rising red tide of communism.

This stamp from Ethiopia, licked by Mussolini in 1935, shows the Fascist alliance of Hitler and the Italian dictator. The slogan says, "Two peoples, one war."

In 1922, Mussolini took the reins of government. "Il Duce" went straight to work, filling the government with Fascists, organizing the strong-man "squadrisi" to "encourage" Italians to support him, and building a strong, super-nationalistic, self-sufficient Fascist Italy.

Although Mussolini's government had its problems, it was the only strong rule Italy has functioned under in this century. As a tourist you will drive on a system of super-freeways, "autostrada," commissioned by Il Duce's government. Many of Rome's buildings, including the Olympic Games complex and the futuristic suburb of EUR, are Fascist in style. (EUR, ten minutes by subway from Rome's Colosseum, with its bold and powerful architecture, is well worth exploring.)

Fascist art and architecture from Mussolini's planned futuristic suburb, EUR (a short subway ride from downtown Rome).

Hitler

The rise of Hitler and Nazism in Germany is fascinating. Although there are not a lot of "Hitler sights," the era of Hitler is a part of Germany's history that cast its shadow across all of contemporary Europe.

The roots of Adolf Hitler's success lie in Germany's anger. After World War One, when Germans hated the Treaty of Versailles and the Weimar government and when inflation ripped ever deeper into Germany's moral fabric, Hitler and his party leaped into the news. When the value of the mark went from four to the U.S. dollar to four trillion in 1923, the hardworking German middle class lost faith in society. All debts, savings, and retirement funds were wiped out. (It took a wheelbarrow full of paper marks to buy a pretzel.) People wanted to believe the promises of a charismatic madman.

Like Mussolini, Hitler was a master of capitalizing on society's problems; when he couldn't find a solution, he found a scapegoat. His party boomed until Germany did. When Germany entered its happy-go-lucky cabaret years in the mid-'20s, people wrote off Hitler and other political extremists as lunatics on the fringe.

When the Great Depression hit in 1929, Hitler rose again. With his political genius, terror tactics, scapegoating of the Jews, and the support of the rich elite of the day (who saw fascism as the only defense against communism), Hitler became Germany's dictator.

Nazi campaign poster
This political ad tells voters they can free Germany from its chains—by voting for Hitler.

The promises of a charismatic "führer" were just what an angry, frustrated, post-World War I Germany wanted to hear.

In 1933, he proclaimed that his "Third Reich" would last a thousand years. (The first two "reichs" were pre-World War I Germany, 1871-1918, and the medieval Holy Roman Empire.) Hitler tried to turn Germany into a monolithic slab of nationalistic rock. There were to be no states, no parties, no classes, and no questions. There was to be only Germany. The Nazi party was purged, the Gestapo kept the flags waving, concentration camps were filled with dissenters who weren't killed, and Nazism became the religion of state.

Nazi propaganda
Translation: "Judaism is criminal." Signs like this were commonplace in Hitler's Germany. Someone had to take the blame for Germany's problems. The Jews were a traditional scapegoat.

In his own frothing way, Hitler was a genius. Germany prospered. The economy boomed, everyone was employed, and complete self-sufficiency (necessary to wage a world war) was right around the corner.

Hitler said, "Space must be fought for and maintained. People who are lazy have no right to the soil. Soil is for he who tills it and protects it. If a nation loses in the defense of its soil, then the individual loses. There is no higher justice that decrees that a people must starve. There is only power, and power creates justice.... Parliaments do not create all of the rights on the earth; force also creates rights. The question is whether we wish to live or die. We have more right to soil than all the other nations because we are so thickly populated. I am of the opinion that in this respect, too, the principle can be applied; God helps him who helps himself."

And people followed him.

Totalitarianism was the fastest-growing form of government in Europe in the 1930s, gaining power in Germany, Italy, and Spain as

Nazi mass meeting, Nuremberg, 1937
Fifty thousand Nazis attend a rally to hear Hitler rant and rave in a setting with the air of a grandiose Hollywood epic. Like Napoleon earlier, Hitler dreamed of a reunited Roman Empire.

well as in the Stalinist USSR. In *The Origins of Totalitarianism*, Hannah Arendt describes this harsh form of government:

> The very ethics of totalitarianism were violent and neopagan. It declared that men should live dangerously, avoid the flabby weakness of too much thought, throw themselves with red-blooded vigor into a life of action. The new regimes all instituted youth movements. They appealed to a kind of juvenile idealism, in which young people believed that by joining some kind of squad, donning some kind of uniform, and getting into the fresh air they contributed to a great moral resurgence of their country. Young men were taught to value their bodies but not their minds, to be tough and hard, to regard mass gymnastics as patriotic demonstrations, and camping trips as a preparation for the world of the future. Young women were taught to breed large families without complaint, to be content in the kitchen, and to look with awe upon their virile mates. The body-cult flourished while the mind decayed. The ideal was to turn the German people into a race of splendid animals, pink-cheeked, Nordic, and upstanding. Contrariwise, euthanasia was adopted for the insane and was proposed for the aged. Later, in WW II, when the Nazis overran Eastern Europe, they committed Jews to the gas chambers, destroying some 6,000,000 human beings by the most scientific methods. Animals were animals; one bred the kind one wanted and killed the kind one did not.

World War II

The peace in Europe following the Treaty of Versailles was unstable. It couldn't last. World War II was inevitable.

While most of Europe between the wars was pacifist and isolationist, Hitler waged a careful campaign of "gradual encroachment." Each year he ranted and raved and threatened to go wild. When he would take just a little, the world felt relieved and hoped he was satisfied.

But even the most naive pacifist couldn't ignore Germany's invasion of Poland in 1939. England and France declared war and it was one big pigpile all over again.

In the first year, Hitler's "Blitzkrieg" was very successful. Hitler conquered most of central and northern Europe with these ingenious Nazi lightning attacks.

Dachau Concentration Camp
The twentieth century saw slaughter and suffering on an unprecedented scale. Modern totalitarian governments proved they could turn people into meaningless numbers.

Winston Churchill took the English helm offering "nothing but blood, toil, tears, and sweat . . . but a faith in ultimate victory." He successfully inspired and led England through the furious "Battle of Britain," when German bombers almost leveled London.

Frustrated by British planes and the English Channel, Hitler turned eastward and sank his iron teeth deep into vast Russia. The Soviets suffered, but a harsh winter and the Russian "scorched earth" policy thwarted the Nazis just as they had foiled Napoleon's army 130 years earlier.

The war raged in Africa as well, while in Asia, Japan grabbed a million square miles. After Japan's unprovoked attack on Pearl Harbor, the United States joined in the melee. America's fresh forces and underestimated industrial might turned the tide.

The Allies took North Africa and invaded Italy. They crossed the English Channel to Normandy on D day (1944), gaining a vital toehold in France from which to attack Germany. Russia made great advances while the Allies gained complete air control of German skies, bombing its cities almost at will. By May 1945, Hitler was dead and Germany was quiet, smoldering, and exhausted.

The tourist today sees very few sights produced by the World Wars—what is important is what the tourist doesn't see. You won't see the wonders of Dresden, Germany, at one time one of the most beautiful medieval cities in Europe. You won't see the lovely churches and architecture of old Berlin, Cologne, or Rotterdam. Air raids leveled all these cities during World War II, and the survivors rebuilt them in a modern style.

The best reminders of this terrible war are found in the resistance museums in Oslo and Copenhagen, at Anne Frank's house in Amsterdam, at the concentration camps at Dachau (near Munich) and Auschwitz (in Poland), and in the memories of older Europeans.

World War II, Fascist, and Nazi Sights:

Concentration Camps: Dachau (near Munich); Mauthausen, Austria; Auschwitz, Poland; Buchenwald, Germany; and others

Hitler's Eagle's Nest, Berchtesgaden, Bavaria

Mussolini's planned city, EUR, Rome

Haus der Kunst (exterior), Munich

Oradour sur Glanc (bombed and burned memorial ghost city), near Limoges, France

Anne Frank's House, Amsterdam

Corrie Ten Boom's "Hiding Place," Haarlem, Netherlands

Kaiser Wilhelm Memorial Church, Berlin

Jewish Archives and museum, Prague

D day landing sights, Normandy

Bayeux WW II museum, Normandy

Cabinet War Rooms, London

Imperial War museum, London

Resistance (against the Nazis) museums in Oslo and Copenhagen

Hitler's first Autobahn rest stop, at U.S. army hotel on Lake Chiemsee, between Munich and Salzburg

Deportation Monument, behind Notre Dame, Paris

Montecassino, Italy

Europe Since 1945

World War II left much of Europe in ruins. Even before the shooting stopped, it was evident that a postwar world would be bipolar, dominated by an American sphere and a Soviet sphere. Scrambling to pick up the broken pieces of earlier powers, each side did what it could to grab the technology and great minds of Germany and turn former enemies into economic and political allies. The Soviets "liberated" the Eastern European nations from the Nazis, installing Moscow-trained governments in each capital. Germany was split in two, with the eastern half of each controlled by the Soviets. The "Iron Curtain" was lowered, ushering in a forty-five-year period of strict Soviet control over the nations it figured it needed as a buffer zone against another attack from the West.

The United States funded the rebuilding of Western Europe by means of its very successful Marshall plan. The Soviet Union sank huge amounts into its defense and space programs. Western Europe's economy lurched and then boomed while Eastern Europe lagged under its controlled Soviet-style economy. The NATO (West) and Warsaw Pact (East) alliances were formed.

The Cold War began. The USSR blockaded West Berlin (1948). With the help of an American airlift, this island of the capitalist West, which provided a painful contrast to the bleak Eastern economies, remained free. (The West German government subsidized this contrast by providing many perks—tax breaks, cheap flights, draft deferments, and so on—to anyone who would live, travel, and work in West Berlin.) The USSR, under the guise of a Warsaw Pact peacekeeping force, crushed revolutions in Hungary (1956) and Czechoslovakia (1968). To keep their people in, the East German government built what it called the "anti-fascist barrier"—what we called the Berlin Wall (1961).

Superpower tensions were on the mind of all Europeans, who were leery of nuclear arsenals capable of destroying Europe's windmills, castles, pubs, and people many times over. The horrors of two devastating wars in their recent past confronted Europeans, with many one-legged pensioners and tombstone-covered hills as reminders. As "evil empire" rhetoric raged between the flagbearers of the planet's two bulkiest ideologies, Europeans felt powerless. Many thought their homeland would be the fighting ground for World War III.

But in the 1980s, the Cold War began to thaw. The rise of the Polish labor movement, Solidarity under Lech Walesa, made a powerful impression on workers across Eastern Europe. Then in 1985 came

Mikhail Gorbachev, the first modern, truly post-Stalin, post-World War II Soviet leader. His reforms and personal charisma made him the man of the decade. I "heart" Gorby pins were common across the Warsaw Pact countries as the Soviet leader ended the Brezhnev doctrine, saying, basically, If you want to split and do your own thing economically, good luck, but we'll need to maintain foreign policy control (as in Finland) for defensive purposes. (With its economic fuel tank on "E," the USSR was backed into a corner by American economic might and Reagan's threat of a battle of economic attrition—called Star Wars.)

And split Eastern Europe did. Like dominoes, the tumultuous revolutions of 1989 and 1990 toppled Communist regime after Communist regime. East German Communist leaders were tried and convicted for abuse of power and corruption. The dictator of Romania and his wife were executed. A playwright became the president of Czechoslovakia. Every time we turned around, another nation raised its grass roots to the sky, tossed out its outdated Communist party, and threatened to join the Eurail club. It was exciting to live in 1989, a year that will be on our children's history tests.

As democracy takes hold in Eastern Europe and one end of yesterday's bipolar world restructures itself to fit into our ever-smaller planet, let's hope for farsightedness and wisdom on the part of the United States, in Europe, and in the rest of the world. One stumble in this delicate sprint for freedom and we could be talking war bonds instead of peace dividends.

Travel in Eastern Europe? Don't jump in quite yet. These countries have miserable tourist industries despite their rich cultures and warm, curious people. Their gray economies will only get worse in the short term, offering a frustrating contrast to independent tourists accustomed to the very efficient Western European tourist industry.

Local tourist information offices in Eastern Europe are so bureaucratic, inefficient, and tied to the high-rise expensive side of hotels and restaurants that they're often more trouble than they're worth. Hotel rooms have never been plentiful, and with any kind of tourist rush, they'll be even less so. Local economic programs will not give tourism a high priority just yet. English is less understood east of what was the Iron Curtain. (German is the handiest second language.)

Much of the thrill of traveling in the Eastern Bloc will fade. Instead of being gray, inefficient, and mysterious, it will now be simply gray and inefficient. Don't get us wrong. We love traveling in the Eastern Bloc, but for the next few years, the average tourist who didn't care to go before the age of Gorbachev might get a piece of the Wall but the thrill will last about as long as the fizz in his Polish cola.

Meanwhile, in Western Europe, countries have been working out other problems. No European country has perfect homogeneity. Small nationalities—without a nation—are struggling for independence, or survival. France, for instance, has the Basques, the Corsicans, and the Celtic people of Brittany, many of whom see themselves as un-French parts of a French empire ruled from Paris. The George Washingtons and Nathan Hales of these little, neglected nationalities are making news in Europe. Terrorism filled headlines throughout the 1970s and 1980s, and there's no reason to think that patriots will stop regretting that they have only one life to give for their countries.

A silent victim of modern times, the environment, was finally recognized in the 1980s. The Green party, whose platform was primarily environmental, effectively raised many issues that many chose not to see in spite of the diseased forests, dead rivers, and radioactive reindeer in their midst. Nuclear accidents, acid rain, ozone problems, and chemical spills are awakening a continent notorious for treating its Mediterranean Sea like its own private cesspool, and even politicians who support big business are beginning to realize that you can't exploit the poor on an uninhabitable planet.

Twentieth-Century Art— Reflecting a World in Turmoil

Why is modern art so bizarre? Better to ask, Why is the modern world so bizarre? The world changed by leaps, bounds, and somersaults during the twentieth century. Strange as some art might seem, it's often an honest representation of our strange world.

The world wars devastated Europe. No one could have foreseen the extent of the senseless slaughter. People, especially artists, were shocked, disgusted, and disillusioned. As old moral values were challenged by the horror of war and our rapidly changing society, so were artistic ones.

Twentieth-century art is such a confusing pile of styles and theories that only two generalizations can be made: (1) none of it looks like the real world, and (2) my dog could do better work on the carpet for a fraction of the price.

But as we learned from ancient Egyptian art, you can't judge art simply by how well it copies reality. Artists distort the real world intentionally. Especially in twentieth-century art, some of the messiest and least-organized-looking works ("It looks like a child's scribbling!") are very sophisticated and based on complex theories requiring knowledge of many art styles. If you don't understand it, you can't judge it. Learn about art first, understand the artist's purpose, and then you can appreciate—or criticize—with gusto.

Speculating on Heroic Death, The Dachau Museum, 1934
The artist predicts the coming world war.

Speaking in very general terms, modern artists portray the "real" world in two different ways. One, the "expressive" way, is to depict the real world but exaggerate things to make them express an emotion— the style of van Gogh. The other, "abstract" way is to abandon the visible world altogether, making basic lines and patches of color that reflect not real objects but a more basic beauty.

Expressionism

The best example of the "expressive" distortion of reality is a style called, incredibly enough, "expressionism." Expressionism carries van Gogh's emotionalism to the extreme. In _The Scream_, the Norwegian artist Edvard Munch (pronounced "MOONCH," 1863-1944) bends and twists everything into a landscape of unexplained terror.

We "hear" the scream in the lines of the canvas—up from the twisted body, through the terrified skull, and out to the sky, echoing until it fills the entire nightmare world of the painting.

Munch, *The Scream* (Oslo)—1893
The Norwegian Edvard Munch led the way into the artistic movement aptly called expressionism. These artists distorted reality to express the horror of the modern world. The museum in Oslo dedicated to Munch's work is excellent.

We can appreciate the power of modern art by comparing *The Scream* with an earlier work, Gericault's *Raft of the Medusa* (see page 215). Both are a terror on canvas. But whereas Gericault's terror arises from a realistic portrayal of a grotesque event, Munch simply distorts the appearance of an everyday scene so that we see it in a more powerful way, from a different emotional perspective.

Expressionism flourished in Germany from 1905 through 1935. Artists show us the horror and injustice of the war years they experienced. The garish colors, twisted lines, and masklike faces stress emotion over realism.

Woodcut by Kirchner, 1917
The expressionist sees a distorted, twisted world—and shows it to us that way.

Social Realism

The totalitarian governments of postwar Eastern Europe and the USSR attempted to control everyone and everything. They used whatever they could to achieve that end, including the media and art.

Soviet propaganda poster "Social realism" art was intended to rouse nationalist and class feelings against the "threat" of the capitalist West. Here the workers are shown victorious through passionate dedication to their state, industry, and military. Soviet art has been a broken record of "worker triumph" propaganda.

Their art was propaganda. Called social realism, the style draws repeatedly on a few Socialist or Marxist-Leninist themes. (For example, the noble, muscular worker is depicted bashing the chains of capitalism and overcoming the evils of the bourgeois world.) The art portrays family ideals, Socialist morality, flags blowing heroically in the wind, and undying respect for the fathers of the ideology (and, of course, the imperial power behind the ideological cloak, Russia). Russia is featured as the liberator—from the Turks, from the Nazis, and from the evil Western world.

Although art as propaganda is nothing new, only in the sphere of the Soviet Union was creativity channeled so effectively into one purpose. Abstract art, which serves no purpose in inspiring the masses, was discouraged. Even artistic mediums as nebulous as music were censored for what they did or did not promote.

Abstract Art

The second strain of twentieth-century art, "abstraction," is less understood than the "expressive" distortion employed by Munch and van Gogh. Abstraction is simplification. For example, when an artist paints a tree, he or she can never capture the infinite details of any individual tree. So the artist simplifies, using lines and colors to show enough details to make the canvas look like a tree. In this sense all art is to some extent an abstraction, or simplification, of the real world.

Throughout history, artists had denied this fact, trying to make their two-dimensional canvases look as real as the three-dimensional world they painted. But by the twentieth century, the camera had been accepted as the captor of reality. Artists began to accept the abstract and artificial nature of paintings. In fact, they emphasized and enjoyed this abstraction to the extent of neglecting the subject itself. They were free to experiment with the devices used to portray the subject—lines, colors, and shapes. Not concerned with representing the real world, this art is called "nonrepresentational."

Abstract artists are like children with a set of brightly colored building blocks. Rather than use the blocks to build a house or some recognizable object, children are fascinated by the blocks themselves. They spend hours placing them in patterns that are pleasing for their own sake, not because they add up to something else.

This is how abstract artists use lines and colors—their "building blocks." But unlike children, abstract artists generally have years of training with which to plan the best arrangement of the "blocks."

The Card Players, Paul Cézanne, 1892

Card Players, Theo van Doesburg, 1916

Here is a progression of realism to abstraction based on Cézanne's post-impressionist painting, which is more or less realistic (top left).

(Top right) The figures are flattened, the canvas reduced to a composition of geometric shapes. The subject matter is still apparent.

(Below right) This later painting carries the process of abstraction further. Simplified into a jumble of puzzle pieces, the card players are barely recognizable. The blocks of line and color themselves become the subject.

Card Players, Theo van Doesburg, 1917

So to approach, appreciate, and judge modern art, the viewer needs to know the rules—especially if the art can't be compared to reality.

Abstract Art = Visual Music

It's helpful to compare abstract art to pure instrumental music. Some music is designed to imitate a sound heard in nature, such as a storm or the call of a bird. Other music is intended to express an emotion, such as the sadness caused by the death of a friend. But most music is the perfect audio equivalent of abstract visual art. It simply plays with the beautiful "shapes and colors" of sound, the harmonious relationship of tones. Our ears don't demand to know what the sounds are supposed to represent.

In the same way, art explores the relationships of lines and colors. The rules of these relationships are visible to the trained eye just as the rules of music are audible to the trained ear. But to the average viewer (or listener), abstract art (or music) is to be enjoyed, not analyzed. Music is enjoyable even if you don't understand the meter and scale on which it's built. The same is true of visual abstract art. It's just plain nice to look at. (Notice the similarity between the titles of abstract artworks and musical compositions—"Composition with Red, Yellow and Blue," "Sonata for Piano and Violin No. 1.")

Kandinsky, *Composition 238: Bright Circle*—1921
Reality is tossed out the window as the artist calls on us to enjoy more basic shapes and colors. We hope this is right side up.

In the colorful geometric patterns painted by Piet Mondrian there is no attempt whatsoever to represent reality. The work is simply a study of the relationships between geometrical segments of color. What appears to be symmetrical regularity between shapes—what anybody with a pen and ruler could draw—was actually drawn freehand. The squares aren't exactly square, and the segments aren't exactly balanced. Mondrian must have agonized over just the right relationship between these blocks of color, following his own set of "rules."

Abstract artists have been criticized for avoiding reality—for playing with their building blocks and making patterns that only they can understand. Artists such as Mondrian, Paul Klee, and Wassily Kandinsky have replied that what they painted was reality—not the fleeting reality of the visible world, the reality that changes and passes away, but the eternal, unchanging world of geometrical relationships. (Plato again.) The abstract artist simplifies the world into timeless shapes and colors. Are your eyes as open-minded as your ears?

Primitives and Wild Beasts

Most modern art styles are a mix of pure abstraction and expressive distortions of reality. One such style is called "primitivism," a return to the simplified (and therefore "abstract") style used in prehistoric cave paintings and stylized, early Greek art. Primitivists tried to paint the world through the eyes of primitive people, with a calculated crudeness. Paul Gauguin was their inspiration; Gauguin had rejected the sterile, modern, industrial world (and its sterile art) for the expressive and magical power of primitive images.

Matisse, *Joy of Life*—1905
Matisse simplifies reality so we can see it better—through primitive eyes. The two-dimensional flatness shows Gauguin's influence.

The "Fauves" (French for "wild beasts," pronounced "foavs") shocked the modern-art world with their exuberant use of elements of primitive art—strong outlines; bright, barbaric colors; and two-dimensional "flatness." The Fauves distorted the visible world so we could see it through more primitive eyes.

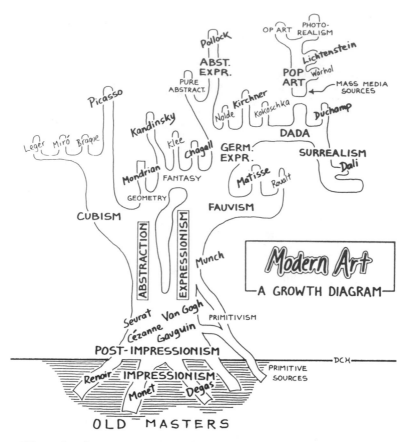

Their leader was Henri Matisse (pronounced "mah-TEES," 1869-1954), a master of simplicity. Each of his subjects is boiled down to its essential details and portrayed with few and simple lines and colors.

Even though Matisse's work looks crude, his classical training is obvious. The "flat," primitive look is actually carefully planned 3-D. The bright colors that seem so bizarre are purposely placed to balance the composition. And despite the few lines, his figures are accurate and expressive.

Picasso and Cubism

The works of Pablo Picasso (1881-1973) reveal both the expressive and the abstract. His long, prolific career spans several decades and art styles. Picasso was an innovator and provides us with prime examples of many things characteristic of twentieth-century art.

When he was 19, Picasso moved from Barcelona to Paris to be where the artistic action was. (An exciting collection of his early works is displayed in his house in Barcelona.) Picasso's early paintings—of beggars and other social outcasts—are touching examples of expressionism done with the sympathy and understanding of an artist who felt, perhaps, as much an outcast as his subjects. Picasso painted these early works in what has come to be called his Blue Period (c. 1905), so called because their dominant color matches their melancholy mood.

Picasso, _The Frugal Meal_—1904
Picasso, like most "far-out" modern artists, first mastered "normal" realism. He then explored beyond what the eye sees, evolving through several stages. This stage was melancholy, a style of expressionism called Picasso's "Blue Period."

Picasso was jolted out of this style by the abstract methods of the Fauves. Intrigued with the paradox of painting a three-dimensional world on a two-dimensional canvas but disliking the 2-D flatness of Fauvism, he played with the "building blocks"—line and color—to find new ways to reconstruct the real world on canvas.

The solution Picasso worked out with his fellow painter Georges Braque is known as cubism (c. 1910) because the painting looks as though it was built with blocks. Chunks of light and shadow seem to stand out in 3-D like shards of broken glass reflecting light. In fact, Picasso experimented with actual three-dimensional collages, pasting everyday materials (such as rope, newspaper clippings, and wallpaper) onto the canvas in place of paint. The materials are as interesting in themselves as what they are meant to represent.

Picasso was still tied to the visible world. The anatomy might be jumbled, but it's all there. Picasso shattered the real world, then pieced it back together on canvas—in his own way.

In his monumental mural, *Guernica*, Picasso blends the abstract and the expressive. In the 1930s, Spanish, Nazi-backed fascists destroyed the Spanish town of Guernica. Picasso captures the horror of the event not through a realistic portrayal but through expressive images. The ambiguous, abstract nature of *Guernica* elevates the painting to a statement about all wars. There are some clearly recognizable images of the agony of war: the grieving mother with her dead child (a modern Pietà); the dying warrior clutching a broken sword; the twisted horse's head. But the real power of the work comes from the disjointed anatomy typical of early cubist works—as if the bombs had shattered every belief and decimated every moral principle, leaving civilization in a confused heap of rubble.

Picasso, *Guernica* (Prado annex, Madrid)—1937
This masterpiece combines cubism, surrealism, and abstractionism in black, gray, and white to show the terror of the Fascist air raid on a defenseless town during the Spanish Civil War. Today it is a virtual national monument of Spain and a comment on the futility and horror of war.

Picasso Sights:

Picasso Museum, Paris
Picasso Museum, Barcelona, Spain
Guernica, Prado annex, Madrid
Grimaldi-Picasso Museum, Antibes
Tate Gallery, Pompidou, and many other modern art galleries

Dada

The Jazz Age of the 1920s, when Europe tried to drown the memory of the war in wine and cynicism, produced dadaism. The name was purposely nonsensical and childish—made up to poke fun at the pompous art styles, theories, and "-isms" of prewar times. The one rule of the dada theory is that there are no rules. The Mona Lisa with a moustache, a snow shovel signed by the artist, a collage of shredded paper dropped on a canvas—these were the dadaists' contribution to Art, a summation of the rebelliousness and disgust of the Roaring Twenties.

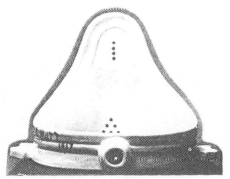

Duchamp, _Fountain_—1917
Marcel Duchamp, the daddy of dada, placed this urinal in a New York exhibit. By taking a common object, giving it a title, and calling it art, he makes us think about the object in a new way.

If a snow shovel is art, what is art? With mass production, the lines began to blur. Handmade art became an economic dinosaur as it became possible for rich people to buy beautiful objects and furnishings right off the production line. Artists found themselves on the outside of an industrial society that was interested more in utility than in aesthetics.

Without a patron to please, modern artists had no one to please but themselves and fellow artists. They turned to subjects of interest to the highly educated—studies in color, brushwork, and textures. Originality and innovation became more important than beauty.

Modern artists face the same challenge as Michelangelo's successors: to be original at all costs. If you can't please the public, shock it.

Surrealism and Beyond

Dada's successor for shock value was surrealism. (The name implies "beyond realism"—as if reality isn't weird enough already.) Inspired by the psychiatric theories of Sigmund Freud, surrealism explores the inner world of the subconscious mind. The canvases of Salvador Dali are "dreamscapes"—landscapes of primal, troubling, dream images. In dreams, objects appear in weird combinations, constantly changing in shape and meaning. A cat becomes a woman, the viewer becomes the cat, and so on.

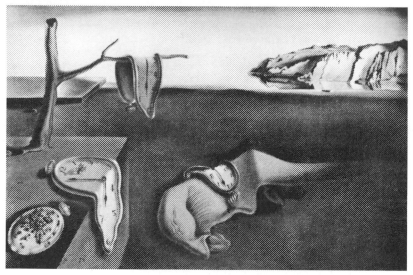

Dali, *The Persistence of Memory*—1931
This tiny work (9" by 13") sums up the surrealists' attempt to shock us by taking familiar objects and placing them in an unfamiliar context.

Marc Chagall (pronounced "shuh-GAWL," 1887-1985), although not a surrealist, used the same scrambling of images. Born in Russia, Chagall layered in his art memories of the folk life of his childhood. His paintings reveal a colorful fantasy of images.

Chagall, *Self-Portrait with Seven Fingers*—1912

While surrealists painted recognizable objects (though often in a twisted or unusual setting), other artists produced purely abstract works. As Europe struggled to rebuild and recover after World War II, the focus of art shifted to the United States.

Jackson Pollock (1912-1956) explored the power of paint. His canvases are dripped and splattered with paint that appears to be tossed on almost at random. When we look at these paintings, we think of Pollock slopping, hurling, and dripping, maybe even dancing around his studio, brush in hand. What was going through his head at the moment of creation? The canvas is the record of that moment. Pollock let the elements of chance and spontaneity create art through him.

Pollock, *Peinture*
"Jack the Dripper" attacks convention with a can of paint. His canvases are not a "window" to see through but a "tray" of interesting patterns and textures.

Pop Art

"Pop Art" of the 1950s and 1960s, like dada of the Jazz Age, challenges the old rules of what constitutes art. The everyday products of commercial society—such as toothpaste, soup cans, comic books, and advertisements—are displayed as art. The viewer is forced to examine these objects in a new way, reflecting on the value our society places on them.

Modern artists experiment with modern materials. From initial experimentation with cubist collages, artists began replacing paint with all kinds of things. The resulting mixed-media creations stimulate all the senses—in some cases, even smell—and fuse the mediums of painting and sculpture.

Lichtenstein, *Whaam!* (Tate Gallery, London)—1963
A child's comic book becomes a 70-square-foot piece of art—"Pop Art." What would Raphael think?

Painting has been the most dynamic of the visual arts in this century, but sculpture followed some of the same trends. The primitivism of the Fauves influenced Constantin Brancusi, whose sculptures are the equivalent of Matisse's "minimal" paintings. Brancusi altered the shape of the original stone only slightly.

Far-out Modern Art Sights:

Pompidou, Paris
Stedelijk, Amsterdam
Tate Gallery, London
Guggenheim Gallery, Venice
Louisiana, north of Copenhagen
Kroller Muller Museum, near Arnhem, Netherlands
Art of the Criminally Insane (Collection de l'Art Brut),
   Lausanne, Switzerland
Modern Museum, Stockholm
Kunst Museum (lots of Paul Klee), Bern, Switzerland
Wallraf-Richartz Museum, Köln, Germany
Dali Museum, Figueres, Spain
Foundation Maeght, St. Paul, French Riviera
Many galleries on the French Riviera (Matisse, Chagall, Picasso)
Commercial galleries selling contemporary art in all major
   cities
Temporary exhibits all over Europe all the time. Often, one
   wing of the museum is reserved for temporary exhibits.
   Check local periodical entertainment guides, tourist in-
   formation offices, posters around town.

Modern Architecture

"Form follows function" was the catchphrase of early twentieth-century architecture. While painters and sculptors have to concern themselves primarily with how good their artwork looks (its form), architects must also be concerned with how their buildings work (function).

At the turn of the century, the ready availability of the steel frame, reinforced concrete, and high-quality, mass-produced glass gave architects the tools to build almost any style of building they wanted. Architects began stripping buildings down to their barest structural elements, letting the function dictate form.

The international style that developed in the 1920s followed the lead of the Bauhaus, a German art school. This blocky building emphasized industrial design and functionalism in architecture. Rectangular outlines, flat roofs, no ornamentation, white walls, and lots of glass were Bauhaus "favorites." When the Nazis closed the Bauhaus, its director moved to the United States and tall, boxlike, steel-and-glass skyscrapers soon became the standard U.S. urban skyline.

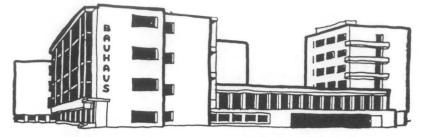

Gropius, Bauhaus (Dessau, Germany)—1925
Modern architecture—more functional than good looking. This purely geometric building set the style for almost every skyscraper since.

Fast-growing U.S. cities, such as Chicago and New York, provided solid foundations for the international style. Frank Lloyd Wright, an important twentieth-century American architect, blended these ideas with his own organic roots.

Scandinavian architects such as Alvar Aalto from Finland developed their own style based on simplicity and clean lines. These traits carry over into the Scandinavian furniture and lighting designs popular in America today.

Scandinavia is Europe's pioneer in planned suburbs. Outside Stockholm you'll find Vallingby and Farsta striving for the ultimate in Swedish order and efficiency. Tapiola, east of Helsinki, is Finland's attempt at a futuristic utopia.

Le Corbusier was a major force in twentieth-century European architecture. An innovative leader in city planning, he popularized putting buildings on pillars to create space below. One church he

Le Corbusier, Chapel at Ronchamp, France—c. 1955
A far cry from Gothic, this highly expressive church is one of the gems of modern architecture. Located atop a hill in the Vosges Mountains.

designed, in Ronchamp, France, has become a pilgrimage site for students of architecture.

As they dealt with the large-scale reconstruction of European cities flattened by World War II, architects busied themselves with plans for towns, housing, and schools. Rotterdam and Cologne are two examples of cities rebuilt from scratch after the war.

Contempory European architecture has branched in several directions. An extreme example of form following function is the Georges Pompidou Center in Paris. This huge, exoskeletal structure has its "guts" on the outside. All plumbing, heating ducts, and wiring are brightly color coded and in full view, freeing the interior space for its expansive modern art museum.

Munich also has its modern architectural treats. The buildings for the 1972 Olympic games are an interesting experiment in tent forms. The BMW headquarters and museum occupy a futuristic, cylindrical, glass skyscraper across the street.

The streets of Europe's cities are becoming people places. Most large cities (such as Copenhagen and Florence) have traffic-free pedestrian areas full of shops and cafés, providing a perfect opportunity for that great European pastime—people-watching.

Faced with ever-dwindling space, rising populations, and dynamic societal changes, European architects and city planners have come up with some creative ideas. Today's architecture is—as it has been from the caveman to Egypt and from Rome to the Renaissance—a product of available materials and technology, climate, and the needs of the people.

Modern Architecture Sights:

Temppeliaukio Church, Helsinki, Finland
The "Cube" at La Defense, Paris
Chapel at Ronchamp, near Mulhouse, France
Planned suburbs of Stockholm (Vallingby and Farsta) and
  Helsinki (Tapiola)
Termini Station, Rome
Forum/Les Halles shopping mall, Paris
Berlin housing projects (Kreuzberg district), Berlin
Pyramid entrance to the Louvre, Paris
Georges Pompidou Center, Paris
Works of Alvar Aalto, Finland (museum in Jyraskyla)
Rotterdam—the whole city

1992—One Europe?

As Europe grapples with problems concerning the environment, international terrorism, superpower politics, and competition in a global market, it is recognizing the growing necessity of speaking, trading, and legislating with one voice. Even with recent setbacks, the question of a Federal Europe is no longer "if," but "when."

Several decades ago Belgium, the Netherlands, and Luxembourg (BeNeLux) united economically. The Common Market or European Economic Community (EEC) is an ever-expanding version of this trade agreement. Twelve countries (BeNeLux, Great Britain, Germany, France, Italy, Denmark, Ireland, Greece, Spain, and Portugal) are now members. With a population of more than 300 million, the EEC is a potentially powerful force. The economic success of this union, the demands of continental problems that recognize no borders, and the pressure of competition in a global market have convinced most Europeans that some degree of unification is a good idea.

In 1992, all borders between EEC countries were dissolved for commerce. A uniform EEC passport is already in use, and a uniform driver's license is in the works. A single currency, the European common unit (ECU) exists now for intra-EEC transactions, and a common currency is likely to replace the various national currencies sometime soon.

Free trade throughout Europe is obviously worth pursuing, but just how far should unification go? Many worry about the homogenization of the cultures as well as the impact of "party crashers" coming in from the poorer eastern fringe of Europe. What impact will a freer Eastern Europe, with its pent-up capacity to consume and produce, have? What about the reunification of Germany, which in itself could create a new economic superpower? What about the foreign policy and defense of a united Europe?

Many expect the unification of Europe to include a series of widening circles, with a core union functioning almost as a single country, a second circle containing Great Britain, a wider circle containing Austria, Scandinavia and Switzerland, and an outermost circle getting Turkey and Eastern Europe in on some of the trade fun.

The Superpower Bowl

Region	Population	GNP (1987)	Trade Balance (1988)
EEC	325 million	$4,100 billion	+ $ 19 billion
US	250 million	$4,500 billion	− $126 billion
Japan	125 million	$2,350 billion	+ $ 95 billion

As you feel the fjords and caress the castles, remember that Europe is alive—coping, groping, and more interested in its future than in its past.

As visitors, we often forget that quaintness, cute, thatched-roof houses, and yodeling are not concerns of the average European. Sure, it's exciting to find odd remnants of Europe's old world that somehow missed the twentieth-century bus. But much of what we see touted as the "real thing" culturally is actually just a pile of cultural clichés kept alive for the tourist. As you travel, seek out contemporary Europe as well as its past. Educate yourself about the concerns and issues of today.

As the world hurtles toward 100 billion McDonald's hamburgers served, Europe is looking more and more like the United States. Fast food, American rock 'n' roll, English phrases, international corporate media blitzes, and Hollywood are bombarding European culture. It seems that when all the wrinkled old ladies in black are gone, they are destined to be replaced by a Europe of Coca-Cola, skyscrapers, Air Jordans, computers, and the global pop culture.

The most encouraging aspect of our future is that as the world grows smaller, more people will travel and rub shoulders. As this happens and we begin to view our globe as the home of five billion equally precious people, we'll all feel a little less American, British, Japanese, French, or whatever and a little more like a member of humankind. With this sort of grassroots understanding of our very human world, we will capitalize on the promising events of recent years and make this fragile world a less frightening place for our children to inherit.

The lessons of history apply—even today. It's easy to think that we are in a grand new age with no precedent, one that follows no rules. But every generation has thought that of their era, and we're just the latest in a long line of "pioneers."

History is happening now, and plenty of excitement awaits. If we see ourselves in historical perspective, see how yesterday shaped today, and learn less from the news media and more from our travels, we will better understand—and shape—the events of tomorrow.

Part II
Tangents

Britain

Ancient Britain

The Isle of Britain was a mysterious challenge to General Julius Caesar as he prepared for his invasion. Curtained in mist, separated from the civilized Continent by an arm of ocean, peopled by strange, savage tribes who painted themselves blue and sacrificed human beings to their gods—this was nearly all that was known of merry olde England when Caesar set sail in 55 B.C. to conquer it.

The 45-year-old general had conquered Gaul (modern France) but wanted one more conquest to impress the folks back home so that when he returned to Rome they would invite him to rule the empire. His invading ships approached Dover to find the cliffs lined with screaming, war-painted, spear-carrying Britons. After beaching, Caesar led a swift charge, driving the Britons back. The Romans huddled near the coast and waited for reinforcements, which were delayed by stormy weather. They were harassed by daring native solders driving war chariots, who would dash up to the camp balanced on the yoke, wreak havoc, and ride away.

As soon as new ships arrived, a weary Caesar packed up and returned to Gaul. His conquest of 200 meters of beach was hailed as a triumph in Rome; the Senate proclaimed an unprecedented twenty days of public thanksgiving.

The next year, better prepared, Caesar tried again, this time marching inland as far as modern London. He won battles, took hostages, exacted tribute, and made treaties. He left England having brought the mysterious land into its first contact with "civilization."

Celts (500 B.C.–A.D. 43)

The Celtic (pronounced "KELL-tik" except in Boston) tribes Caesar found weren't as barbarous as Caesar had expected. There were perhaps 100,000 Britons scattered in small, isolated tribes. A number of towns had 500 people; present-day Colchester, with 1,000, was the largest. Still, most were rural farming/hunting/herding tribes united under a local chieftain. Overland trade routes were a few rough paths (Icknield Way is still visible), and there was some trade with the Gauls across the channel. Most buildings were small and made of wood, but there were a few large castles, notably Hod Hill and Maiden Castle, both in Dorset.

The Celts (who included Gaels, Picts, Scots, and many smaller peoples and tribes) migrated to England and Ireland from the Continent beginning around 500 B.C. They conquered and blended with the prehistoric inhabitants (those even more mysterious people who built Stonehenge with huge rocks quarried 100 miles away and traded goods as far as ancient Greece). The Celtic language survives today in modern Gaelic (Scotland), Erse (Ireland), Welsh (guess), and Breton (Western France). About half of present-day Great Britain is of Celtic-Pictish blood. (The other half is Pakistani, I think.)

The Celts' nasty reputation in the Roman mind came from the Druids. These witch-doctor priests presided over rituals to appease the gods, spirits, and demons that inhabited the countryside. There were ghosts and spirits everywhere; one could feel them in the gloom of a dark forest or in the power of a rushing waterfall. The Druids, painted blue, sacrificed and decapitated animals and occasionally humans, offering the head to a local god or to one of the more powerful fertility or war gods. Then they tore the body apart, using the disposition of the guts to predict the future. They also practiced voodoo magic, cursing someone by making a statue of them and then mutilating it.

The Romans, tolerant as they were, drew the line at Druidism. Because the Druids were also tribal aristocrats trying to preserve tradition, they posed a political threat to the Romans. The Druids maintained power for a century after Caesar's brief invasions.

Romans (A.D. 43-500)

Then, in A.D. 43, the Emperor Claudius ordered a massive invasion that overwhelmed the courageous but outmatched Celts. Claudius personally rode north from Rome for the victory procession through Colchester, accompanied by the Praetorian Guard, a host of Roman aristocrats and the imperial elephant corps to impress the natives. The Romans had arrived.

Claudius left after two weeks with the simple order, "Conquer the rest." It took forty years, but finally all the lowland areas of

England and Wales, plus lower Scotland, were in Roman hands, where they would remain for four centuries. The fiercely independent herdsmen of the Scottish highlands, though nominally Roman, never were assimilated into "civilized" Roman society (and, some would say, have yet to be assimilated into British society).

The conquest wasn't without resistance. In A.D. 60, after a dispute with a local kingdom, Roman soldiers took the palace, flogged the queen, raped her daughters, and seized the royal treasury. The outraged Celts banded together under Queen Boadicea and set out burning and looting Roman towns. The rebels took "Londinium" (London), burned it to the ground, and offered the Romanized inhabitants as human sacrifices to the Celtic god of war. Blood-hungry with success, the rebellion spread. It took months for the Romans to quiet the Celts. The winter was a bleak one for Britain as the Romans wreaked violent revenge. To escape reprisal, Boadicea and her family took poison. (Boadicea is honored with a statue across the street from Big Ben, in London.)

The Romans learned a lesson, however, and instituted policies to keep the Celts happy. Government was in the hands of a Roman, but he allowed local chieftains to retain power as long as they cooperated with him. Local customs and religious practices were generally accepted.

Around their forts the Romans planned towns in the familiar Roman pattern—a rectangular street plan with the forum (marketplace) and basilica (courthouse) in the center, temples, baths, and a piped water system. Later, earthwork walls were built, defining their growth limit through the Middle Ages. Some towns grew to have as many as 1,000 inhabitants.

To connect towns and forts and to facilitate trade and communication, the Romans built roads, many of which still stand. Latin was taught, and soon it was as popular (in urban centers) as Celtic. When marriage was legalized for Roman soldiers, they often married local girls, and their sons grew up to join the ranks. The line between "Roman" and "Briton" grew fuzzier and fuzzier. By A.D. 200, the urban centers of southeast England were as "civilized" as any part of the empire. The population of Roman Britain grew to two million.

Londinium was the Roman center of the country, the capital, trade center, and the hub of the road system. It was surrounded by a stone wall (parts of which are still visible). From here, Britain traded with the Continent, exporting wool, metals, hunting dogs, corn, and oysters. In return, they got all the luxuries of the Roman world: pottery, wine, glassware, lamps, jewelry, silverware, furniture, the latest fashions in clothes, and so on.

The northern tribes of Scotland weren't very impressed with what the Romans had to offer, preferring independence to the niceties of Latin culture. Roman soldiers had to protect their settlements from periodic raids by the highlanders. They conquered as far north as the present border of Scotland and then built a wall to keep the Scots out. Hadrian's Wall (built while Hadrian was emperor, around 130) stands 20 feet high and 8 feet thick (wide enough to hold a chariot), stretching from coast to coast across northern England. It was manned by 20,000 soldiers in forts spaced one mile apart ("mile castles") all along the wall. For more than three centuries it kept the Scots at bay, and much of it stands today, a tribute to Roman military engineering.

(Hadrian's Wall is well worth a visit. The best-preserved section is in Northumberland National Park, along Military Road between Chollerford and Gilsland. A youth hostel called Once Brewed is just a short walk from a Roman mile castle with the best museum about the wall.)

Christianity arrived with the Romans. Rome, always tolerant of local religions, accepted many of the local Druid gods, giving them new Latin names. (The superstitious Roman soldiers, assigned to a distant outpost near a dreary forest, were careful not to offend any fierce spirits that might have dwelled there.) The sterile Roman religion, with its abstract gods and reverence for the state, didn't really "do it" for the locals, so the Britons, like many Romans throughout the empire, turned to Eastern religions such as Mithraism, the Cult of Isis, and Christianity.

(Legend has it that Christianity was brought by Joseph of Arimathea, the man who paid for Jesus' burial, and that he converted the Britons with a miracle: he planted his staff in the ground and it took root, becoming a thorn tree in Glastonbury that is said to bloom every Christmas.)

Christianity became a powerful force—probably the number-one religion—during the Roman occupation. But Celtic, Roman, and Eastern religions were also a part of Roman Britain. As late as A.D. 400, Celtic temples were built, and many Druidic rituals survived among the peasants up until modern times.

As Rome fell, so fell Roman Britain. The combination of internal decay and external enemies that caused Rome's collapse forced them to slowly withdraw troops and administrators from Britain. Over the centuries, even the Roman governors and generals became "Britonized" and drifted away from Rome. Some generals went so far as to secede from the empire, declaring themselves kings of Britain. Without Rome's strength and organization, the island was easy prey for invaders. In A.D. 409, the emperor in Rome was forced to completely abandon Britain.

The Anglo-Saxons (A.D. 400-800)

The invaders came from Germany and Denmark, tribes called Angles, Saxons, Jutes (and worse names by the Britons). They came not as conquerors but as refugees, leaving behind a crowded, bleak homeland for the fertile farmlands of Britain. As early as 250, small groups in longboats began arriving on the northeast coast. The Roman Britons fought them off when they could and tolerated them when they couldn't. As Roman support waned, the invasion/migrations increased. The sixth century saw the Anglo-Saxons pushing the Celts and Romanized Britons westward. This is the period of the real King Arthur, most likely a Christian Romanized British general valiantly fighting the invading tribes.

By 600, the southeast part of the island was "Angle-land" (England), the land of the Angles. The Roman world slowly crumbled; the towns dwindled and the roads fell into disuse. The invaders were a rough, savage people compared to the Romans, with no central government or economy. Each tribe had its own chief and council of elders. The society was bound by a code of hierarchy and personal loyalty similar to that of the later medieval feudal system.

England had entered the Dark Ages. The economy was weak, life was harsh, and justice was severe. The "wergild," a system worked out to financially compensate relatives for people murdered in feuds, gives us a look at the value placed on human life in those harsh times. If a noble was killed, the murderer's clan had to pay the victim's clan 1,200 shillings; a "thane" (knight) was worth 300; a "churl" (free peasant), 200; killing a serf required no recompense at all. Women of equal position were worth less than their male counterparts. Hmmmm.

The Anglo-Saxon pagan religion replaced Christianity in many places. Some of these Norse gods are familiar to us today: Tiw, Woden (King of the Gods), Thor (with his hammer), Frig. Not familiar? How about "Tiw's-day," "Woden's-day," "Thor's-day," and "Frig's-day"? They also celebrated a spring festival to the goddess Eostre (Easter).

Christianity reentered England with missionaries from both Ireland and Rome. When the Saxon King Aethelbert of Kent was converted (around 600), the tide was turned. Within a hundred years, England was again mostly Christian, though not by much. Pagans continued to rule in many kingdoms throughout the Dark Ages.

One of the Christian kings, Offa (c. 780), brought some stability to the warring Anglo-Saxon tribes. The time of peace brought a renaissance of learning, and the English language took its earliest form. The poem "Beowulf," written in England but incorporating Norse mythology, was written at this time. (You can see a manuscript in the British Museum, London.) Offa printed coins with his portrait on them, advancing the notion that the many Anglo-Saxon tribes were part of a single nation. Offa also built a trench to separate England from the Celtic Welsh. This "moat," the length of the English-Welsh border, is called "Offa's Dyke" today and is a popular hike among young locals.

Only Two Invasions to Go (A.D. 800-1066)

True unity didn't come until after another set of invasions—this time from the Vikings, the Anglo-Saxons' distant cousins from Denmark. The two groups warred, made peace, and mingled during the next few centuries. This was the period of rulers with names such as Harold Harefoot, Eric Bloodaxe, Edgar the Peacock, Ethelred the Unready, and Edward the Confessor (Edward commissioned Westminster Abbey).

The stew of peoples that make up present-day England was nearly complete—from prehistory to the Celts, the Romans, the Anglo-Saxons and finally the Danes. Next came the Normans, from northern France (present-day Normandy). William the Conqueror invaded from across the channel, defeating the Saxon king Harold at the Battle of Hastings (1066). This battle marks England's escape from the Dark Ages and her entry into the High Middle Ages.

English Kings and Queens

"For God's sake, let us sit upon the ground
And tell sad stories of the death of kings..."
—_Richard II_, Shakespeare

The history of England's royalty is full of violence, corruption, treason, sex, scandal, power, and greed. Remarkably, the country survived its rulers.

England's Alfred the Great

Alfred (849-899), an enlightened and compassionate ruler, is considered the first king of a united "England." He rallied the scattered Anglo-Saxon tribes of England to ward off the Viking invaders. After establishing peace, he turned to matters closer to his heart. Having had an older brother, he never expected to become king, so he'd studied poetry and Latin, even visiting Rome in his teens.

When he was called upon to lead the Anglo-Saxons, Alfred took it as his personal responsibility to defeat the Vikings (who were believed to be a punishment from God) and educate his people so they could learn God's will. He reformed the government and built schools, teaching English as well as Latin. Alfred deserves his reputation as the model English king—strong, learned, and kind.

"French" Kings, the Normans

William the Conqueror crossed the channel from Normandy and defeated the Saxon forces at Hastings. He was crowned King of England on Christmas Day, 1066, in London's Westminster Abbey, where future kings and queens would be crowned. A harsh but efficient ruler, he united the British lords and established a feudal society. (Construction of the complex of buildings known as the Tower of London, where so many leaders were later executed, was begun during William's reign.)

The Tower of London
The prison and execution site for those accused of crimes against the monarchy. Admission tickets include a very informative and entertaining tour by a Beefeater. (Executions available by reservation only.)

Neither he nor his Norman successors were ever very popular with the common people. They were foreign invaders who spoke French and followed French customs.

His son, William II, called "Rufus" (the Red) because of his ruddy complexion, was even less well liked. A vain, arbitrary tyrant, he made no attempt to mix with the English people. He died in a hunting "accident"—an arrow in the back. His brother Henry just happened to be in the hunting party, behind him. Henry immediately rode to Winchester, seized the treasury, and was crowned king the next day.

More "French" Kings, Angevins

The French kings expanded their empire. By the time Henry II took power (1154) at the age of 21, his Angevin Empire stretched from Scotland to northern Spain. His long and hard-fought rule consolidated the empire.

Henry was a good soldier, a fair diplomat, well read (for a king), and was possessed with restless energy and a violent temper. The beginning of his reign was marked by optimism. He and his wife Eleanor, a beautiful and accomplished lady of the time, established a court where chivalrous knights, ladies, troubadors, and scholars met. Henry built numerous castles throughout the empire.

But then things went bad, and it seemed as though everyone in the world was fighting Henry. He waged war with the Welsh, the Scots, and French rebels. He quarreled with English barons over taxes. His sons, supported by Eleanor, tried to overthrow him. Perhaps the most painful betrayal was that of his close friend and adviser, Thomas Becket, whom he had appointed Archbishop of Canterbury. When Becket's strong, independent policy threatened the king's power, Henry's knights murdered him in Canterbury Cathedral. Becket became an instant martyr to the English people, and the cathedral became a popular pilgrimage site.

Henry II died a broken man, and his son Richard the Lionhearted assumed power. Richard was the model of a chivalrous knight—a good soldier, a poet, a musician, and a handsome, valiant Crusader. He was also a Frenchman. He hated England. (He once said, "I would sell London if I could find a buyer.") During his ten-year reign, he spent only six months in the country he ruled.

Everyone hated Richard's successor, his brother John Lackland. Everyone. He is unanimously considered the worst king England ever had. Devious and weak, he had an uncanny ability to make enemies of everyone—barons, popes, the English, and the French. He murdered his nephew in a drunken rage. He waged war in France and lost miserably. The Angevin Empire collapsed under his rule. He overtaxed and bullied the English barons. All in all, he was very much the evil King John of the Robin Hood legend—perhaps the one true character in the myth.

John's place in history was assured by signing the Magna Carta (Great Charter) forced on him by unhappy barons. This was the first step of many in English history to limit the power of kings and increase that of the nobles and common people. (The Magna Carta is on display in the British Museum, London.)

Royalty on the Rocks—The Troublesome Centuries (1200-1400)

"Some have been deposed; some slain in war;
Some haunted by the ghosts they have deposed...
All murder'd..."
—*Richard II*, Shakespeare

The next two centuries gave Shakespeare enough regicide, rebellion, and treason for eight plays. In that time, four kings were murdered, two died in battle, civil wars were rampant, and two family lines of kings were overthrown.

Edward II, a tyrant, was opposed by Roger Mortimer, his wife's lover. Edward was captured and murdered in a manner so brutal that to describe it would exceed this book's standard of good taste. Well, okay, if you insist. Suffice it to say it involved a red-hot poker, Edward's backside, and a thrusting motion. Ooh.

His son, Edward III (reigned 1327-1377), avenged his father's death in a relatively civilized manner, by merely having Mortimer hanged, drawn, and quartered. Edward's good rule (aided by his chivalrous son, the famous "Black Prince") included early victories in the Hundred Years' War with the French, in which England initially conquered, and then slowly lost, France.

The next monarch, Richard II (reigned 1377-1399), ruled poorly and was finally overthrown by an upstart baron, who locked him in the Tower of London. The long line of French-English kings came to an end.

The House of Lancaster

Henry IV, the Usurper (reigned 1399-1413), of the house of Lancaster, was the first completely English king—the son of English parents who spoke no French. Handsome, athletic, a musician and scholar, he invited the poet Geoffrey Chaucer to his court. Yet like so many others, when he died he was bitter and broken, worn out by years of opposition and civil war.

His son, the "Prince Hal" of Shakespeare's plays, was said to have lived a wasted youth, carousing, gambling, and thieving with commoners and prostitutes. Whether true or not, when he became Henry V he was cold, stern, and very capable. His victory at the Battle of Agincourt (1415) put most of France back under English rule.

All his gains became losses in the weak hands of Henry VI. Henry VI's attempts to hold France were foiled by a young French peasant woman, Joan of Arc. She claimed to hear voices of saints and angels who told her where to lead the French armies. She was eventually captured and burned as a witch by the English but not before the tide was turned.

War of the Roses

The inept Henry VI of the Lancaster family was opposed by the York family, and a long civil war broke out—the "War of the Roses," named for the white and red roses that each family used as its symbol. Edward IV, a York, locked Henry in the Tower of London, later executing him. Edward died young, at the age of 40, reportedly "worn out by his sexual excesses."

Two of Edward's excesses survived him but not by much. His sons, the heirs to the throne, were kidnapped and murdered in the Tower of London by Richard III (Edward's own brother), and both houses decided the bloody war had to end. When a petty noble from the house of Tudor defeated Richard's armies and killed him in battle, all of England was prepared to rally round him as the new king. Henry VII was crowned, a diplomatic marriage was arranged, and England was united.

Tudor Rule 1485-1603

Henry VII (reigned 1485-1509) was shrewd and efficient; he was England's first "modern" chief executive. He united the country and built up a huge treasury. (To protect himself from traitors, he established a royal bodyguard, the Beefeaters.)

His 18-year-old son inherited a nation that was solvent, strong, and at peace. Henry VIII (reigned 1509-1547) was the English version of a Renaissance prince—tall, handsome, athletic, a poet and musician, and well read in secular learning and theology. He was charismatic but could also be arrogant, cruel, gluttonous, erratic, and paranoid.

The most notorious event of Henry VIII's reign was the break with the Catholic church (and his establishment of the nearly identical Church of England). This arose over the Catholic church's refusal to grant him a divorce from his first wife, Catherine of Aragon (the daughter of Ferdinand and Isabella of Spain) and his subsequent marriage to the beautiful and lively Anne Boleyn. Henry was determined to get a wife who could give him a son. For whatever reasons—love, desire for an heir, diplomacy, or sheer lust—Henry went through six wives, divorcing, imprisoning, or beheading them when they no longer served his purpose.

Henry faced enemies in England over his break with Catholicism, and he dealt with them in a characteristic way—with the ax. Among

Henry VIII, by Hans Holbein

those beheaded at the Tower for holding fast to their convictions was Thomas More, Henry's chancellor and author of the famous political tract *Utopia.*

While the Reformation wars raged on the Continent, England had religious troubles of its own. After the brief but weak reign of Henry's long-awaited male heir, the stage was set for Henry's daughters.

Mary I (reigned 1553-1558), the daughter of his first wife, Catherine, had her mother's fanatic Spanish Catholic devotion (the same kind that gave us the Inquisition). She was convinced her mission was to return England to the Roman church come Hell or high water. Neither came but in her zeal, she ordered burned at the stake over 300 men, women, and teenagers and ordered the execution of the innocent, 17-year-old Lady Jane Grey. Compared with the tens of thousands killed in other countries it seems like nothing, but it shocked the English enough that they turned their backs on Catholicism for good and nicknamed their queen "Bloody Mary."

Mary's successor, Elizabeth I (1558-1603), Henry's daughter by the fiery Anne Boleyn, had absorbed the lesson of religious fanaticism. She was a Protestant but a product of a broad Renaissance education. Her tolerant policies and prudent nature brought peace at home and victory abroad, making England a true European power for the first time. Among other conquests, Elizabeth subdued Ireland, beginning that country's centuries of struggle for independence.

Queen Elizabeth I (1558-1603)

The English navy defeated the famed Spanish armada and soon ruled the waves. Explorers and traders probed the New World and Asia, bringing back spoils and luxury goods. (Sir Walter Raleigh introduced tobacco from America to a skeptical Queen Elizabeth.)

Elizabeth was golden-haired, prudent, and a "Virgin Queen," but her cousin Mary, Queen of Scots, was dark, lively, a lover of dance and music, and highly sexed. Mary (not "Bloody Mary"), a Catholic from the Stuart family, represented the opposition to Elizabeth and the Protestant regime. After Mary was implicated in an anticrown plot, Elizabeth imprisoned her for 19 long years. But Mary never bowed.

Fat, wrinkled, and wearing a wig to cover her balding head, she was led to the tower's execution block. "So perish all the Queen's enemies." The ax fell.

The Elizabethan era was England's High Renaissance, especially in literature. Shakespeare, Raleigh, John Donne, Christopher Marlowe, and many others shaped the course of English literature and the English language itself. (The British Museum in London has letters and manuscripts by all of England's great writers.)

The Stuarts

When Elizabeth died, presumably still a virgin and definitely without an heir, the Tudor throne passed to the Stuarts—Mary, Queen of Scots' son, James. James I (reigned 1603-1625) was a capable man who was incapable of proving it—"the most learned fool in Christendom," said one contemporary. He was vain and arrogant, a "foreigner" (from Scotland) and a Catholic to boot who succeeded in alienating both the English people and Parliament.

James insisted that he ruled by "divine right" and was therefore above Parliament and human laws. On the way to his coronation, a man accused of thievery was brought to him. James had him hanged on the spot without trial, thus alienating himself instantly from the commoners.

The one lasting achievement of his reign was the King James version of the Bible, a landmark translation in both theology and literature, the culmination of the Elizabethan Renaissance.

It's said that James steered the state toward the rocks and then left his son to wreck it. Throughout the seventeenth century, the haughty Catholic Stuart kings were at odds with Parliament until Parliament got fed up, rebelled, and established a "constitutional monarchy" that limited, by law, the king's power.

Charles I (reigned 1625-1649) was his father's son in every way, but even more so: he was pompous, vain, anti-Protestant, and anti-Parliament. When Parliament refused to grant him more money, he dissolved the body for over ten years. Parliament (which was made up mostly of nobles) responded by raising its own army and declaring war on the king. Their leader, Oliver Cromwell, vowed, "We will cut off the King's head—with the crown on it." Civil war had begun.

Parliament defeated the troops loyal to the king, deposed him, and set up a Commonwealth ruled by Parliament. Charles was executed as Cromwell had promised. (The one mark of distinction in Charles's undignified reign was that he faced his death with dignity.)

Cromwell, a Puritan gentleman farmer elected to Parliament, soon assumed the powers of a dictator. He was very capable, religiously tolerant, and kept a steady hand in a troubled time. However, he himself suspended Parliament, a la Charles, when it disagreed with him.

When Cromwell died, in order to prevent another civil war in the struggle for power, Parliament invited Charles II to reign—on condition he follow rules set out by Parliament.

(The French experienced a similar cycle 130 years later: The royalty abused its power. Parliament took matters into its own bloody hands, beheading the king. After a dictator's enlightened but harsh rule, the king was invited back. Then he was allowed to rule—with constitutional or parliamentarian limitations.)

Charles II and Restoration

The "Restoration" of the monarchy (1660) was reason to celebrate in England. After decades of civil war and Puritan rule (with all the negative things "puritan" implies), it was nice to have the pomp, ceremony, luxury, and even decadence of the Stuart kings. Charles II (1660-1685) had spent his exile in the magnificent court of Louis XIV. He returned to London with the latest fashions.

Charles had a series of dazzling mistresses who shocked the Puritan Parliament and titillated the public. (There were so many, most of them Catholics, that one of them took to identifying herself: "I'm the Protestant whore.")

During Charles's reign, London was devastated by a plague and burned to the ground in the Great Fire of 1666. The rebuilding, led by architect Christopher Wren, reflects Charles's baroque influence (from Versailles).

Charles's son, James II, lived up to the Stuart name by persecuting Protestants and plotting against Parliament. He was thrown out in the "Glorious Revolution." Parliament invited James's daughter and her husband to rule—again, according to the dictates of Parliament. William and Mary were succeeded by the unremarkable Queen Anne.

The House of Hanover

In 1714, the Stuart line was exhausted, and so were the English people, worn out by religious strife. Parliament chose the king least likely to stir up trouble, George I (reigned 1714-1721) of Germany. George was 54 years old, spoke no English, and had no interest in politics. His chancellor, Sir Robert Walpole, essentially ran the country. George II (1727-1760) was the sequel to this bland state of affairs.

George III (1760-1820) was the first truly English ruler in 50 years. He took the throne with high hopes and then ran right into the

American Revolutionary War, the French Revolution, and Napoleon. The world changed too fast for him, and in 1810, he slipped into madness—diagnosed at the time as "flying gout" that had settled in his brain. England was left with "an old, mad, blind, despised and dying king" (as the poet Shelley put it).

But England was changing rapidly, the Industrial Revolution was creating a whole new society, and England's monarchy knew it would meet the same fate as its French counterpart if it didn't modernize.

Victoria

Fortunately, along came Queen Victoria (reign 1837-1901), the first of England's modern "figurehead" monarchs. She had little interest and less influence in government. Her husband, Prince Albert, took some part in promoting science and industry (especially in organizing the Great Exhibition of 1851), but after his death things were run by Parliament and prime ministers (Disraeli and Gladstone).

Victoria was under 5 feet tall but radiated a regal aura. She was strong, bearing nine children, whom she married off to other European royal houses. (Kaiser Wilhelm and Tsarina Alexandria of World War I fame were her grandchildren.) She hated Georgian excesses and was notoriously prudish (hence, our word "Victorian").

The Victorian period saw England rise to its zenith. Its colonial empire was the largest in the world and its technology was the envy of Europe, yet its pockets of poverty were worse than those of many of its colonies.

Victoria's son, Edward VII (reign 1901-1910), was born and raised in the lap of Victorian luxury but never quite grew up, assuming the throne as a "child" of 60. The Edwardian period before World War I was the last golden (though fading) age of English optimism and civility. The horrors of the Great War shattered that forever.

The House of Windsor

Edward's son, George V of Windsor, ruled in the "modern" style (subservient to law and Parliament) until 1936, when he was succeeded by his son, Edward VIII. Edward (the Duke of Windsor), in the most-talked-about action of modern royalty, abdicated the throne to marry a commoner, the twice-divorced American, Mrs. Simpson. Edward's brother, George VI, ruled until his popular daughter, Elizabeth II, took the throne with her husband, Phillip Mountbatten, Duke of Edinburgh. Charles, Prince of Wales (of *National Enquirer* fame), waits to be our generation's entry in the parade of English kings and queens.

One of your authors mixing it up with Princess Di as Charles
looks on.

As you travel through England, you'll hear plenty of news about
Charles, Lady Di, their royal rug rats, and the British royalty of today.
If you're alert and even if you're not, there's a good chance you'll get
at least a fleeting glimpse of England's busy first family. Although
their kings and queens don't come cheap and are only figureheads,
most British seem to thoroughly enjoy having a royal family.

Victorian London

"It was the best of times, it was the worst of times..."
—*A Tale of Two Cities*, Charles Dickens

Dickens's words best describe his own city of London in the 1800s. With four million people, it was the world's largest. It was the busiest, the richest, the most productive; the hub of the most industrialized nation on earth; and the capital of a colonial empire that covered a fourth of the world's land surface. But the seamy underside of London was like a Third World country—dirty, poor, disease-ridden, and dangerous.

This contrast was everywhere. You could buy any commodity in the world on London's docks—and lose it to a thief just as quickly. It was the center of industrial growth, yet it was choked with coal dust and industrial filth. London hosted the lavish social life of gay Prince Edward as well as thousands of homeless urchins begging, stealing, and sleeping in the streets. Palaces and townhouses contrasted with sagging tenements and well-lit cafés with seedy pubs where the poor indulged in one of their few affordable pastimes, drunkenness.

This was the Victorian period—that is, it occurred within the time of Queen Victoria (1837-1901)—but it might better be called "Albertian" London. Victoria's husband, Prince Albert, from Germany, was handsome, intelligent, progressive, and extremely proper. Victoria adored him. He was the quintessential gentleman.

The Great Exhibition and London's Growth

It was one of Albert's projects that spurred London's remarkable growth. He was fascinated with science and technology and proposed a Great Exhibition "uniting the industry and art of all nations"—in other words, a World's Fair. Held in 1851 in Hyde Park, it was the talk of Europe.

More than six million visitors jammed London's streets. (More than a million bottles of lemonade were sold at the fair.) The main attraction was the amazing Crystal Palace, an iron and glass structure, with 300,000 windowpanes, covering 19 square acres—the symbol of the new and glorious Industrial Age. The Exhibition was a smashing success, and many visitors returned to settle down in London.

The British Empire of the nineteenth century was the biggest, richest, and most powerful in history. Here, John Bull (the British Uncle Sam) is shown selfishly holding his swollen colonial empire.

The Victorian Age was a building time: the Houses of Parliament, the Law Courts on the Strand, railroad stations (to accommodate a revolutionary form of transportation), churches, office buildings, and townhouses went up. Unfortunately, this abundance of building was not accompanied by a similar abundance of good taste. Most were designed in a rather bland neo-Gothic or neoclassical style. The one truly Victorian style was the use of ornamental ironwork, inspired by Joseph Paxton's Crystal Palace. There was wrought-iron everywhere; everything had a railing, whether it needed it or not.

On a typical business day, London traffic moved as fast as the narrow streets would allow. Double-decker buses—horse-drawn in those days—were as vital as their fossil-fuel-burning cousins of today. Efficient, two-wheeled, horse-drawn cabs sped recklessly throught the streets. For the less fortunate, the bicycle brought new mobility. On the streets were merchants of all kinds, many of whom sang a song to advertise their wares—the popular muffin-man, ring-ing his bell to attract children at tea time; the quack doctor hawking his "Elixir of Life"; the fishmonger; the delivery boy; lamplighter; prostitute; pickpocket; and bobbie.

The Rich

On the busy streets, London looked like a real melting pot of humanity, but Victorian society was rigidly hierarchical—rich, middle class, and poor. The rich spent part of their time on their country estates, coming to London only for "the season," the period of socializing and parties. The main purpose of these events was to pretend to have fun while arranging marriages for the children. Most marriages were business deals involving large dowries. The moral code was very strict, almost "Victorian."

Nineteenth-century London was referred to as "two worlds, one rich and one poor." This view of the wealthy at a horse race contrasts sharply with the picture on page 289.

The rich went, dressed in their finest, to the opera, theater, or parties. Women wore skirts that had huge bustles, and they covered themselves almost from head to toe. (Double-decker buses were equipped with "decency boards" on the stairways, so ladies needn't expose even a bit of leg when they climbed up.) The men looked dashing in cloak, cane, top hat, and lavender gloves. In their conversations at these shindigs, they discussed business, gossip, and world affairs or debated the merits of socialism, "free love," or Darwin.

Every rich family had servants. The husband and wife each had personal attendants to dress them, advise them, and keep their social calendar. Besides these, there were the cooks and maids. Cleanliness, like godliness, was a priority.

Middle Class

The middle-class families, while trying to keep up with the wealthy, were most influenced by the example of Victoria and Albert. The royal couple was the model of domestic happiness—proper, hardworking, and devoted to their many children. So it was throughout middle-class London. The wife was lord and master of the house; the husband was lord and master of the wife. He came home from work to find his slippers and velvet jacket warming by the fire. After dinner he'd play with the kids, do some reading aloud, listen to his wife play the piano, and go to bed early.

Some middle-class families aspired to live like the rich. They hired a servant or two and did what they could to squeak their kids into an upper-class college. In fact, one of the characteristics of the Victorian Age was the advance of the middle class. They lived in nice homes equipped with that new-fangled invention, the toilet. They were well-educated and infected with Albert's interest in science and the arts. The popularity of Dickens's works attests to this. Dickens's stories were serialized in pulp magazines that reached literally millions of people.

The Poor

Progress did not trickle down to London's wretched lower classes, however. Even before Reagan, the upper classes were oblivious to the life-style of the urban poor. The lower class lived in a a different world, one that the upper class didn't care to know about.

In the East End (and St. Gile's and Clare Market), people lived in decaying, crowded buildings crawling with rats. Whereas a middle-class family of ten (most Victorians had large families) lived in a spacious, ten-room house, the poorest lived ten to a single room. Human waste lined the streets.

The gas lighting hardly cut through the dark on foggy nights in narrow alleyways where cutthroats lurked. Brothels, gambling dens, and pubs were the major businesses in these districts.

Work was scarce, especially for the hordes of unskilled country folk who packed up their dreams and rushed to the big city. A man might haul garbage, shovel coal, or make deliveries, but that was about it. Women and children labored in the factories for pennies. For those in debt, there was the workhouse, which was much like a prison work camp. For some, the alternatives were drunkenness or the Queen's Army—recruiting sergeants stood outside the pubs with a shilling in their hand as bait for the down and out.

Private charities did little good. It wasn't until major government reforms at the end of the century that the slums got some relief. The reforming spirit got a boost from the writings of Dickens, a poor boy who made good but never forgot where he came from.

Victorian London was a strictly hierarchical society, but all the classes had one thing in common—a spirit of optimism. There was a vitality to the city that even the poor felt. There was a sense that technology could bring about a better life for all, that hard work and right living would be rewarded just as surely as laziness and vice would be punished. London was a busy, hard-driving, shrewd city that maintained an outer face of gentility, grace, and good cheer.

Europeans

A Babel of Tongues

Imagine the confusion if the citizens of each state in the United States spoke their own language. Europe is like that. It wasn't always that way. If you understand how Europe's languages evolved, you might not understand more words, but at least you'll understand better what it is you don't understand. Understand?

Europe's languages can be arranged into a family tree. Most of them have the same grandparents and resemble each other more or less like you resemble your brothers, sisters, and cousins. Occasionally, an oddball uncle sneaks in who no one can explain, but most languages have common roots.

An understanding of how these languages relate to one another can help boost you over the language barrier. The following generalities are useful:

1. Knowing Greek and Latin roots used in our language broadens your English vocabulary and helps you make educated guesses at the meaning of words in other languages.

2. The most valuable second languages to know in Europe are German, French, and Spanish. English is the most widely spoken language in Europe.

3. As you can see from the tree (p. 293), the dominant European family branches are the Romance and Germanic language clans.

Romance Countries—Italy, France, Spain, and Portugal

The Romance family evolved out of Latin, the language of the Roman Empire ("Romance" comes from "Roman"). Certainly, knowing Latin would be a real asset in your travels. But knowing any of the modern

Romance languages helps with the others. For example, high school Spanish will help you read common words in Portugal and Italy.

French, after English, is the most popular second language in Central Europe and the Mediterranean world. In Morocco and other former French colonies, French is the standard second language. Colonial background determines the second language (and sometimes even the first language) of countries all over the world.

French is more international, but knowledge of any one of the Romance languages (including Spanish, Italian, and Portuguese) will help you make some sense of the other languages in this linguistic family.

Germanic Countries—Germany, Scandinavia, and England

The Germanic languages, though influenced by Latin, are a product of the native tribes of northern Europe—the "barbarians" of Roman days.

German is your most valuable second language in Northern and Eastern Europe. It's spoken by all Germans and Austrians and most Swiss. You'll also find German-speaking enclaves in Italy, Czechoslovakia, Yugoslavia, Romania, and other nearby countries. Anyone who went to school during the Nazi occupation (1940-1945) probably studied—and tried not to learn—German.

German is easily the most valuable European language to know in Turkey. It seems every other Turk has "arbeitet in Deutschland für zwei Jahren" (worked in Germany for two years). They love to show off their German, which is probably as broken as yours. You'll get along great.

The people of Holland and northern Belgium speak Dutch (called Flemish in Belgium), which is very closely related to German. A German can almost read a Dutch newspaper.

The Scandinavians (except the Finns) can read each other's magazines and enjoy their neighbors' TV shows. If you speak one Scandinavian language, you can get by in all the Scandinavian countries. Older Scandinavians are very likely to speak more German than English. English is the second-language choice of Scandinavia's youth and is probably spoken better here than anywhere else on the Continent.

Although Norwegians, Danes, and Swedes can understand each other (at least as well as Shakespeare could understand Charlie Brown), the Finns, who are "Scandinavian" only geographically, have not even a hint of "Yah sure ya betcha" in their language. Finnish, like

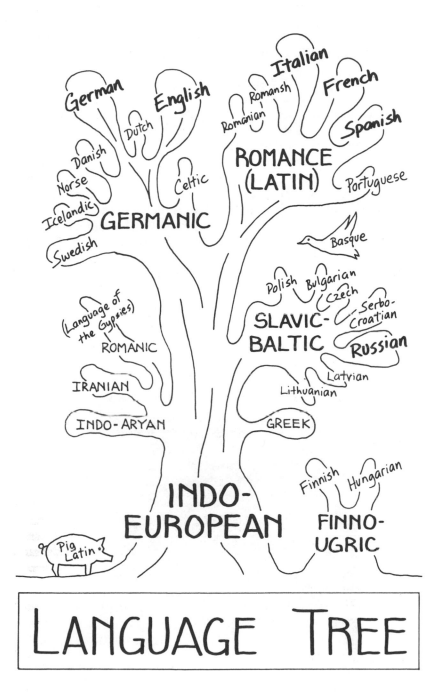

German · Dutch · English · Italian · Romansh · French · Romanian · Spanish

Danish · Norse · Celtic · ROMANCE (LATIN) · Portuguese

Icelandic · GERMANIC

Swedish · Basque

Polish · Bulgarian · Czech · Serbo-Croatian

(Language of the Gypsies) · SLAVIC-BALTIC · Russian

ROMANIC

IRANIAN · Latvian · Lithuanian

INDO-ARYAN · GREEK

Finnish · Hungarian

INDO-EUROPEAN · FINNO-UGRIC

Pig Latin

LANGUAGE TREE

Hungarian and Estonian, was somehow smuggled into Europe from distant Central Asia. More Finns speak Swedish than English.

English is technically a Germanic language, although sometimes it seems as though English shares half its words with French.

Multilingual Regions

Linguistic boundaries are never as cut and dried as political borders. Europe has several offically multilingual states and generally fuzzy borders.

Switzerland speaks four languages: 67 percent of the people speak Swiss German; 20 percent speak French; 12 percent speak Italian; and 1 percent speak Romansch, a language related to ancient Latin. The Romansch-speakers live in remote southeastern Switzerland.

Alsace, another bilingual culture, is a French province on the German border. This chunk of land, whose ownership has often been disputed, happens to lie between the Rhine River (which the French claim is the natural boundary) and the Vosges Mountains (which the Germans claim God created to divide these two peoples). Its people have been dragged through the mud during several French-German tug-of-wars. For the time being, it's a part of France. Still, your German will be much more useful here than English.

The Tower of Babel
A Berlitz nightmare.

Belgium waffles, linguistically, with the southern half speaking French (the Walloons) and the other half speaking Flemish, or Dutch. Brussels, like Belgium itself, is legally bilingual, but the French in Belgium—like those in Switzerland and Canada—often feel tongue-tied and abused linguistically.

Their problems pale, however, beside the linguistic and demographic mess in Yugoslavia, whose citizens speak five different languages.

The Slavic people of Eastern Europe (Poland, Bulgaria, Czechoslovakia, and Yugoslavia) speak languages related to Russian. Until recently, all students had to study Russian. Almost none learn it.

Speaking Russian in Eastern Europe will get you nowhere. You'll be surprised how many English-speaking people you'll meet in the East. There aren't actually all that many, but those who learned it dream West and are eager to meet foreigners like you.

Dying Tongues

The Basques, struggling to survive in the area where Spain, France, and the Atlantic all touch, are well aware that every year five languages die on our planet and that the cards are stacked against isolated groups like theirs.

England is surrounded by a "Celtic Crescent." In Wales, Scotland, Ireland, and Brittany (western France) you'll find bits and pieces of the old Celtic language. These survive mostly as a symbol of national spirit and local determination not to be completely subjugated culturally (as has occurred politically) by England or France. Seek out those diehard remnants of the old culture in militant bookstores (fronts for the autonomy movement in Brittany), Gaelic or folk pubs, and the Gaeltachts (districts, mostly in Western Ireland, where the old culture is preserved by the government).

Small linguistic groups, such as those who speak Flemish or Norwegian, are quicker to jump on the English bandwagon. It's crucial for these cultures to know a major language, and ours is the most major. These cultures are melting more and more into the English sphere of linguistic influence, while large groups such as the Spanish, French, and Germans can get by without grasping English so readily.

Study the family tree of European languages. Imprint it on your mind and take it to Europe. These ideas will enable you to get the most communication mileage out of what bits and pieces of Europe's languages you do pick up.

Money Talks

Countries decorate their coins and currency with their own history and culture. Famous statesmen, authors, royalty, scientists, and even local art, mountains, and animals are honored on foreign money much as Washington, Lincoln, and eagles are on ours.

If you're bored on a long train ride through Germany, pull out a two-mark coin and ask a native, "Who is this?" He'll tell you it's Konrad Adenauer, West Germany's first post-Hitler chancellor.

Here's a quick look at some of Europe's money.

The painter Delacroix with one of his famous works on the French 100-franc note.

France puts "Liberté, Egalité, Fraternité" on just about everything. Liberty, equality, brotherhood, the slogan of the Revolution, is alive and well in the France of today. Among many other great Frenchmen on France's paper money, you'll find the philosopher Voltaire, the scientist Louis Pasteur, and the artist Delacroix.

If you can't get to Holland's great Rijksmuseum, just look at the 10-guilder note. It shows a self-portrait of Frans Hals, a contemporary of Rembrandt and a top Dutch Master. Give the braille dots on Dutch bills a feel.

In Switzerland, coins, bills, stamps, and even license plates refer to the country as "Helvetica," the name of the original Celtic inhabitants conquered by Julius Caesar. "CH," seen on automobile decals all over Switzerland, stands for "Confederation Helvetica."

Italy has fun money. Its 1,000-lire note, called a "mille" (pronounced MEE-lay), worth about 75 cents, features Giuseppe Verdi, the nineteenth-century operatic composer whose stirring music helped inspire Italian unification. Christopher Columbus, born in Genoa, is honored on the 5,000-lire note. Great art as well as artists such as Michelangelo and Leonardo show up on other Italian bills.

Before you pay for your Norwegian cup of coffee look at the Arctic explorer Nansen on the 10-crown note. His boat, the _Fram_, is just across the harbor from Oslo. The same denomination in Denmark portrays Hans Christian Andersen, the author of popular children's stories such as "The Ugly Duckling" and "The Emperor's New Clothes." It will cost you about 10 crowns to visit the Knott's Berry Farm-type Hans Christian Andersen Center in his hometown of Odense.

If you're bored on a long train ride through Germany, pull out a bill and ask your neighbor, "Who is this guy?" If he doesn't know, don't be surprised. Would you know Alexander Hamilton if you saw him on a $10 bill?

Class Struggle

Societies are contained in iron pie tins. When each group in a society is satisfied with or stuck with their slice of the socioeconomic pie, history is put on hold. When existing groups struggle for more pie or new groups enter and need a slice of their own, history is made.

There are times when the pie needs to be resliced. It can be done voluntarily (such as during the biblical jubilee year, every 50 years, when land is redistributed) or it can be done violently (when landless groups take the pie-cutter into their own hands).

In the Dark Ages there were three slices, or estates: the landed nobility, the clergy, and the peasantry. The first two estates liked their slice. The third estate was stuck with its slice. Every issue was decided in favor of the status quo: two to one.

Around the year 1000, cities joined the European quest for pie. The nobility and clergy said, "Welcome to our pie. You can share the slice we gave to the third estate [peasantry]." This was the structure of the Old Regime.

But the merchants, bankers, and lawyers of the cities grew stronger and richer until the pie had to be resliced. It happened in France.

The three estates met rarely—only when the king needed to levy extra taxes. To fund the American "freedom fighters" in their struggle against his and their mutual enemy, Britain, the French king called the General Assembly. He expected a rubber stamp, but it had been about a hundred years since the last meeting, and the city folk in the third estate wanted to make some changes.

In a modest move to restructure the pie, they wanted to vote by a show of hands rather than the predictible, two-to-one vote by house. The first two estates refused. The estate that sat "on the left" replied, "Okay then, we are the government. You're welcome to join us when you want to." The third estate proceeded to legally abolish feudalism. The king sided with "the right," which polarized the situation.

The revolutionary stallion ran its course, and after much bloodshed, the pie was resliced to make room for the city folk. This was the liberal revolution.

As the city classes rose, they had to have someone to walk on. Their doormat was the working class—the proletariat—and the 1800s gave birth to Marx and the Socialist revolution. Through unions, violent revolution, or threat of revolution, this new element of society elbowed its way into history. . . and a respectable slice of pie.

These movements are no longer limited to one geographic region. As our world shrinks and our appetites refuse to be satisfied, a new struggle emerges. The Third World is raising its head. It sees a modern world built on exploitation of the undeveloped world—taking its raw materials, then selling them back as finished product. At the south edge of America's empire, landless peasants are taking the jubilee year seriously. First-world Christians know God was kidding when he spoke of land reform. The United States prefers to view liberation theology-based popular movements in Central America as

Communist conspiracies rather than recognizing the hungry serfs trying to end Yankee-sponsored feudalism.

The developed Western world will have to learn from history and reslice the pie voluntarily or one day the balance will tip, and just as it did in the French Revolution, the blade will fall.

Whose Story Is History?

With all the chaos and suffering on this planet, it's comforting to believe America earned its wealth fair and square. But when 5 percent of the world's people (we Americans) control about a third of its wealth, it makes you wonder. Responsible stewardship of our wealth starts with an honest understanding of where it comes from. Do our history books hide the truth?

I have a degree in history—European history. For kicks and self-righteous chuckles, I used to thumb through the lies and propaganda the students in the USSR call history. My degree implied I really knew my history—or so I thought.

Then I read *The Future in Our Hands*, a book by Norwegian philosopher Erik Dammann. He suggests that European/American society gained the upper hand economically only by the brutal exploitation of what became the most poor, mixed up, and troubled parts of our world. And in the process, thriving cultures were destroyed forever.

This short article will give a few examples of how impressive the "Third World" used to be, explain how Europe could manage to have such a devastating impact on the rest of our world, review the consequences today, and inspire you to broaden your understanding of our planet with some further study. But this article has nothing directly to do with how you and I should handle our wealth. I simply want to stimulate you with a little history—from a different perspective.

When Columbus discovered America, the world's biggest and one of its most beautiful and sophisticated cities was Tenochtitlán, present-day Mexico City. Built out over a large lake with a population of about half a million, it looked a lot like Amsterdam. There were goldsmiths, chemists, barbers, public baths, and bustling market-places. Pre-Columbian Mexico had a system of paved roads, aqueducts, suspension bridges, police, a criminal code and court sys-

tem, doctors capable of performing skull surgery, and a king elected
by a council. Hernán Cortés, the Spanish conquistador who conquered present-day Mexico, wrote, "Discipline and high principles
prevail everywhere. People are well educated and, as far as I can tell,
the form of government resembles that of Pisa or Venice." This is the
Mexico that the Europeans "discovered" and destroyed 500 years ago.
Mexicans don't celebrate Columbus Day.

Many areas of Africa, Latin America, and Asia were just as
morally, ethically, and technically developed as Europe before our
culture expanded. In A.D. 400, while most of Europe was still in skins,
Africans wore Indian cotton and Chinese silk. In 1500, the number
one industry in Timbuktu was books. Africa had intricate networks
of roads, large cities, irrigation projects, and lots of trade. During
these days, when European nations exchanged ambassadors with
their African counterparts, they expressed much respect for African
governments, crafts, and societies. By the 1800s, when artifacts from
these same civilizations were brought to Europe, they were thought
to be from Atlantis or ancient Greece. By this time we had "learned"
that Africans were incapable of creating objects of such quality. In
school we called Africa "the dark continent."

In 1489, Vasco da Gama discovered the route to India—with the
help of Arab sailors and using maps and directions from friendly African merchants along the way. The Indian Ocean already had a busy,
well-balanced, and stable system of trade among Indians, Chinese,
Arabs, and Africans. These people used boats much bigger than those
the Portuguese had arrived in. Their boats were equipped with tools
such as quadrants and compasses.

Everywhere, the Europeans were received warmly. They saw
incredible wealth and spent the next 400 years taking it. Entire cultures vanished as hundreds of millions were enslaved. Literate and
stable societies were colonized, raped, and left illiterate and with no
basis for development. (Before Indonesia and Algeria were colonized
by Europeans, for instance, their populations were 90% literate.
When the Europeans were done with them, they left them with their
independence and 90% illiteracy.) Thousands of tons of gold were
brought to Europe. All this gave Europe and the United States the
resources, surplus wealth, land, and manpower to undergo the most
rapid development in history at the expense of the rest of the world.
The inertia from this period lasts until today, and the wealth still
flows in our favor.

How did this happen? The Europeans were powered by greed and
a love of gold. Exploration was done for profit. And the cultures the

Europeans met were just no match for Western tactics. For instance, African generals always left rear openings so their enemies could retreat if necessary. Battles were normally started in the afternoon so that the weaker side could retreat under the cover of darkness. Before the battle, opposing sides partied together.

In our culture, whether fighting within itself or overtaking more distant peoples, all is fair in love and war. For example, the first president of the United States won fame and a decisive victory by attacking on a Christmas eve when his enemy was drunk and unprepared, an unthinkably dirty trick in Third World battle etiquette.

Within a few years of da Gama's famous voyage, Portugal controlled the Indian Ocean and had destroyed the 500-year-old cultures of East Africa. European memory of a destroyed civilization vanishes conveniently with that culture.

For the next nearly 400 years, the slave trade powered much of the European/American economy. A superprofitable triangular trade system brought slaves from Africa to America and minerals and natural wealth from America to Europe and fueled Europe's Industrial Revolution, providing several centuries of a steady 300 percent profit for the capital investment of European shippers. Huge ports such as Liverpool grew up and boomed with the slave industry. During this period the industrial basis of European/American economic power in the twentieth century was established.

While only about 15 million slaves reached America alive, conservative estimates say Africa lost 50 million of its strongest young men through the European and American slave trade. Four hundred years of steady slavery demoralized and emasculated Africa. For all this, Africa received nothing—except the opportunity to buy European products. African cultures crumbled and were comfortably forgotten. What was left had no confidence and almost no hope. (Those whose wealth was built on slavery find comfort in the thought that slave traders were only capitalizing on an existing institution of inter-African slavery. Slavery in Africa before the Europeans arrived was closer to feudal European serfdom. Only with the European aggressiveness did slavery become big business.)

In the 1800s, when slavery became unprofitable, it was finally thought to be immoral. Europe's leaders met in Berlin and divided up Africa by drawing lines on the map. Cultural and linguistic boundaries were ignored. Now Europe would take freely of Africa's mineral wealth. Colonial powers racked up annual profits of from 50 to 500 percent.

Shortly after its discovery, Central America was given to Spain by Pope Alexander. The ensuing destruction of Mexico from 1519 to

1521 by Cortés and a handful of mercenaries is a fascinating story of greed and power.

According to pre-Columbian Mexico's religion, their Messiah, Quetzalcoatl, was due to arrive wearing a beard and riding a horse (two things very unusual to these people) during the very year Cortés arrived, a bearded man on a horse. Thinking Cortés was Quetzalcoatl, the Mexicans warmly welcomed the Spaniard with "2,000 heavy pieces of gold." Montezuma, the Mexican leader, greeted Cortés, saying, "O Lord, our Lord. . .at last you have come to this land, to your own land and to Mexico your own city. Sit down on your mat, upon your throne which I have kept for you. . .Welcome to our land. Rest yourself now. Rest here for awhile. Rest in our palace— together with your princes, your exalted companions, and all the others."

Cortés thought this was great. He and his men were taken into the king's palace and were so impressed with all the gold and riches that they arrested Montezuma, destroyed the palace, and took all its riches.

Doubting the divinity of Cortés, the citizens asked him to leave and welcomed him to take their treasure with him. But Cortés wanted complete control, so the battle began and the Spaniards destroyed the civilization: 100,000 were killed, and the libraries, temples, art, and literature of this culture were lost forever. Today Montezuma is remembered for his "Halls" and as a kind of diarrhea. His descendants and, ironically, those of the conquistadors, are known collectively as "wetbacks."

Twelve years later, under the Spaniard Pizarro, gold-hungry Europe moved into South America. Europeans looted for 100 years before mining was even necessary. The Indians were beasts of burden. Africans were imported to fill in when populations shrank. (A hundred years of war and new diseases cut Mexico's population by 50 percent.) By 1800, about half of the populations of Venezuela and Brazil were Africans imported by European businessmen. For 300 years, Spain milked Latin America until, in the early 1800s, independence was won. Then in 1824, British Foreign Minister Channing said, "Latin America has won its freedom. If we play our cards right, this part of the world will be ours!" France, Britain, and the United States moved in—if not politically, then economically. When looked at honestly, Central America under the USA today is more of the same.

Asia fared no differently. The European attitude to the rest of the world is summed up nicely in this quote from Germany's Emperor Wilhelm as he sent 20,000 troops in to put down a Chinese peasant uprising: "Remember, when we meet the enemy, there will be no quarter, and no prisoners will be taken. Use your weapons in such a way that for 1,000 years no Chinese will dare look at a German. Pave the way for civilization once and for all."

Until now this story would provide little more than the foundation for a moral crusade. Morality aside, today's world is a complex interdependent system. In our hair-trigger age, peace, stability, and environmental stewardship aren't niceties. They will determine future standards of living.

The story continues. Today's global tensions are basically more of the same—struggles for material wealth, often cloaked in ideologies. The inequities of the past enable the "developed" world to grow richer while the other end of the global teeter-totter sinks deeper into poverty and the chaos that accompanies it.

And we churn on, stoking our material appetites, promising ourselves we can have it all, and cementing our feelings with fears of the enemy and soothing reassurances of how only our system works. Perhaps it's a good time to stop. Ah yes, stop, step back, rise above the maze, and examine the place history gave us. Think about the part we play.

They say the wise learn from history. The value of what they learn depends on the quality of the history they study. "Whose story is history?"

—Rick Steves

Art Appreciation

*"Only through art can we get outside ourselves and
know another's view of the universe."*
—*Marcel Proust*

To Know Art Is to Love Him

Getting to know art is like getting to know another person. First
impressions mean a lot, but true understanding comes only after a
long relationship. By opening your mind to the other's viewpoint, you
become fast friends.

In art, as with people, it's wrong to judge something before you
understand it. As they say, "Don't criticize what you can't under-

stand." Learn about it first. Then you can really run it into the ground. This section looks at the two-step process of appreciating art— understanding it and then judging it.

Every work of art has two different "subjects": (1) the subject itself (a chair, a nude woman, a country landscape), and (2) the mood or message it conveys to the viewer. To understand the artist's purpose, we need to see both subjects.

The artist might purposely change or distort reality (the actual subject matter) to enhance the mood (subject number two). We can't judge the work by simply how realistic the portrayal is. We must understand the reason for the distortion of reality—the mood that distortion creates in us.

We see the world through the artist's eyes, with his or her perspective and emotions, like looking through someone else's prescription glasses.

Knowing a little something about artists' lives makes their art more interesting and sometimes easier to understand. Find out where the artist was and what the inspiration was for a certain painting. A simple painting of crows in a wheat field takes on new meaning when you know that, shortly after painting it, van Gogh shot himself.

Each artist has a style as individual as a signature. Learn to spot the common features of your favorite artist.

Techniques

When you look at a painting, what catches your eye? Artists know what will attract your attention. They use this knowledge to punch the right emotional buttons to get their message across. (Modern advertisers have made a science of this; they know that pink makes you happy, red is sexy, which kinds of images make you feel tense, and so on—to persuade you to buy their detergent.) Here are some of the techniques used to attract your attention and produce an emotional response.

Composition

Composition, the layout of the main figures, is the skeleton of the work. Imagine a painter planning out a scene on grid-lined graph paper. He calculates how big the main characters will be and where to place them. Let's say the artist decides to arrange the figures into a geometrical pattern, say a pyramid like this:

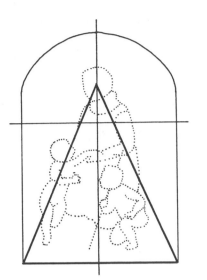

It doesn't look like much in rough form, but flesh out this skeleton composition with neat lines and real-life colors and you have Raphael's _La Belle Jardiniere_. The geometrical composition is what makes the picture so harmonious and pleasing to the eye.

(Note: Look at this skeleton pattern. See how much forethought has gone into the composition, how orderly and "beautiful" the shapes are. Imagine these rough shapes colored in. It would look something like modern art, no? Can you see the appeal of abstract art, which uses the same rules of composition, line, and color but doesn't portray real-life subjects?)

You can find the compositional scheme of any painting. Put a blank piece of paper over your favorite work and trace the major geometrical patterns and lines. (Don't try this in the Louvre.)

Line

The eye will naturally follow the curve of a line until it's broken by a line running in another direction. The artist uses this eye movement to create movement and rhythm in the scene—which, in turn, creates a mood of tension or rest in the viewer. At their own pace, trained artists guide you from one figure to the next.

In the Isenheim Altarpiece, Grünewald directs all the motion toward Christ's agonized face. From John's pointing finger, your eye travels to the face, up Christ's arm to the crossbar, out to the end, down to the grieving figures at the left, down their slanted bodies to the kneeling Mary, and up her arm, pointing again to Christ's head. Grünewald moves our attention full circle, always returning to the central figure of Jesus, where the lines intersect.

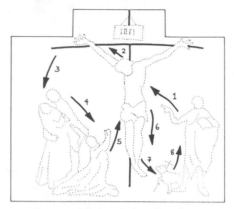

Grünewald's *Isenheim Altarpiece*

Perspective

Lines are governed by the laws of perspective, that is, how to paint three-dimensional objects on a two-dimensional surface. When you draw receding lines to turn a square into a 3-D box, you've followed the laws of perspective. If the lines of the box were continued, they'd eventually converge on the horizon at what is called the "vanishing point."

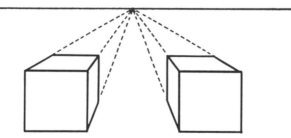

Perspective and the vanishing point

Using perspective and the vanishing point, an artist can place the viewer of a painting right in the middle of the action. Think of the picture frame as a window through which you are viewing the painted scene. Where are you in relation to the main figures? The artist lets you know, subconsciously, with the vanishing point.

Look for the vanishing point, the point where all the receding parallel lines of the painting would converge if they were extended (like those in the box illustration). This is eye level. Some of the figures are above this imaginary line, others below. You can judge your position and distance from them by reference to this subtle vanishing point.

Looking down.

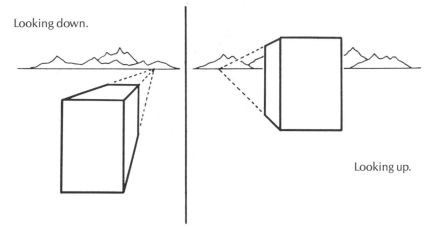

Looking up.

The vanishing point is also the compositional center of the work. In Leonardo's famous *Last Supper,* the lines converge at the center of the canvas, which is the emotional focus—Christ's head. All the linear motion flows to and from this center of calm. (See page 126.)

Architecture usually employs a vertical line that serves as the center of order, dividing the building into symmetrical halves, left and right.

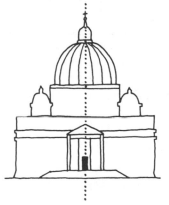

In sculpture, there is a center of gravity, too, and a "frame" like a picture frame. The imaginary square block of marble (or wood, or other material) from which the sculpture was carved serves as a "frame" surrounding the figure.

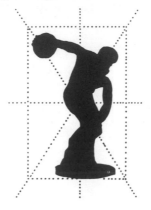

One final aspect of line technique is brushwork. Some painters make broad outlines of figures, then fill them in with smooth color (like a coloring book). Giotto demonstrated this technique. Van Gogh, however, used almost no outlines whatsoever. His paintings are more like a mosaic of minute patches of color applied by quick strokes of the brush.

Color

Color is the flesh on the compositional skeleton, bringing the figures to life. Yet it too plays a role in bringing order to art. When we choose clothes, we make sure the colors don't clash. In art, they must go together as well. The artist can make the picture peaceful by using harmonious colors or tense by using colors that clash.

Red, yellow, and blue are the primary colors; we get the rest by blending these three. Red is associated with passion, action, intensity. Yellow is warmth, the sun, peace. Blue is melancholy, thoughtful, the sea and sky. Some colors complement each other (red and green), while others contrast (yellow and orange). Obviously, the various combinations and moods available to the artist are endless.

Understanding Is Appreciation

When people, admitting their ignorance of art, say, "But I know what I like," they usually mean, "I like what I know." It's easier to like something that's familiar and understood. Baseball is the most boring game in the world if you don't understand the rules or players. Good wine is best appreciated by people who've made a point of understanding the art of winemaking. You can't appreciate the classic lines of a '56 Chevy if you don't know a Volvo from an Edsel. If you like what you know, you can usually increase your liking by simply increasing your knowing.

When you understand an artist's intention and techniques, you can _appreciate_ the work even if you don't _like_ the result. In baseball, you can appreciate a well-turned double play even if you don't like it (it made your team lose). In art, you may not like what was painted—it might be an unusual, startling, or bland scene—but you might appreciate the artist's composition or use of line and color.

Learn as much as you can about art history, artists, styles, theories, and so on, but remember that the best aid to art appreciation is simply an open mind.

Check out a book with nice color prints from the library. Relax in your favorite chair. Light a fire. Open some wine. Then, alone or with a friend, leaf slowly through the book. Don't bother much with names, dates, or commentary. Just look for a painting or two you like. Play a game where you pick your favorite from each chapter, and then compare notes with a friend. (If, after two glasses of wine, you still can't find anything you like, don't push it. Turn on the TV.)

Once you find a good one, ask yourself _why_ you like it. Is it the bright colors? The story it tells? The emotional effect on you? Does it make you feel good? Or sad? Or angry? _Any_ reason for liking art is a good one. Just try to recognize what it is.

Look for other works by an artist you like. If you like a similar work maybe that means you like that style. What do the two works have in common?

Try to understand what went through the artist's mind while painting the scene in that way. Even if you don't see anything of worth, assume that he put a lot of thought and sweat into the work. Assume the artist is pleased with his creation. Try to understand why.

Museum-going

Europe is a treasure chest of great art. Many of the world's greatest museums will be a part of your trip. Here are a few hints on how to get the most out of these museums.

Some studying before the trip makes the art you'll see in Europe much more exciting. It's criminal to visit Rome or Greece or Egypt with no background in the art of those civilizations. I remember touring the National Museum of Archaeology in Athens as an obligation and being quite bored. I was convinced that those who looked as if they were enjoying it were actually just faking it. Two years later, after taking a class in ancient art history, that same museum was a fascinating trip into the world of Pericles and Socrates—all because of some background knowledge.

A common misconception is that great museums have only great art. A museum such as the Louvre, in Paris, is so big (the building was, at one time, the largest in Europe) you can't possibly cover everything properly in one visit, so don't try. Be selective. Use a guide or guidebook to show you what is considered the best two hours of viewing in a museum. Brief guide pamphlets recommending a basic visit are available in most of Europe's museums. With this selective strategy, you'll appreciate the highlights while you are fresh. If you have any energy left, you can explore other areas that you are specifically interested in. For me, museum-going is the hardest work I do in Europe, and I'm rarely good for more than two or three hours.

Our book *Mona Winks* (Santa Fe, N.M.: John Muir Publications, 1989) gives you fun and easy-to-follow self-guided tours through twenty of Europe's top museums.

Victim of the Louvre

If you are determined to cover a large museum thoroughly, the best strategy is to tackle one section a day for several days. If you are especially interested in one piece of art, spend half an hour studying it and listening to each passing tour guide tell his or her story about David or the Mona Lisa or whatever. They each do their own research and come up with different information to share. There's really nothing wrong with this sort of tour freeloading. Just don't stand in the front and ask a lot of questions.

Before leaving I always thumb through a museum guidebook index or look through the postcards to make sure I haven't missed anything of importance to me. For instance, I love Dali. I thought I was finished with a museum, but in the postcards I found a painting by Dali. A museum guide was happy to show me where this Dali painting was hiding. I saved myself the agony of discovering after my trip was over that I was there but didn't see it.

Most museums are closed one day during the week. Your local guidebook or tourist information should know when. Free admission days are usually the most crowded. In some cases, it's worth the entrance fee to avoid the crowds.

Art Patronage

The Lowly Artist and Church and State

It's only recently that artists have claimed the right to paint just what they want, just how they want it. In the ancient world, the artist had a low social status and was expected to do as he was told. Anyone who worked with his hands was simply a "common laborer," like a brick-layer. The ancient Egyptians, with their need for funerary art, encouraged painters and sculptors and paid them well for their services but never gave them any special respect. (Architects had higher social status; they worked with their heads, not their hands. Imhotep, who designed the first pyramid in 2650 B.C., was actually deified.)

In early Greece, most artists were slaves. Again, the wealthy free-men didn't want to get their hands dirty. Gradually, though, artists gained respect. By the Golden Age they had begun to sign their works, rising above the level of the anonymous craftsman. Still, even the great sculptor Phidias was criticized for vanity when he tried to include his self-portrait (and that of Pericles) in one of his works on the Acropolis.

By the time of Alexander the Great, however, artists were freer to express their individual tastes. For the first time we see the private patron financing an artist to make works that are merely pleasing to the eye. Artists became respected and admired in the community. Alexander showered wealth and favors on his favorites. He once offered the great artist Apelles one of his own mistresses, he was so pleased with a painting.

The more practical Romans thought their artists should be paid but not pampered. As Seneca put it, "Art should be enjoyed—artists should be disdained." Nevertheless, their society gave artists plenty of work: government buildings, temples, monuments to emperors and conquerors, coins, household goods, graven images of gods, and portraits. Roman artists were treated as anonymous skilled crafts-men who couldn't compare with the classical Greeks. Rich Romans were most interested in buying copies of Greek masterpieces.

Medieval Guilds

With the Fall of Rome and the resulting economic and cultural decline, there were no strong states and few wealthy individuals. What little art there was was in the hands of the church. Monks illus-trated manuscripts of the Bible and sacred writings. For lay artists, virtually the only market for their talent was in churches and monasteries. "Lodges" of journeymen masons, carvers, sculptors, and the like traveled from town to town building religious structures.

Artists fought for economic security against the unstable patron-age of the Middle Ages by forming guilds. Half union, half co-op, guilds trained artists, regulated quality standards (as well as moral standards), and served as middlemen between the artists and prospec-tive buyers. In a sense, the guild often was the artist's patron: it told him where and when to work and gave him his percentage of the fee when the completed product was approved. As late as 1570 in Italy, artists were required to be members of a guild.

The guild underlined the artist's role as craftsman. The Guild of St. Luke in Holland included painters, carvers, and goldsmiths as well as plumbers, slate layers, printers, and lantern makers. Most commis-sions were collaborations between guild members—one covered the walls, another painted a design on them, another carved the orna-ments, and so on.

Private Patrons—The Artist Triumphant

With the economic growth of the later Middle Ages, there were more patrons willing to spend more money. Individual artists were in high demand and art flourished. We see the same pattern throughout history—a culture prospers by economic or military expansion, creating a class of patrons with a taste for decoration. In ancient Egypt, this class was the ruling kings and priests who used art to maintain the political and religious status quo. Greece and Rome added a new class of wealthy people who appreciated art apart from its propaganda purposes. In the early Middle Ages, the church was the only patron, producing art only for its limited, spiritual purposes.

In the Renaissance, all three patrons—church, state, and private individuals—competed with their growing wealth for a few artists.

This climate of healthy competition not only made artists wealthy, famous, and respected, but it also, for the first time in history, allowed them freedom to create art on their own terms, not according to the patron's specifications. With Michelangelo, the modern idea of the artist as a divinely inspired genius had arrived.

Dürer, *Self-Portrait in a Fur Coat* (Alte Pinakothek, Munich) In 1500, it was a bold statement to paint yourself at all— much less looking as proud as this. Dürer's message: it's time to start respecting all people, especially artists.

Patronage and artist prestige reached its height during the baroque period. Rubens and Bernini lived like princes, courted by kings, cardinals, and intellectuals alike.

This contrasted with the financial picture in the Northern European countries. In northern trading cities a large middle class of merchants and bankers controlled the wealth. A steady patronage by the church and monarch was not available because the North was Protestant and more democratic. Northern artists had to turn to scenes that would interest the buying public: landscapes, domestic scenes,

Vermeer, *Kitchen Maid* (Rijksmuseum, Amsterdam)—1658 Vermeer, sensitive to the taste of a new art market, captured stillness and simple ordinary beauty.

humorous incidents. They still did some works made-to-order, but more and more they began to complete works for display at trade fairs, hoping to find a buyer. This set the precedent for modern patronage.

In the time of absolute monarchs such as Louis XIV of France, artists were compelled to work for the king alone. Louis established the Royal Academy to train young artists for his service. They had less independence than their counterparts in free-market Holland and England but more formal training and financial security. France soon became the center of European art.

The Modern, Independent Artist

The French Revolution was the (symbolic if not final) end of the "Old Regime" of church, state, and aristocrats which had financed most of Europe's great art since the Middle Ages. Increasingly, artists worked alone, independent of the institutions that had previously supported them. They turned away from the propaganda art of church, kings, and even so-called lovers of freedom such as Napoleon.

In the nineteenth century, art retreated into the museums and galleries. Artists didn't wait for a specific commission to decorate a particular palace, church, or public square. Instead, they created what they wanted, then looked for a place to exhibit it. The impressionists and the painter Courbet had to arrange their own exhibitions when the conservative galleries refused their controversial work. Some artists (such as Cézanne) rejected all outside patronage or official schooling by financing themselves or by simply refusing to sacrifice their artistic principles to the demands of the buying public. The bohemian artist, starving but true to himself, was born.

Of course, some forms of official patronage have filled the vacuum. Churches still commission artists and architects (the church at Ronchamp, France, by Le Corbusier is one modern example). And governments are some of the steadiest sources for an artist. Until recently, Eastern European countries have used art for propaganda purposes, with huge monuments and murals dedicated to Marxist leaders and ideals. In the West, large corporations fund the arts for P.R. purposes and tax write-offs.

For all this "official" patronage, however, the modern artist insists on independence from a meddling patron. The artist's income usually comes from unknown buyers who negotiate through a middleman. Art buying has become a major investment area for businessmen with no interest in the art itself.

As you enjoy Europe's art, remember, it wasn't designed to embellish a museum. Some patron probably paid to employ that artist for a particular self-serving purpose.

Common Subjects and Symbols in Art

In a quick jaunt through any church, palace, or museum, you're bound to see many of the same subjects painted and sculpted in different ways by different artists. A little knowledge (a dangerous thing, but we'll trust you) of these common themes helps you appreciate the art much more.

The inspiration for most European art comes from the Bible and Greek/Roman mythology. For general background I'd recommend reading the Book of Matthew in the New Testament (about 35 pages long) and a children's book of Greek myths.

Christian Themes and Symbols

Jesus of Nazareth (c. 4 B.C.-A.D. 29)

The life of Jesus is the most popular source of material. Here's a thumbnail sketch.

Born in a stable under miraculous circumstances, he was visited by shepherds and Wise Men. His religious mission had earlier been announced to his mother, Mary, by the angel Gabriel. He was raised to be a carpenter, but even at an early age he proved his teaching powers.

At 30, he left home to preach the word of God, choosing twelve disciples, or apostles. He preached, performed miracles, healed people, and antagonized the religious establishment.

On a visit to Jerusalem, Jesus celebrated Jewish Passover with his disciples. Later that night he was arrested by the Roman and Jewish authorities, betrayed by one of his own followers. Arraigned before the Jewish elders and the Roman governor, Pilate, and mocked and

Four artists of four eras tackle the same subject in four different ways

Medieval: This fourteenth-century crucifix concentrates on the agony of Christ—his twisted, tortured body and drooping head.

Renaissance: Masaccio's Christ is solid, serene, and triumphant—part of a majestic architectural setting presided over by God the Father.

Baroque: Rubens captures the drama and human emotion of the moment with the expression on Christ's face and the rippling energy of the surrounding figures.

Modern: Rouault breaks up the scene into its basic geometrical "abstract" forms. The only emotion is in the tilt of Christ's head. The heavy outlines and blocks of color are almost a return to medieval stained glass.

whipped by Roman soldiers, he was given a crown of thorns and sentenced to die by crucifixion. They made Jesus carry his own cross to the execution site.

Crucifixion was a Roman specialty. The victim often hung for days before dying. They stabbed Jesus in the side for good measure. Above the cross were the Roman initials I.N.R.I. for "*Jesus of Nazareth—King (Rex) of the Jews.*" Mary was comforted at the foot of the cross by John, one of the disciples. After his death, the body was taken down and placed in a tomb.

After three days, Jesus came alive again and visited many of his friends and disciples. Finally, he ascended into heaven.

Stained-Glass Checklist

Here's a handy list of some of the most popular scenes from Jesus' life, with Bible references:

• **Annunciation**—The angel Gabriel announces the birth of a son, Jesus, to Mary. (Luke 1:26-38)

• **Madonna and Child**—Mary and the baby Jesus. (Luke 2:6,7)

• **Holy Family**—Mary and Jesus with Mary's husband Joseph, mother Anne or others. When two children are shown, they're usually Jesus and Johnny the Baptist.

• **Adoration of the Magi**—Three wise kings follow a bright star from the East and bow down to worship the baby Jesus (Matt. 2:1-12). Tradition says that one king was from Ethiopia; he is usually depicted having black skin.

• **Flight to Egypt**—Mary's husband, Joseph, is warned to flee from King Herod. Herod, wanting to be sure that the newborn boy predicted to be greater than he (Jesus) will die, has ordered that all male infants be killed. Joseph and Mary take Jesus to Egypt. (Matt. 2:13-23)

• **Slaughter of the Innocents**—King Herod kills the children in and around Bethlehem, where Jesus was born. (Matt. 2:16-18)

• **Baptism of Jesus**—John the Baptist pours water over Jesus in the Jordan River as a symbol of cleansing. God the Father is represented in the scene as an eye or a voice and God the Holy Spirit is represented as a dove. (Matt. 3:13-17)

• **Resurrection of Lazarus**—Jesus raises his friend Lazarus from the dead. (John 11:1-45)

• **Last Supper**—Jesus celebrates the Jewish festival of Passover by having one final meal with his disciples. That same night he was arrested. (Mark 14:1-31, John 13:1-17:26)

• **Garden of Gethsemane**—Jesus is arrested while praying in a garden. (Mark 14:32-53)

• **Crucifixion**—Jesus is nailed to a cross and dies. (Matt. 27:27-54, Mark 15:16-39, John 19:16-37)

• **Pietà**—Mother Mary with the dead body of Jesus. (no clear reference)

• **Resurrection**—On the third day after his burial, Jesus rises from the dead and appears to many people, including his mother, Mary Magdalene, his disciples, and two men on the road to Emmaus. (Matt. 28, Mark 16, Luke 24, John 20-21)

• **Ascension**—Jesus leaves the earth by rising into the clouds (ascending) to return to his rightful place beside his Father in heaven. (Acts 1:9-11)

• **Last Judgment**—Jesus returns to the earth to sort out the good people and the bad. Angels float the good to heaven and demons drag the bad to hell. Bodies rise from their graves to find out how they will fare.

• **Assumption of the Virgin**—Angels hoist Mary up through the clouds to heaven.

Old Testament

The Old Testament tells the history of the Israelite people, from the creation of the world to the coming of Jesus.

• **Creation of the World, Man, and Woman**—God creates the world and all living things out of nothing. Adam (the first man) is lonely, so God creates Eve (the first woman) from Adam's rib. (Gen. 1:1-2:25)

• **Fall of Man and Banishment from Eden**—A serpent convinces Eve to eat the one fruit God told her not to, and she in turn convinces Adam to have a bite. This is his first sin, and Adam and Eve are banished from the lush garden because of it. (Gen. 3:1-24)

• **Cain and Abel**—Adam and Eve have two sons. Abel becomes a keeper of sheep and Cain, a farmer. Both make sacrifices to God, but God accepts only Abel's sacrifice. Cain becomes angry, kills his brother, and is banished forever.

• **Abraham Sacrifices Isaac**—God makes a pact with the wanderer Abraham, promising him many descendants even though he is old and his wife is childless. Abraham believes God, and his faith is rewarded by the birth of his son, Isaac. But then God tests Abraham's faith by asking him to sacrifice Isaac. Abraham intends to obey, but God stops him just before he kills Isaac. Isaac becomes the father of the Jewish nation; one of his descendants is Jesus. (Gen. 22:1-18)

• **Exodus from Egypt**—The people of Israel are captives of the Egyptians, but Moses rises up to lead them to freedom. They are promised a new land, but because they disobey God, they are first forced to wander in the desert for 40 years. (Exodus 1-15)

• **Moses and the Bronze Serpent**—The people of Israel disobey God again while they wander in the desert, so God sends snakes to bite them. He tells Moses, though, to make a bronze snake and put it on a pole, and that all who keep their eyes on it will live.

• **Moses and the Ten Commandments**—In order to tell the people of Israel how He wants them to live, God gives Moses on Mt. Sinai ten "thou-shalt-nots" written on tablets of stone.

• **David and Goliath**—The people of Israel are challenged in battle by the Philistines, who have a mighty giant warrior, Goliath. Of all the Israelis, only a young shepherd boy named David is bold enough to fight him (David later becomes king). David uses rocks and a slingshot to bring Goliath down, then cuts off the giant's head. (1 Samuel 17:1-51)

The Saints

Holy people were venerated by the European faithful. Though we don't know what they really looked like, we can tell who's who by their symbols.

• **Peter**—The most important saint, a disciple of Jesus. The name Peter means "rock." Jesus said, "On this rock I will build my church." St. Peter's Basilica, in Rome, is built upon the grave of St. Peter. Usually shown in middle age with a bushy beard, keys, or an upside-down cross in hand.

• **Paul**—The second most important saint, Paul was primarily responsible for establishing Christianity through his missionary journeys. He wrote half of the books of the New Testament. Shown bald-headed and bearded, gripping a sword and a book.

• **Matthew, Mark, Luke, and John (The Four Evangelists)**—Wrote the first four books of the New Testament, which chronicle the life of Christ. Symbols: Matthew, an angel with a book; Mark, a lion; Luke, a winged bull; and John, an eagle with a book.

• **John the Baptist**—Shown as an emaciated prophet dressed in animal skins, carrying a long cross, a lamb, and often a scroll bearing the words "Ecce Homo." Spent many years preaching that Jesus was coming into the world, then eventually baptized him.

• **Mary Magdalene**—A prostitute whom Jesus forgave of her sins. She became a follower of Jesus and was at the cross when he died. Usually shown having long hair and carrying a jar of ointment.

• **Michael, the Archangel**—Shown in armor, with a sword, standing over or fighting with a dragon; also sometimes shown with a set of scales. The most important of the angels, Michael cast Satan out of heaven and will one day lead the forces of Good at the last great battle on Judgment Day. He will blow the waking trumpet on Judgment Day.

• **Anne**—The mother of the Virgin Mary, the grandmother of Jesus, shown with the Virgin Mary and usually also with the baby Jesus.

• **Francis of Assisi**—A medieval monk noted for his vow of poverty and love of God. The most important monk of all time, Francis founded the Franciscan order and lived in Assisi, Italy. He is usually shown in brown Franciscan habit, on his knees, with a winged Christ in the sky sending down the "stigmata" (the nail marks from Jesus' body with which to mark his body).

• **Sebastian**—A soldier in the army of Roman emperor Diocletian. Although Diocletian loved him, when it was discovered he was a Christian he was ordered tied to a tree and shot with arrows. Legend says he survived to confront Diocletian . . . only to then be beaten to death with clubs. Usually depicted naked, tied to a tree and pierced by arrows.

• **George**—The subject of many legends, George saved a town from a dragon to which the townspeople were sacrificing their children. He was a chivalrous knight, usually shown on horseback spearing a dragon while the king's daughter, Cleodolinda (who was next to be sacrificed) looks on.

• **Jerome**—A hermit who translated the Hebrew Bible into Latin, producing the Vulgate, the standard text of the Catholic church through modern times. His symbols vary, but he is often shown with a lion, from whose foot he extracted a thorn.

• **Bartholomew**—A first century A.D. missionary. Tradition says he was captured in Armenia and flayed alive, then crucified for being a Christian. Bartholemew is usually shown with a book and knife or holding his skin. He is sometimes depicted being skinned.

• **Denis**—Sent by the Pope on a missionary journey to Paris, Denis became the first Bishop of Paris and was eventually beheaded there for his faith. You'll see him all over Paris holding his head in his hands.

• **Theresa**—Lived in the sixteenth century, reformed the Carmelite monastic order. She wrote many religious works. Theresa is usually shown with her heart pierced by an angel's arrow, or in ecstasy while praising God.

• **Christopher (the patron saint of us travelers)**—A third-century man who went out in search of someone to serve. He wandered aimlessly for years and ended up ferrying people across a river while waiting for Christ to appear to him. Christ finally appeared as a child whom Christopher carried across the river. Shown as a giant carrying a child and holding a staff.

These stories are found in pictures and stained glass in churches throughout Europe. The masses were usually illiterate, so church paintings were their Bible.

Much Christian art is symbolic. During medieval times, every animal, fruit, flower, color, and number had some meaning. Apes symbolized man's baser nature; bees were a symbol of industriousness ("busy as a . . ."); a lamb was a sacrificial animal (like Jesus); a dolphin carried the soul of the blessed to heaven. Mythical beasts had meaning, too: dragons (Satan), griffins (power), unicorns (purity), and phoenixes (resurrection). Numbers had symbolic meaning; 7 was a lot, 77 was a heck of a lot.

It's interesting to compare two different paintings or stained glass of the same subject. There are literally thousands of Crucifixions, but no two are the same. Some artists concentrate on Jesus' agony, some on his serenity. For some, it's a gruesome moment of defeat, for others, a glorious triumph over sin.

Jesus is portrayed in different ways to emphasize different virtues. In one picture, he is the Good Shepherd—a handsome, kindly young man caring for men as a shepherd cares for his sheep. In another, he is a wise teacher. Or he might be a king, crowned in majesty. He may even be a warrior. These differences tell a lot about how people viewed the Christian message at the time of the painting.

If you see a face in a crowd of saints, church fathers, and Bible figures that you don't recognize, chances are it doesn't really belong in such holy company, anyway. Patrons of works often insisted that they be included in the work—praising the Virgin Mary or what have you. If money couldn't buy them a spot in heaven, at least it could put them in a picture of heaven.

The Stars of Greek and Roman Mythology

The Greek gods were bigger-than-life human beings. They quarreled, boasted, loved, and hated just as mortals do, yet they controlled the fates of men. Classical mythology tells how the gods dealt with each other and with the mortals who asked them for favors. (The Greeks must have enjoyed hearing their own weaknesses glamourized, just as we do through our Hollywood stars.)

Later, the Romans adopted most of the Greeks' gods and gave them new names. Still later, Renaissance artists revived them, using them as symbols of Christian virtues and vices. After centuries of painting the same old God, it must have been a great sense of freedom to paint new ones—and a whole pantheon of them, to boot.

Here are the most important Greek gods and how to recognize them (Roman name in parentheses):

• **Zeus (Jupiter)**—Ruled as King of the Gods in their court on Mount Olympus. He divided up his realm among his sisters, brothers, and children. Bearded, sometimes carries a spear. Zeus had a nasty habit of turning himself into some earthly form to hustle unsuspecting females. You're as likely to see him portrayed as a bull, a cloud, a swan, or a shower of gold as in his majestic human body.

• **Hera (Juno)**—Wife of Zeus.

• **Poseidon (Neptune)**—King of the Sea. Holds a trident.

• **Hades (Pluto)**—King of the Underworld. Bearded and sad, carries a staff.

• **Apollo**—Ruler of the Sun, God of Music and Poetry. Drives the flaming chariot that is the sun across the sky each day. Major symbol is the sun.

• **Hermes (Mercury)**—Messenger of the Gods. His helmet and shoes have wings. Carries a lot of flowers these days.

• **Ares (Mars)**—God of War. Dresses in war garb and carries a spear.

• **Dionysus (Bacchus)**—God of Wine (and college fraternities). Holds grapes, wears a toga and a wreath of laurel leaves. Sometimes shown as a chubby little boy.

• **Athena (Minerva)**—Goddess of Wisdom. A virgin, born from the head of Zeus. Carries a spear.

• **Artemis (Diana)**—Goddess of the Moon and Hunting. Carries a bow and arrow.

• **Aphrodite (Venus)**—Goddess of Love and Beauty. Often shown partially naked, with Cupid nearby.

• **Eros (Cupid)**—God of Desire. Usually shown as a baby with wings, wielding a bow and love arousing arrows.

Other characters and miscellaneous beasts:

• **Pan (Faun)**—A lesser god of shepherds. Top half man, bottom half goat. Carries a pan flute.

• **Hercules**—Son of Zeus born to a mortal woman. Strongest man in the world. Performed many feats of strength. Often wears a lion's skin.

• **Odysseus (Ulysses)**—The lead character *The Odyssey*, the story of his 10-year journey home from the Trojan War.

• **Helen of Troy**—The most beautiful woman in the world. Her kidnapping started the Trojan War, the subject of *The Iliad*. Hers is "the face that launched 1,000 ships."

• **Satyrs**—Top half man, bottom half goat. Horny.

• **Centaurs**—Top half man, bottom half horse. Wise.

• **Griffins**—Winged, lionlike beasts.

• **Harpies**—Birds with human female head and seductive voice.

- **Medusa**—Woman with hair of snakes and a face that, when glimpsed, turns people to stone. Slain by Perseus.

- **Pegasus**—Winged horse.

- **Minotaur**—Beast with the head of a bull. Lived in the labyrinth (maze) in the palace on Crete.

Even if you know zero about art, if you know who's in a painting and what they're doing, your interest level jumps 50 percent. Learn something about Christian and classical mythology, and your trip will be much more enjoyable.

Historical Scenes

Modern artists, in search of new subjects, turned to famous scenes from history, trying to capture the glory or emotion of the moment. In the early 1800s romantic artists tapped the patriotic fervor of their audiences with scenes of heroics against oppressors. Goya's *Third of May* shows the murderous execution of Spanish nationals by Napoleon's troops. Delacroix painted a battle scene from a French antimonarchy uprising. J. L. David, a neoclassicist, chronicled (and "romanticized") the French Revolution and reign of Napoleon.

Still Lifes

Scholars debate whether "art imitates life" or "life imitates art," but to a great extent, "art imitates art." Artists often choose a subject already done by many previous artists in order to carry on and extend the tradition—to both learn from earlier masters' versions and try something new.

Perhaps the best example is the "still life," a painting of a set of motionless, common objects—fruit, cups, a knife, a chair, curtains, and so on. It's a simple form, often undertaken by students practicing their drawing and simple composition, yet many great artists have shown their ingenuity by turning it into great art. Each successive artist is challenged to make the old style new again.

Landscapes

Other styles involve painting of places: landscapes, seascapes, domestic and rural scenes. The place may be completely different in two different paintings, but it is still interesting to compare each artist's approach.

El Greco, *Landscape of Toledo*

Baroque artists often decorated churches with an appropriate "landscape"—heaven. Ceilings seem to open up to the sky, gloriously busy with angels, chariots, and winged babies (called "putti").

Portraits

Portraits are, of course, supposed to be accurate renditions of the person, but many try to glorify the subject, even at the expense of accuracy. Different portrait artists take different views in this matter. It's interesting to compare. Two particular types of portrait sculpture are the "bust" (neck and head only) and "equestrian" (riding a horse).

The "nude" is another particular kind of portrait, concerned more with the shape of the body than specific identifying features. A good nude is not necessarily of the most beautiful body. It's up to the artist to pose the body just right—reclining or standing—to capture the most interesting and harmonious lines.

A classical style, the "contrapposto" (Italian for "counterpoise"), is a painting or sculpture of someone standing, resting their weight on one leg. The faint S-like curve of the body attracts the eye as much as any individual body features. (Michelangelo's David is contrapposto.)

Three
Different
Nudes

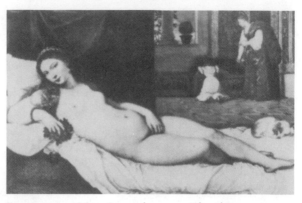

Renaissance, Titian: Sensual curves, rich colors, sexy gaze.

Neoclassical, Ingres: Pure, cool lines of the body blending with the lines of the drapes and sheets.

Modern, Picasso: Minimum number of lines necessary to capture the nude form.

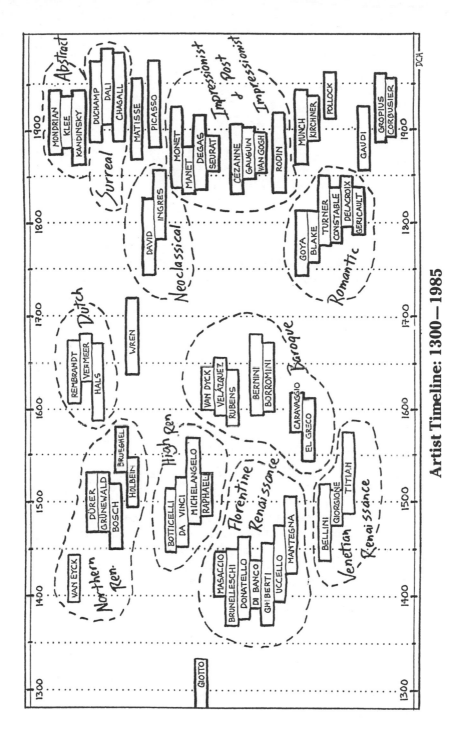

Artist Timeline: 1300–1985

Music Appreciation

Music, like all art forms, is shaped by the cultural mood and environment of the time. It's easy to trace the course of musical history as it marches arm in arm with painting, architecture, sculpture, philosophy, and life-styles in general—from baroque to neoclassical to romantic to impressionistic and into the "no holds barred" artistic world of our century.

As we trace this evolution of musical styles through post-Renaissance history, let's use this section as a review of the progression of art styles in general since the baroque days of Louis, Bernini, and Bach.

The baroque world was controlled exuberance, glory to man and his God-blessed accomplishments. In other words, "Let's shine and enjoy our success—without rocking the boat." Music, like art, was brilliant, bright, alive, and decorated with trills, flutters, and ornamentation—like the powdered wigged, perfumed, and elegantly gowned musicians who wrote and performed it.

But the frills rested on a strong foundation. While a two-part Bach invention, Handel's *Messiah*, or a Scarlatti sonata may sparkle with bright and happy ornaments, they are carefully based on a solid mathematical structure. An analysis of Bach's work shows many patterns, staircase-type series, and a grand plan, tying all the musical ribbons and bows together. Bach, Handel, and Scarlatti, all born in 1685, were the great musical masters of the baroque period.

The neoclassical movement was a "back to pure, clean basics" movement artistically and culturally. It was a stern reaction to the "clutter" of baroque. Buildings were built with clean and true domes, circles, and squares. The age of reason had arrived, and beauty was simple. A good example of how music played along with the neoclassical movement is found in the art of Mozart. This classical composer wrote pieces of powerfully simple beauty. Grand and frilly were out. The better a Mozart sonata is played, the easier it sounds to play. Classical music, like the dome on our capitol building, is a search for basic, pure beauty. Its beauty is its simplicity.

The romantic movement refused to stifle its heart and emotions to logical, realistic, calculated, T-square beauty. Music's grand metronome had swung back again. The romantics were awestruck by the wonders of nature and strove to be overcome by its power and immensity. They expressed emotions—good and bad—for the sake of emotions. Orchestras grew in size to add more punch. A series of pieces by Chopin, Wagner, or Schumann can take you through an emotional wringer. The pieces, often with names reflecting their heart-felt story ("Ase's Death", "Pleading Child", "Raindrops Prelude," "Dreaming"), are an effort to affect the listener more than to merely entertain.

In the 1800s, reason and logic were dethroned and Nature and emotion became a religion. Grieg's fjord hideaway, Verdi's nationalism, and Chopin's battered heart all inspired the masterpieces of this era.

As painting reached beyond mere realism, we enter the impressionist era. While Monet and Renoir were catching sunbeams, leafy reflections, and the fuzzy warmth of that second glass of wine, composers such as Debussy and Ravel were doing the same thing on the keyboard or with orchestras. Artists struggled to capture basic shapes, colors, and moods. A blue moment, the crashing sea, a fleeting rainbow, or an enchanted cathedral were targets of the artist's mind, the painter's brush, and the composer's pen. And just as painters created a scene with many small dabs of different-colored paint, impressionist composers built a mosaic of sound, blending scattered notes from many instruments.

Frustration over a mass-produced world, techno-fascism, and our current media madness (with public tastes shaped by Madison Avenue), led many artists of the twentieth century to give up on pleasing the people, enjoying instead the personally stimulating works of artistic esoterica. Paintings are abstract, and music is atonal.

Atonal music is freed from tonality and worry about "what key are we in?" There is no key, no meter or consistent beat pattern (such as $\frac{2}{4}$ or $\frac{3}{4}$ time), and the only real rule is that artists should not be bound by the rules of others.

Recognizing that music is only organized sounds, modern composers experiment with new sounds and new organizations, even doing away with the common scale. As with modern visual art, it's hard to tell just what "style" will come next—when the artists are trying so hard to reject the rules of style altogether.

Appendix

Best of Europe Sightseeing Lists

Offbeat Europe:

Paris Sewers tour
A million skeletons in Paris Catacombs
Parco dei Mostri, near Viterbo, Italy
L'Art Brut (art of the criminally insane), Lausanne, Switzerland
Legoland, Bilund, Denmark
Porthmeirion (Italian city), Wales
Homage to Stravinsky fountain (near Pompidou Center), Paris
Hundertwasser Haus, Vienna
Garden of Trick Fountains, Hellbrunn Castle, Salzburg, Austria
Cappucin crypts (bones), Rome and Palermo, Italy
World's second-largest McDonald's, Rome
Thimble Museum, Creglingen (near Rothenburg), Germany
Medieval Crime and Punishment Museum, Rothenburg, Germany

Favorite Festivals:

Salzburg Music Festival, end of July through August
Edinburgh, late August through early September
Dafni Wine Festival, mid-July through early September (near Athens)
Munich beerhalls, June 1st through May 31st
Oktoberfest, late September to early October, Munich
Each country's national holiday (like French Bastille day, July 14, and Swiss
   Independence day, August 1).
Palio, Siena, Italy (July 2 and August 16)
Carnevale, Venice (February)
Fasching, Germany (especially Köln), in February
Kinderfest, Dinkelsbühl, Germany (3rd weekend in July)
Avignon, France (July)

Rick's Favorite Works of Art:

Garden of Delights, Bosch, Prado
Isenheim Altarpiece, Grünewald, Colmar
Primavera, Botticelli, Florence
Guernica, Picasso, Madrid
Pietà, Michelangelo, Vatican
David, Michelangelo, Florence
Virgin of the Roses, Schongauer, Colmar
Swiss Alps, God
Sainte-Chapelle church, Paris
St. John the Baptist, Donatello, Venice
Self-Portrait, Dürer, Prado
Death of Murat, David, Brussels
Hand of God, Milles, Stockholm
Weeping Virgin Altarpiece, Seville
Pietà Rondanini, Michelangelo, Milan
Orsay Museum building, Paris
Temppeliaukio church, Helsinki

Gene's "Lucky 13" Picks (with apologies to no one):

Isenheim Altarpiece, Grünewald, Colmar
The Tempest, Giorgione, Venice
Head of Christ Mosaic, Dafni, Greece
Interior of My Studio, Courbet, Louvre
Burial of Count Orgaz, El Greco, Toledo, Spain
School of Athens, Raphael, Vatican Palace
Moses, Michelangelo, S. Pietro in Vincoli, Rome
Last Supper, Leonardo, Milan
Intrigue, James Ensor, Royal Museum, Antwerp
Descent from the Cross, Roger van der Weyden, Prado
Grande Odalisque, Ingres, Louvre
Jacob Wrestling with the Angel, Gauguin, National Gallery, Edinburgh
St. Francis in Ecstasy, G. Bellini, New York

Most Overrated Sights:

Manneken-Pis, Brussels
Stonehenge, England
Atomium, Brussels
Athens, Greece
Glockenspiel, Munich
Mermaid, Copenhagen
Hitler's Bunker, Berlin
Spanish Steps and Trevi Fountain, Rome
Blarney Stone, Ireland
Land's End, England

Loch Ness Monster, Scotland
Cannes
Champs-Elysees, Paris' hamburger row

Most Underrated Sights:

Ostia Antica, Rome's ancient port
Bath, England's finest city
Toledo Cathedral Sacristy, Spanish Renaissance
Chantilly Chateau, near Paris
Vaux-le-Vicomte Chateau, near Paris
Schatzkammer (Treasury), Munich
Glasgow
Bern
Pisa Baptistry and Church (not Tower)
Brussels
Bulgaria

Most Underrated Museums:

Vatican Museum (before the Sistine Chapel)
Unterlinden Museum (_Isenheim Altarpiece_ and more), Colmar
Chagall Museum, Nice
Groeninge Museum, Brugge
York Castle Museum, York
Costume Museum, Bath (closed through 1991)
Fitzwilliam Museum, Cambridge
Museo del Duomo (Donatello and Michelangelo), Florence
Museo Borghese (Titian, Caravaggio, Bernini), Rome
Museo de Santa Cruz (El Greco), Toledo
Kunstmuseum, Bern
Kroller-Muller, Arnhem, Netherlands

Favorite Churches:

Charlemagne's chapel, Aachen
Sacré-Coeur, Paris
St. Peter's, Vatican
Toledo Cathedral, Toledo
Sainte-Chapelle, Paris
Orvieto, Italy
Santa Maria della Autostrada, freeway exit, Florence

Best Evening Scenes:

Seville, flamenco and paseo street scenes
La Dolce Vita stroll, Via del Corso, Rome
Piazza Navona, Rome
Mathauser's Beerhall, Munich

Jazz clubs, Paris
"Pub Crawl," back streets of Venice
Empty St. Mark's Square at midnight, Venice
Tivoli, Copenhagen
Anyplace with a Europe Through the Back Door tour guide
Any Italian hill town after the tour buses have left
Passegiata/Paseo, almost every Italian/Spanish town in evening
Son-et-Lumiere, Versailles, France
Breakwater, Vernazza, Cinque Terre, Italy

Musical Sights:

State Opera Houses, Vienna, Milan, and Paris
Mozart's birth house, Salzburg
Musee Carnavalet (Chopin), Paris
Ringve Musical history museum, Trondheim, Norway
Beethoven's birth house, Bonn
Europe's greatest organs: Passau (Germany), Haarlem (Holland)
Sibelius monument, Helsinki
Beatles Museum, Liverpool
Grieg home, Troldhaugen, Bergen, Norway

Royal Jewels:

Crown Jewels, Tower of London
Schatzkammer, Vienna and Munich
Apollo Gallery, Louvre, Paris

Cemeteries:

Cappuchin crypts (oodles of bones), Rome and Palermo
Pere Lachaise (Chopin, Jim Morrison, Edith Piaf, Oscar Wilde)
Central Cemetery (Beethoven, Brahms, Mozart, etc.), Vienna
U.S. cemeteries in Normandy (France) and Bastogne (Belgium)

Sports and Games Sights:

Olympics museums, Innsbruck and Lausanne
Olympic stadium, Berlin, Athens
Olympic Village, Munich
Ski jumps in Innsbruck, Garmisch
Ski museum, Holmenkollen ski jump, Oslo
Hurling match, anywhere, Ireland
Hang gliders and parasailers, throughout the Alps (especially Chamonix,
    Tegelberg near Füssen, and the Schilthorn)
Luge rides near Reutte, in Tirol, Austria, and Chamonix, France
Autoworld museum, Brussels
Casinos in Baden-Baden (Germany) and Monte Carlo
Cousteau aquarium, Monte Carlo
Summer Olympics: 1992, Barcelona

Assorted Military Sights:

The medieval armory, Graz, Austria
Museé do l'Armée, Invalides, Paris
Medieval Crime and Punishment Museum, Rothenburg
Valley of the Fallen, near Madrid
Wasa, Swedish warship, Stockholm
Armory (medieval weapons), Doge's Palace, Venice
Gibraltar
Waterloo (fans only), Brussels, Belgium
Imperial War Museum, London

Artists and Dates

Bernini, 1598-1680 Baroque grandeur.
Blake, William, 1757-1827 Mystical visions.
Bosch, Hieronymous, 1450-1516 Crowded, bizarre scenes.
Botticelli, Sandro, 1445-1510 Delicate Renaissance beauty.
Braque, Georges, 1882-1963 Cubist pioneer.
Brunelleschi, Filippo, 1377-1446 First great Renaissance architect.
Brueghel, Pieter, ca. 1525-1569 Netherlands, peasant scenes.
Caravaggio, 1573-1610 Shocking ultrarealism.
Cézanne, Paul, 1839-1906 Bridged impressionism and cubism.
Dali, Salvador, 1904-1989, Father of surrealism.
Degas, Edgar, 1834-1917 Impressionist snapshots, dancers.
Donatello, c. 1386-1466 Early Renaissance sculptor.
Dürer, Albrecht, 1471-1528 Renaissance symmetry with German detail; "the Leonardo of the north."
El Greco, 1541-1614 Spiritual scenes, elongated bodies.
Fra Angelico, 1387-1455 Renaissance techniques, medieval piety.
Gauguin, Paul, 1848-1903 Primitivism, native scenes, bright colors.
Giorgione, 1477-1510 Venetian Renaissance, mysterious beauty.
Giotto, 1266-1337 Proto-Renaissance painter (3-D) in medieval times.
Goya, Francisco, 1746-1828 Three stages: frilly court painter, political rebel, dark stage.
Hals, Frans, 1581-1666 Snapshot portraits of Dutch merchants.
Ingres, Jean Auguste Dominique, 1780-1867 Neoclassical.
Leonardo da Vinci, 1452-1519 A well-rounded Renaissance genius who also painted.
Manet, Edouard, 1823-1883 Forerunner of impressionist rebels.
Mantegna, Andrea, 1431-1506 Renaissance 3-D and "sculptural" painting.
Matisse, Henri, 1869-1954 Decorative "wallpaper," bright colors.
Michelangelo, 1475-1564 Earth's greatest sculptor and one of its greatest painters.
Mondrian, Piet, 1872-1944 Abstract, geometrical canvases.
Monet, Claude, 1840-1926 Father of impressionism.
Munch, Edvard, 1863-1944 Led the way into expressionism.

Picasso, Pablo, 1881-1973 Master of many modern styles, especially cubism.
Pollock, Jackson, 1912-1956 Wild drips of paint.
Raphael, 1483-1520 Epitome of the Renaissance — balance, realism, beauty.
Rembrandt, 1606-1669 Greatest Dutch painter, brown canvases, backlighting.
Renoir, Auguste, 1841-1919 Impressionist style, idealized beauty, pastels.
Rodin, Auguste, 1840-1917 Rough-finish "impressionist" sculpture.
Rubens, Peter Paul, 1577-1640 Baroque, fleshy women, violent scenes.
Steen, Jan, 1626-1679 Slice of life everyday Dutch scenes.
Tiepolo, Giovanni Battista, 1696-1770 3-D illusions on ceilings.
Tintoretto, 1518-1594 Venetian Renaissance plus drama.
Titian, 1485-1576 Greatest Venetian Renaissance painter.
Turner, Joseph Mallord William, 1775-1851 Messy "impressionist" scenes of nature.
Uccello, Paolo, 1396-1475 Early 3-D experiments.
Van Eyck, Jan, 1390-1441 Northern detail.
Van Gogh, Vincent, 1853-1890 Impressionist style plus emotion.
Velázquez, Diego, 1599-1660 Objective Spanish court portraits.
Vermeer, Jan, 1632-1675 Quiet Dutch art, highlighting everyday details.
Veronese, Paolo, 1528-1588 Huge, colorful scenes with Venetian Renaissance backgrounds.

A New Enlightenment Through Travel?

Thomas Jefferson said, "Travel makes you wiser but less happy." We think he was right. And "less happy" is a good thing. It's the growing pains of a broadening perspective, a tearing off of the hometown blinders. It exposes you to new ways of thinking and to people who have a completely different set of "self-evident" truths. We've shared with you a whole book of our love of travel. Now allow us one page to share some thoughts on how travel has given us new ways of thinking.

On any trip, the biggest culture shock can occur when you return home. America is a land of unprecedented material wealth. Though comprising only 5 percent of the world's people, we control over 30 percent of the global economic pie. We've built a wall of money around our borders, insulating ourselves from world problems. We can't see that our rampant pursuit of wealth, both as individuals and as a society, has global repercussions—long-term damage to the earth, impoverishment of weaker nations, and military aggression to maintain our disproportionate standard of living. Only by traveling can we see ourselves as others see us and see how our life-style affects others.

For us (Rick and Gene), travel has brought a new perspective. Like the astronauts, we've seen a planet with no boundaries. It's a tender green, blue, and white organism that will live or die as a unit. We're just two of five billion equally precious people. And by traveling we've seen humankind as a body that somehow must tell its fat cells to cool it . . . because nearly half of the body is starving and the whole thing is threatened.

Returning home, we've found that you can continue the mind-expanding aspect of travel by pursuing new ideas. Expose yourself to some radical thinking. Books such as *The Fate of the Earth* (Schell), *Food First* (Lappe), *Small Is Beautiful* (Schumacher), *The Future in Our Hands* (Dammann), and *Bread for the World* (Simon) and the newsletters of small peace groups are just a few sources that have opened our eyes and made us think globally.

A new enlightenment is needed. Just as the French Enlightenment led us into the modern age of science and democracy, a new enlightenment must teach us the necessity of realistic and sustainable affluence, global understanding, peaceful coexistence, and controlling nature by obeying her.

We hope that your travels give you a fun and relaxing vacation or adventure . . . and also that they'll make you an active patriot of the planet. The future is in our hands.

Rick and Gene

General Index

Geographical Index

*A list of references by country, city, and region,
for planning your trip*

About the Authors

Rick Steves

Rick has gained notoriety as a guru of alternative European travel. Since 1980 he has led "Back Door" tours of Europe and written ten travel guidebooks including the classic *Europe Through The Back Door*, which started a cult of people who insist on washing their socks in sinks and taking showers "down the hall" even when not traveling. Rick also publishes the "Back Door" travel newsletter, writes a weekly newspaper column, and gives travel lectures throughout the United States. As a native of Seattle, Washington, he graduated from the University of Washington with degrees in European History and Business Administration.

Gene Openshaw

Gene is a writer and a composer. After graduating from Stanford University, he promptly put his degree to work by writing joke books and performing stand-up comedy. He also has worked as a travel guide, schoolteacher, roofer, movie projectionist, musician, and political pamphleteer. As a composer, his works include a few minor classical pieces, music for theatrical productions, an obscure album of songs, and an opera.

Send Me a Postcard—
Drop Me a Line . . .

It's our goal to make this book the most helpful 368 pages of European history and art any traveler can read. Any suggestions, criticisms, or feedback from you would really be appreciated (send to 120 4th N., Edmonds, WA 98020). Any correspondents will receive our Back Door travel newsletter and we'll be happy to send a free copy of our next edition of *Europe 101* to anyone whose advice helps shape it. Thanks and happy travels.

Rick

Rick Steves' BACK DOOR CATALOG

All items field tested, highly recommended, completely guaranteed, discounted below retail and ideal for independent, mobile travelers. Prices include tax (if applicable), handling, and postage.

The Back Door Suitcase / Rucksack $70.00

At 9"x22"x14" this specially designed, sturdy functional bag is maximum carry-on-the-plane size (fits under the seat) and your key to foot-loose and fancy-free travel. Made of rugged water resistant Cordura nylon, it converts easily from a smart-looking suitcase to a handy rucksack. It has hide-away padded shoulder straps, top and side handles and a detachable shoulder strap (for toting as a suitcase). Lockable perimeter zippers allow easy access to the roomy (2,700 cubic inches) central compartment. Two large outside pockets are perfect for frequently used items. Also included is one nylon stuff bag. Over 40,000 Back Door travelers have used these bags around the world. Rick Steves helped design and lives out of this bag for 3 months at a time. Comparable bags cost much more. Available in navy blue, black, or grey.

Moneybelt $8.00

This required, ultra-light, sturdy, under-the-pants, nylon pouch is just big enough to carry the essentials (passport, airline ticket, travelers checks, and so on) comfortably. I'll never travel without one and I hope you won't either. Beige, nylon zipper, one size fits nearly all, with "manual."

Catalog FREE

For a complete listing of all the books, travel videos, products and services Rick Steves and Europe Through the Back Door offer you, ask us for our 64-page catalog.

Eurailpasses . . .

...cost the same everywhere. We carefully examine each order and include for no extra charge a 90-minute Rick Steves VHS video Train User's Guide, helpful itinerary advice, Eurail train schedule booklet and map, plus a free 22 Days book of your choice! Send us a check for the cost of the pass(es) you want along with your legal name (as it appears on your passport), a proposed itinerary (including dates and places of entry and exit if known), choice of 22 Days book (Europe, Brit, Spain/Port, Scand, France, or Germ/Switz/Aust) and a list of questions. Within 2 weeks of receiving your order we'll send you your pass(es) and any other information pertinent to your trip. Due to this unique service Rick Steves sells more passes than anyone on the West Coast and you'll have an efficient and expertly-organized Eurail trip.

Back Door Tours

We encourage independent travel, but for those who want a tour in the Back Door style, we do offer a 22-day "Best of Europe" tour. For complete details, send for our free 64 page tour booklet/catalog.

All orders will be processed within 2 weeks and include tax (where applicable), shipping and a one year's subscription to our Back Door Travel newsletter. Prices good through 1993. Rush orders add $5. Sorry, no credit cards. Send checks to:

**Europe Through The Back Door ● 120 Fourth Ave. N.
Box 2009 ● Edmonds, WA 98020 ● (206) 771-8303**

Other Books from John Muir Publications

Adventure Vacations: From Trekking in New Guinea to Swimming in Siberia, Bangs 256 pp. $17.95

Asia Through the Back Door, 3rd ed., Steves and Gottberg 326 pp. $15.95

Belize: A Natural Destination, Mahler, Wotkyns, Schafer 304 pp. $16.95

Bus Touring: Charter Vacations, U.S.A., Warren with Bloch 168 pp. $9.95

California Public Gardens: A Visitor's Guide, Sigg 304 pp. $16.95

Costa Rica: A Natural Destination, 2nd ed., Sheck 288 pp. $16.95

Elderhostels: The Students' Choice, 2nd ed., Hyman 312 pp. $15.95

Environmental Vacations: Volunteer Projects to Save the Planet, 2nd ed., Ocko 248 pp. $16.95

Europe 101: History & Art for the Traveler, 4th ed., Steves and Openshaw 372 pp. $15.95

Europe Through the Back Door, 11th ed., Steves 448 pp. $17.95

Europe Through the Back Door Phrase Book: French, Steves 112 pp. $4.95

Europe Through the Back Door Phrase Book: German, Steves 112 pp. $4.95

Europe Through the Back Door Phrase Book: Italian, Steves 112 pp. $4.95

Floating Vacations: River, Lake, and Ocean Adventures, White 256 pp. $17.95

A Foreign Visitor's Survival Guide to America, Baldwin and Levine 224 pp. $12.95

Great Cities of Eastern Europe, Rapoport 256 pp. $16.95

Guatemala: A Natural Destination, Mahler 288 pp. $16.95

Gypsying After 40: A Guide to Adventure and Self-Discovery, Harris 264 pp. $14.95

The Heart of Jerusalem, Nellhaus 336 pp. $12.95

Indian America: A Traveler's Companion, 2nd ed., Eagle/Walking Turtle 448 pp. $17.95

Interior Furnishings Southwest: The Sourcebook of the Best Production Craftspeople, Deats and Villani 256 pp. $19.95

Mona Winks: Self-Guided Tours of Europe's Top Museums, 2nd ed., Steves and Openshaw 456 pp. $16.95

Opera! The Guide to Western Europe's Great Houses, Zietz 296 pp. $18.95

Paintbrushes and Pistols: How the Taos Artists Sold the West, Taggett and Schwarz 280 pp. $17.95

The People's Guide to Mexico, 9th ed., Franz 608 pp. $18.95

The People's Guide to RV Camping in Mexico, Franz with Rogers 320 pp. $13.95

Ranch Vacations: The Complete Guide to Guest and Resort, Fly-Fishing, and Cross-Country Skiing Ranches, 2nd ed., Kilgore 396 pp. $18.95

The Shopper's Guide to Art and Crafts in the Hawaiian Islands, Schuchter 272 pp. $13.95

The Shopper's Guide to Mexico, Rogers and Rosa 224 pp. $9.95

Ski Tech's Guide to Equipment, Skiwear, and Accessories, ed. Tanler 144 pp. $11.95

Ski Tech's Guide to Maintenance and Repair, ed. Tanler 160 pp. $11.95

A Traveler's Guide to Asian Culture, Chambers 224 pp. $13.95

Traveler's Guide to Healing Centers and Retreats in North America, Rudee and Blease 240 pp. $11.95

Understanding Europeans, Miller 272 pp. $14.95

Undiscovered Islands of the Caribbean, 3nd ed., Willes 264 pp. $14.95

Undiscovered Islands of the Mediterranean, 2nd ed., Moyer and Willes 256 pp. $13.95

Undiscovered Islands of the U.S. and Canadian West Coast, Moyer and Willes 208 pp. $12.95

A Viewer's Guide to Art: A Glossary of Gods, People, and Creatures, Shaw and Warren 144 pp. $10.95

The Visitor's Guide to the Birds of the Eastern National Parks: United States and Canada, Wauer 400 pp. $15.95

2 to 22 Days Series
Each title offers 22 flexible daily itineraries that can be used to get the most out of vacations of any length. Included are not only "must see" attractions but also little-known villages and hidden "jewels" as well as valuable general information.

22 Days Around the World, 1993 ed., Rapoport and Willes 264 pp. $13.95

2 to 22 Days Around the Great Lakes, 1993 ed., Schuchter 192 pp. $10.95

22 Days in Alaska, Lanier 128 pp. $7.95

2 to 22 Days in the American Southwest, 1993 ed., Harris 176 pp. $10.95

2 to 22 Days in Asia, 1993 ed., Rapoport and Willes 176 pp. $10.95

2 to 22 Days in Australia, 1993 ed., Gottberg 192 pp. $10.95

2 to 22 Days in California, 1993 ed., Rapoport 192 pp. $10.95

22 Days in China, Duke and Victor 144 pp. $7.95

2 to 22 Days in Europe, 1993 ed., Steves 288 pp. $13.95

2 to 22 Days in Florida, 1993 ed., Harris 192 pp. $10.95

2 to 22 Days in France, 1993 ed., Steves 192 pp. $10.95

2 to 22 Days in Germany, Austria, & Switzerland, 1993 ed., Steves 224 pp. $10.95

2 to 22 Days in Great Britain, 1993 ed., Steves 192 pp. $10.95

2 to 22 Days in Hawaii, 1993 ed., Schuchter 176 pp. $10.95

22 Days in India, Mathur 136 pp. $7.95

22 Days in Japan, Old 136 pp. $7.95

22 Days in Mexico, 2nd ed., Rogers and Rosa 128 pp. $7.95

2 to 22 Days in New England, 1993 ed., Wright 192 pp. $10.95

2 to 22 Days in New Zealand, 1993 ed., Schuchter 192 pp. $10.95

2 to 22 Days in Norway, Sweden, & Denmark, 1993 ed., Steves 192 pp. $10.95

2 to 22 Days in the Pacific Northwest, 1993 ed., Harris 192 pp. $10.95

2 to 22 Days in the Rockies, 1993 ed., Rapoport 192 pp. $10.95

2 to 22 Days in Spain & Portugal, 1992 ed., Steves 192 pp. $9.95

2 to 22 Days in Texas, 1993 ed., Harris 192 pp. $10.95

2 to 22 Days in Thailand, 1993 ed., Richardson 180 pp. $10.95

22 Days in the West Indies, Morreale and Morreale 136 pp. $7.95

Parenting Series
Being a Father: Family, Work, and Self, *Mothering* Magazine 176 pp. $12.95
Preconception: A Woman's Guide to Preparing for Pregnancy and Parenthood, Aikey-Keller 232 pp. $14.95
Schooling at Home: Parents, Kids, and Learning, *Mothering* Magazine 264 pp. $14.95
Teens: A Fresh Look, *Mothering* Magazine 240 pp. $14.95

"Kidding Around" Travel Guides for Young Readers
Written for kids eight years of age and older.
Kidding Around Atlanta, Pedersen 64 pp. $9.95
Kidding Around Boston, 2nd ed., Byers 64 pp. $9.95
Kidding Around Chicago, 2nd ed., Davis 64 pp. $9.95
Kidding Around the Hawaiian Islands, Lovett 64 pp. $9.95
Kidding Around London, Lovett 64 pp. $9.95
Kidding Around Los Angeles, Cash 64 pp. $9.95
Kidding Around the National Parks of the Southwest, Lovett 108 pp. $12.95
Kidding Around New York City, 2nd ed., Lovett 64 pp. $9.95
Kidding Around Paris, Clay 64 pp. $9.95
Kidding Around Philadelphia, Clay 64 pp. $9.95
Kidding Around San Diego, Luhrs 64 pp. $9.95
Kidding Around San Francisco, Zibart 64 pp. $9.95
Kidding Around Santa Fe, York 64 pp. $9.95
Kidding Around Seattle, Steves 64 pp. $9.95
Kidding Around Spain, Biggs 108 pp. $12.95
Kidding Around Washington, D.C., 2nd ed., Pedersen 64 pp. $9.95

"Extremely Weird" Series for Young Readers
Written for kids eight years of age and older.
Extremely Weird Bats, Lovett 48 pp. $9.95
Extremely Weird Birds, Lovett 48 pp. $9.95
Extremely Weird Endangered Species, Lovett 48 pp. $9.95
Extremely Weird Fishes, Lovett 48 pp. $9.95
Extremely Weird Frogs, Lovett 48 pp. $9.95
Extremely Weird Insects, Lovett 48 pp. $9.95
Extremely Weird Primates, Lovett 48 pp. $9.95
Extremely Weird Reptiles, Lovett 48 pp. $9.95
Extremely Weird Sea Creatures, Lovett 48 pp. $9.95
Extremely Weird Spiders, Lovett 48 pp. $9.95

Masters of Motion Series
For kids eight years and older.
How to Drive an Indy Race Car, Rubel 48 pages $9.95
How to Fly a 747, Paulson 48 pages $9.95
How to Fly the Space Shuttle, Shorto 48 pages $9.95

Quill Hedgehog Adventures Series
Green fiction for kids. Written for kids eight years of age and older.
Quill's Adventures in the Great Beyond. Waddington-Feather 96 pp. $5.95
Quill's Adventures in Wasteland, Waddington-Feather 132 pp. $5.95
Quill's Adventures in Grozzieland, Waddington-Feather 132 pp. $5.95

X-ray Vision Series
For kids eight years and older.
Looking Inside Cartoon Animation, Schultz 48 pages $9.95
Looking Inside Sports Aerodynamics, Schultz 48 pages $9.95
Looking Inside Sunken Treasure, Schultz 48 pp. $9.95
Looking Inside Telescopes and the Night Sky, Schultz 48 pp. $9.95
Looking Inside the Brain, Schultz 48 pages $9.95

Other Young Readers Titles
Habitats: Where the Wild Things Live, Hacker & Kaufman 48 pp. $9.95
The Indian Way: Learning to Communicate with Mother Earth, McLain 114 pp. $9.95
The Kids' Environment Book: What's Awry and Why, Pedersen 192 pp. $13.95
Kids Explore America's African-American Heritage, Westridge Young Writers Workshop 112 pp. $8.95
Kids Explore America's Hispanic Heritage, Westridge Young Writers Workshop 112 pp. $7.95
Rads, Ergs, and Cheeseburgers: The Kids' Guide to Energy and the Environment, Yanda 108 pp. $12.95

Automotive Titles
How to Keep Your VW Alive, 15th ed., 464 pp. $21.95
How to Keep Your Subaru Alive 480 pp. $21.95
How to Keep Your Toyota Pickup Alive 392 pp. $21.95
How to Keep Your Datsun/Nissan Alive 544 pp. $21.95
The Greaseless Guide to Car Care Confidence: Take the Terror Out of Talking to Your Mechanic, Jackson 224 pp. $14.95
Off-Road Emergency Repair & Survival, Ristow 160 pp. $9.95

Ordering Information
If you cannot find our books in your local bookstore, you can order directly from us. If you send us money for a book not yet available, we will hold your money until we can ship you the book. Your books will be sent to you via UPS (for U.S. destinations). UPS will not deliver to a P.O. Box; please give us a street address. Include $3.75 for the first item ordered and $.50 for each additional item to cover shipping and handling costs. For airmail within the U.S., enclose $4.00. All foreign orders will be shipped surface rate; please enclose $3.00 for the first item and $1.00 for each additional item. Please inquire about foreign airmail rates.

Method of Payment
Your order may be paid by check, money order, or credit card. We cannot be responsible for cash sent through the mail. All payments must be made in U.S. dollars drawn on a U.S. bank. Canadian postal money orders in U.S. dollars are acceptable. For VISA, MasterCard, or American Express orders, include your card number, expiration date, and your signature, or call (800) 888-7504. Books ordered on American Express cards can be shipped only to the billing address of the cardholder. Sorry, no C.O.D.'s. Residents of sunny New Mexico, add 5.875% tax to the total.

Address all orders and inquiries to:
John Muir Publications
P.O. Box 613
Santa Fe, NM 87504
(505) 982-4078
(800) 888-7504